D0884236

More Praise for *Derivatives Demystified*

"A concise presentation, devoid of off-putting jargon, that offers corporate officers and risk managers important information about derivative instruments and trading strategies."

> Minali Misra
> Senior Risk Management Officer
> International Finance Corporation
> Washington, D.C.

"Over the past two decades, the Wall Street community has produced a seemingly endless variety of new and complex financial instruments. In *Derivatives Demystified: Using Structured Financial Products*, John Braddock explains in everyday easy-to-read language, the purpose and use of many of these products as well as the buzzwords that frequently confound the nonfinancial investor or executive."

> Alger B. "Duke" Chapman
> Chairman and CEO of The Chicago Board
>   Options Exchange
> Chicago

"This balanced and comprehensive treatment of derivative products provides a very timely counterpoint to those that decry the perceived abuses of derivatives without an understanding of the long history and many uses of these types of financial products."

> Michael Fitzgerald
> Partner specializing in corporate
>   and derivative securities issuances
> Brown & Wood
> New York

DERIVATIVES
DEMYSTIFIED

DERIVATIVES DEMYSTIFIED

Using Structured Financial Products

John C. Braddock

JOHN WILEY AND SONS, INC.

New York • Chichester • Weinheim • Brisbane • Singapore • Toronto

For Charles, Philip, and Kathy

This text is printed on acid-free paper.

Library of Congress Cataloging-in-Publication Data:
Braddock, John C., 1954–
    Derivatives demystified : using structured
financial products / John C. Braddock.
        p.   cm. — (Wiley series in financial engineering : 6033)
    Includes index.
    ISBN 0-471-14633-1 (cloth: alk. paper)
    1. Structured notes.   2. Securities.   3. Financial engineering.
    I. Title.   II. Series.
    HG4651.5.B73   1997
    332.64'5—dc20   96-44904

Printed in the United States of America

10 9 8 7 6 5 4 3 2 1

PREFACE

Given the degree to which the concept of "derivatives" has burst onto the international financial scene in recent years, it is worth remembering that structured financial transactions involving derivative instruments are not new. They have occurred throughout history. Thirteenth century shipping merchants in Venice during the time of Marco Polo are reputed to have bought and sold option contracts to protect their investments in or speculate on the value of cargoes enroute by ship to and from Asia. Confederate states during the U.S. Civil War are said to have issued bonds whose interest payments were indexed to cotton prices and then entered into swap contracts with England, exchanging agricultural commodities for armaments. American Depositary Receipts, whose values are derived from the common stocks of non-U.S. companies, have been traded on U.S. securities exchanges since the 1920s.

The advent of computerized option pricing models and standardized option contracts in the early 1970s led to the development and growth of a variety of option and futures contracts on U.S. government securities, stock indices, and currencies in the 1980s. The evolution of structured derivative products continues in the 1990s, ranging from exchange-listed instruments that offer retail investors opportunities once available only to investment professionals to private over-the-counter contracts that cater to the specific needs of institutional and high net-worth investors. The types of structured products and available payoff profiles range from principal preservation to speculation.

In recent years, structured derivative financial products have been the source of a great deal of controversy among government regulators, politicians, the media, the public, and corporations. Derivatives are blamed for a number of financial problems, such as an increase in global stock market volatility, the financial collapse of certain U.S. municipalities, and the large financial losses suffered by market professionals who claim ignorance about the kinds of derivative instruments they buy and obligations they incur. Many investors, members of the public, financial market professionals, and political leaders presume that it is only a matter of time before derivatives cause the meltdown of the world's financial markets, where one institution after another fails from the uncontrollable unwinding of a daisy chain of derivative-based transactions.

It appears, however, that derivatives are often the scapegoat for a number of more fundamental financial missteps. Here are a few of the more notorious business misfortunes that have been blamed on derivatives:

The Collapse of Barings Bank: The collapse of Barings Bank appears to have occurred through a combination of unauthorized activities of a rogue trader in Singapore, lax regulatory and compliance oversight, and inadequate operational controls.

The Bankruptcy of Orange County: The U.S. municipality of Orange County, California, among others, provided a very high level of public service for years despite the steady decline in California property values and related tax revenues. Taxes in Orange County remained low for years, due, in large part, to above-average returns the county received from very risky interest rate derivatives it purchased with taxpayer funds. Orange County's appointed financial managers bet aggressively on the direction of interest rates. Unfortunately, after years of winning with derivatives, interest rates abruptly reversed direction in early 1994 (due to interest rate increases by the U.S. Federal Reserve) and the county lost over $1.7 billion. Orange County's treasurer, instead of acknowledging his incomplete awareness of the risks inherent in the types of highly speculative financial obligations he had incurred on behalf of the county, blamed "derivatives" for the financial crisis and the Wall Street dealers who sold them.

Financial Losses at Several U.S. Blue-Chip Corporations: Several blue-chip corporations (e.g., Procter & Gamble, who has raised a number of legal concerns about the structured derivative products it has purchased from Bankers Trust, as has Gibson Greetings Company) have used structured derivative products regularly as an efficient means of protecting their global business revenues from, among other things, currency and interest-rate risk. Financial problems in such industrial corporations appear to arise, however, when managers and corporate treasurers, in search of profits, move beyond their risk management capabilities into speculative trading activities often involving a variety of complex derivative instruments and structured financial products.

Of course, dealers are not without fault. The concerns expressed by regulators and politicians about how various derivative instruments are marketed to investors, risk and financial disclosure, customer suitability, and capital adequacy, among others, have a great deal of merit. It is important, however, to recognize that derivatives and the structured financial products created from them appear to have contributed to the global financial markets becoming more efficient. There are those who argue that "... a broad consensus [exists], both in the public and private sectors, that derivatives provide numerous and substantial benefits. . . ."* It is unlikely, however, that a favorable consensus of opinion on derivative securities will emerge until more broadly identifiable benefits are realized from them.

Structured products and the derivative securities engineered into them, because of the financial leverage they often employ, can be highly sensitive to market valuation changes. They often act like the leading edge or "fingertips" of world financial markets, providing valuable pricing information about many types of financial assets, sometimes before the underlying cash markets respond. They can provide investors with the first hints of market moves and valuable pricing information about the interrelationships of various financial assets trading in global markets. They can alert investors to international market behavior, facilitate the movement of risk exposure into and out of investment portfolios, and allow risk be shifted efficiently from investors who want it to those who do not. Investors who might avoid or liquidate certain investments because of risk concerns may use derivative securities and the structured financial products made from them to implement specific strategies, often without transaction costs, tax obligations, or the sale of the underlying assets. Structured derivative

---

* *Derivatives: State of the Debate*, an unpublished study by Donald L. Horwitz and Robert J. Mackay, October 1995.

products can also be used by corporations to raise capital at lower funding costs. Despite widespread misperceptions about the nature, use, and applications of derivative instruments, "the ingenuity of the financial markets has transformed the patterns of volatility in the modern age into risks that are far more manageable . . . than would have been the case under any other conditions."*

The central goal of this book is to advance the development of a favorable consensus of opinion on derivative securities so that needed improvements occur in how they are structured, sold, and regulated, and so that their benefits to the world financial markets become more clearly known to broader segments of the national and international investment community and the public at large.

ACKNOWLEDGMENTS

I wish to offer sincere thanks to my friends and colleagues, David A. Dami and Paul Sclafani at Oppenheimer & Co., Inc.; Michael F. Fitzgerald at the law firm of Brown & Wood; Paul M. Gottlieb at Union Bank of Switzerland; and Jeffrey J. Hass at New York Law School. They each have provided a great deal of substance to the legal and technical discussions in this book. Bill Feingold and Dalip Awasthi at PaineWebber Incorporated deserve thanks for clarifying the discussion on convertible securities. Bill's comparisons of convertibles to baseball and options to basketball are particularly entertaining. I would also like to thank Dr. Jack Marshall of St. John's University for encouraging me to write this book and for introducing me to Myles Thompson at John Wiley & Sons, Inc. Also, Jacqueline Urinyi at Wiley provided many good suggestions and a much appreciated firm hand in guiding my preparation of the manuscript. Lastly, I would like to thank Mary Daniello at Wiley and Bernice Pettinato at Beehive Production Services for their superb editing and production efforts.

JOHN C. BRADDOCK

New York, New York
January 1997

---

*Peter L. Bernstein, *Against the Gods: The Remarkable Story of Risk* (New York, Wiley, 1996), p. 323.

CONTENTS

INTRODUCTION

This book examines categories of structured financial products and investment strategies in use among qualified retail investors, sophisticated high-net-worth individuals, investment professionals, corporations, and financial institutions. Most important, in an area of finance that can be highly quantitative and full of technical jargon, this book provides corporate and financial managers, brokers, investors, bankers, traders, lawyers, regulators, government officials, and business students with clear explanations, insights, and examples of derivative-based structured financial products.

It is divided into four parts: an introduction to structured products (Chapters 1–4), specific types of structured products (Chapters 5–12), various trading strategies and capital-raising approaches (Chapters 13, 14, and 15), and an extensive resource guide. Chapter 1 provides a concise orientation as to the variety of structured products discussed in this book, including what they are, why they are used, and who uses them. On Wall Street, the term *structured product* refers to financial instruments designed or engineered to meet specific financial or investment objectives. Business activities related to the creation, marketing, and valuation of the structured products discussed herein are collectively referred to as *financial engineering*. *Structuring* refers to a nontraditional process of creating and fabricating a wide variety of financial products whose values are linked to or derived from one or more underlying assets, such as equities, bonds, commodities or currencies, or other economic interests.

Structured products are often referred to as *derivatives*, a generic term used to describe a wide variety of financial instruments ranging from stan-

1

dardized, exchange-listed products, such as options and futures, to custom-tailored, over-the-counter instruments to those whose values are linked to or are derived, in whole or in part, from the price or value of one or more underlying assets, including equity indices, exchange rates, interest rates, or commodity prices. Elemental derivatives are the building blocks of structured products and can be fabricated into a diverse array of innovative financial instruments. Elemental derivatives fall into two general categories: *forward-based*, such as forward contracts, futures, and swaps; and *option-based*, including put and call options, caps, floors, and collars (see display).

FORWARD-BASED AND OPTION-BASED ELEMENTAL DERIVATIVES

Forward-Based

- Forward Contracts
  Forward Rate Agreements (FRAs)
  Forward Foreign Exchange Contracts
  Forward Commodity Contracts
- Futures Contracts
  Interest Rate Futures
  Equity Index Futures
  Currency Futures
- Swap Transactions
  Averaging Swaps
  Basic Swaps
  Commodity Swaps
  Currency Swaps
  Forward Start Swaps

Option-Based

- Warrants
- Put and Call Options
- Cap and Floor Agreements
- Equity Options
- Interest Rate and Currency Options
- Exotic Options

The ability to design and sell structured financial instruments offers some potential benefits, specifically:

- Facilitating investor demand for timely, innovative, researched-backed investment products designed to exploit global market opportunities.

- Providing the potential for above-average returns and portfolio protection to investors.

- Lowering funding costs to corporate and governmental issuers and favorably increasing their visibility in the international capital markets.

- The ability to engage in hedging, trading, and underwriting activities that can generate profits, sales credits, and other benefits to broker–dealers through increased sales revenues and order flow to stock loan, investment banking, syndicate, and research departments.

- Advantages to broker–dealers in recruiting internal sales people and a significant marketing, development, and retention edge with corporate, institutional, and individual clients.

Compared to traditional financial instruments, many structured derivative products have other unique, as well as controversial, characteristics, including:

Lack of Regulation.   Although many of the products discussed herein are some of the most heavily regulated securities in the world, many structured derivative transactions occur outside of established regulatory regimes. This characteristic enhances the unfettered creativity that has been the hallmark of numerous derivative products around the world and is currently the subject of a great deal of controversy, study, and debate.

Borderless International Transactions.   Given their birth during the globalization of the capital markets, derivative instruments can be denominated in almost any currency, structured within almost any legal and regulatory environment and around almost any obstacle. They are designed to exploit market inefficiencies within, across, or between international political borders.

Innovation.   From unleveraged and principal preserving to highly leveraged and speculative, from "plain vanilla" to "exotic," structured products continue to be developed with features and nuances that cater to the specific needs of investors around the world.

Lack of Secondary Trading Liquidity.   Other than standardized derivative securities and structured products that are listed on securities exchanges around the world, many such instruments trade over-the-counter and have no established market for secondary trading, other than "upstairs" markets made for clients by originating broker–dealers.

Off-Balance Sheet Accounting.   Because they often fall outside traditional regulatory and accounting categories, many structured derivative products are treated as off-balance-sheet items and, other than financial footnotes, are not always reflected in traditional disclosure materials and financial ratios used by investors to analyze the performance of corporate users and issuers of such instruments.

Financial Leverage.   Using derivatives and structured instruments, end users can achieve almost any degree of financial leverage or "gearing" desired in pursuing financial objectives; relatively small capital outlays can finance products that produce potential cash surpluses and deficits and positions that have tremendous potential to appreciate as well as depreciate.

Organizations successful in structuring and trading derivative financial instruments integrate such activities into their firm's strategic business plans and usually have managers who understand and support such activities. Chapter 2 highlights many of the responsibilities of officers and directors overseeing structured product activities and a sampling of the regulations (proposed, pending, and adopted) affecting derivatives. Some firms enter the derivative business without taking a systematic approach toward trading, structuring, and risk management. Occasionally, companies have entered, abruptly exited, and later reentered the business over the course of several years. The nature of organizational support for structured product trading, origination, and risk management should include the features explained in the accompanying display on the facing page.

Structured derivative products typically undergo significant financial and legal scrutiny. Positions relating to and used to offset or hedge the risk

ORGANIZATIONAL SUPPORT FOR STRUCTURED PRODUCT TRADING

1. Management commitment to and support of structured products as a component of ongoing business strategies.

2. Research, pricing, and computer modeling capabilities to support derivative and structured product valuation and pricing.

3. Trade execution, risk management, and computerized audit and management reporting capabilities.

4. The establishment of international "shelf" registration programs for timely exploitation of worldwide market opportunities in equity, debt, commodity, and currency asset classes.

5. Use of the parent corporation's balance sheet as the issuer of and for credit backing for structured product offerings.

6. Access to retail and institutional distribution channels.

7. Access to syndicate resources and syndicate awareness of structured products to assist and expand marketing and underwriting capabilities.

8. Operational, administrative, computer, and back office support and safeguards relating to derivative trading and structured product origination.

9. Legal, compliance, and investor suitability safeguards and procedures.

10. Access to offshore booking facilities in order to obtain favorable capital reserve treatment and related economic benefits pertaining to the issuance of structured products.

associated with issuing various structured derivative products often comprised combinations of exchange-listed options, futures, options on futures, and cash securities that produce virtually no credit risk to the issuer of structured products. Exchange-traded derivative instruments and contracts are issued by securities or futures exchanges and are regulated by government agencies.

Structured derivative product positions are generally valued and marked-to-market daily by financial control personnel assigned within firms managing the market price risk related to such positions. They monitor and prepare regular management reports on derivative trading activities and positions. To the extent back-to-back, over-the-counter options (i.e., nonpublic or nonstandardized options) are purchased from third parties to hedge market risk relating to the issuance of structured products, they are typically purchased from counterparties whose creditworthiness, among other factors, undergoes a formal credit review. Also, exchange-listed structured products in the United States, for example, must be registered with the U.S. Securities and Exchange Commission where they undergo a particularly stringent review process. They are listed on securities exchanges[1] under specific derivative listing and investor suitability standards. Chapter 3 discusses the origination process and the legal and marketing activities that comprise new product creation. Chapter 4 illuminates some of the basic quantitative aspects of new financial product development.

Chapters 5 through 12 review the general characteristics of various categories and permutations of structured products available to investors around the world, such as warrants, structured notes, and exotic options. Chapter 13 discusses structured financial products and strategies available to shareholders seeking to monetize or hedge large equity positions or restricted stock holdings. Chapters 14 and 15 relate to certain structures available to corporations for their capital-raising activities.

It is important to note that structured derivative products require the involvement of an issuer (e.g., a corporation, government, or government agency, etc.) who is the ultimate obligor to whom investors look for fulfillment of the terms of each particular transaction. Structured products must also be supported by risk management capabilities that are employed to reduce or eliminate various market risks that influence an issuer's obligations to perform under such offerings. Risk management capabilities are fulfilled by entities (either affiliated or unaffiliated with the issuer) with the trading, quantitative, and other financial engineering skills necessary to engage in capital market activities that act as a counterbalance to the issuer's performance obligations under a portfolio of structured product liabilities. Issuers of structured products often hedge their balance-sheet exposure to such

---

[1]Securities exchanges include stock (e.g., the American, New York, Pacific et al.) and option (e.g., CBOE et al.) exchanges, most of which have similar rules for listing and trading structured financial products.

obligations using their own in-house derivative trading desks or by purchasing such market protection from creditworthy counterparties through
identical, back-to-back transactions. Issuers then fund their obligations to
investors by periodically unwinding or monetizing a portion of their hedge.

For example, a public corporation that issues a combination of stock
and bonds uses the proceeds to fund its particular operating capital and investment needs. However, an issuer and obligor of a structured derivative
product uses a substantial portion of the proceeds from such an offering
for hedging[2] purposes or for "immunizing" itself from exposure to the risk
of price fluctuations relating to the market or asset on which the structured product is based. Such hedging activity requires the continuous buying and selling of options, futures, cash securities, and other instruments
and investment contracts, often around the clock and in financial markets
around the world, using some or all of the proceeds generated from an offering. The success of a risk manager is, in large part, a function of the
costs incurred and the amounts of offering proceeds consumed in hedging
a portfolio of structured product obligations. Profitability is a function of
the level of success in managing position risk and retaining as much of
such proceeds as possible over the life of the position. The securities that
constitute the hedge often include instruments with shorter or even longer
terms than the structured products sold to investors. This mismatch of
terms and instruments in the hedge with those related to the structured
product generates risks (e.g., gap risk, roll risk, and tracking error, as defined in Chapter 3) that must be closely managed by the obligor and its risk
managers.

The extensive Resource Guide at the end of this book provides a great
deal of background and reference material that supports the information
contained in Chapters 1–15. Sample structured product presentations to

---

[2]Hedging is the management (i.e., buying and selling) of elemental derivative and cash market
positions associated with proprietary derivative trading portfolios (i.e., investments made by
firms for their own account) and structured product obligations sold to investors. Issuers of
structured products may hedge their price risk exposure to structured product obligations
using in-house derivative trading desks, they may choose to minimize internal risk exposure
by purchasing back-to-back hedges from outside hedge-writing firms (i.e., financial contracts
written by other dealers under terms similar or identical to instruments sold to investors), or
they may use a combination of internally and externally managed hedges. Elemental derivative positions and those embedded in structured products are often segregated into discrete
asset categories and monitored daily by financial control personnel, derivative traders, and
business managers.

management, information about offering expenses, the activities of structured product working groups, legal, marketing, and pricing information are included. There are also sample term sheets supporting many of the types of products discussed in this book. A glossary of terms is also included.

The format of much of the material is intended to provide concise summations of the material in a readable form which, when combined with the text, enhances immediate comprehension and understanding without assuming an extensive knowledge of derivatives and structured products.

PART ONE

Introducing Structured Financial Products: Definition, Responsibility, Product Development and Marketing, Risk Management

1
SUMMARY OF STRUCTURED PRODUCTS

WHAT ARE STRUCTURED FINANCIAL PRODUCTS?

Investors considering investments that are most appropriate for their needs often focus on the payoff pattern expected from each potential opportunity—appreciation, income, a combination of both? Assume, for example, that an investor has a diversified portfolio of stocks and income-producing bonds. A structured derivative product a conservative investor may consider is called a *principal protected note*. In lieu of coupon payments, payoff at maturity equals the return of the principal investment plus any appreciation that may result from price changes of the underlying asset on which the instrument is based, including perhaps an asset that would normally be too risky for the investor, such as currency exchange rates or the stocks of an emerging market economy. On the other hand, a speculative investor may seek short-term returns from warrants or exotic options that are many times greater than his or her initial investment with the knowledge that such an investment could expire worthless.

Structured products are financial instruments and contractual obligations that are designed, created, bundled, issued, and sold to investors to meet specific investment objectives. The term *structuring* or *financial engineering* refers to a process of creating a wide variety of financial products whose payments are linked to or based on one or more underlying assets, such as U.S. and international stock prices and interest rates, currency exchange rates, commodity prices, and indices.

The linkages between assets can take the form of:

- Absolute price levels or index values (up or down)
- Spreads between individual securities, baskets, sectors, indices, and markets
- Correlations between two or more asset classes
- Yield curve shapes, convergence, or divergence

The next section outlines reasons for using structured financial products.

WHY USE STRUCTURED FINANCIAL PRODUCTS?

Investors around the world use structured products to:

- Address financial objectives with instruments that provide greater flexibility than the alternatives offered by traditional exchange-traded stocks, bonds, futures, and options.
- Enhance the potential returns from international markets or protect against market price volatility.
- Secure returns based on the performance of broad-based benchmark indices or specific custom-made industry sectors.
- Defer, avoid, or reduce transactions costs, capital gains taxes, or management fees associated with buying and selling securities.
- Obtain returns from potentially higher yielding and otherwise unavailable investments by combining elements of different asset classes into hybrid instruments (e.g., trust units or equity-linked notes).

- Limit, reduce, or virtually eliminate downside exposure to price fluctuations in cash investments by using structured derivative products that are linked to similar or identical assets (e.g., portfolio replicated put protection); risk of loss is usually limited to the dollar amount invested in and the creditworthiness of the issuer of the derivative instrument.

- Participate in the returns of international markets with less cash exposure (downside risk can be limited to the dollar amount invested).

- Diversify into international markets, reduce exchange rate exposure, defer taxation, or minimize regulatory risks.

- Invest in internationally linked structured instruments that trade in the investor's home market during normal trading hours rather than during trading hours in other time zones.

SPECIFIC USERS OF STRUCTURED FINANCIAL PRODUCTS

Structured financial products are used by a wide variety of investors, including:

1. Retail investors with the appropriate investment experience and financial goals

2. Sophisticated, high-net-worth investors that satisfy customer suitability criteria established by regulators and by internal policies

3. Fund managers (pension funds, mutual fund investment advisors, asset managers, and hedge funds)

4. Insurance companies (including separate accounts)

5. Governments and government agencies

6. Corporations and corporate executives

7. Financial intermediaries

8. Arbitrage accounts

9. Investment and commercial banks

TYPES OF STRUCTURED FINANCIAL PRODUCTS

The types of structured products and investment strategies discussed in this book include warrants, index- and other asset-linked notes, convertible securities, equity-linked notes, exotic options and warrants, swaps, investment trusts, over-the-counter private placements, monetization and hedging strategies for restricted stock and other concentrated equity positions, equity-linked capital market transactions for corporations, and a structured shelf registration and equity distribution program for corporate issuers and affiliated shareholders.

CONCLUSION

One way to convey complex concepts is by linking them to familiar ones. Most investors are familiar with traditional mechanisms for financial wealth accumulation and preservation—stocks and bonds. Structured products are like stocks and bonds with new features attached—similar to purchasing a new automobile and adding a few extras such as power windows, cruise control, and a computerized braking system.

As a backdrop to discussions about various types of structured products and how they are created, Chapter 2 sets an important tone for the book. It highlights many of the responsibilities of officers and directors overseeing structured product development, trading, and risk management activities.

2

RESPONSIBILITIES OF OFFICERS AND DIRECTORS OVERSEEING STRUCTURED DERIVATIVE PRODUCT TRANSACTIONS

Although many individuals and organizations relish the unfettered pursuit of financial transactions around the world, it is clear that preserving investor confidence in the integrity of worldwide capital markets is of paramount importance. This chapter reviews risks, obligations, and certain key questions that should be asked regarding structured derivative product transactions. It outlines some recommendations of governmental finance and regulatory officials, senior representatives from international financial institutions, and academicians about derivative practices and principles, and it discusses a suggested framework for voluntary oversight of such activities.

This chapter is based in part on unpublished seminar material prepared by and used with the permission of Seward & Kissel entitled "Managing Derivatives: Responsibilities of Officers and Directors Overseeing Derivative Transactions," October 25, 1995.

Senior managers of organizations that successfully engage in structuring and trading derivative products are committed to and support derivative trading and structuring activities as an integrated component of their strategic business plans. Such support is provided with the knowledge that operational procedures exist to provide management with the requisite understanding and control over those aspects of derivative structuring, hedging, and trading in which the firm is involved. (See the sample management presentations in the Resource Guide.)

The following information includes brief descriptions of certain derivative risks, certain minimum standards of management oversight for officers, directors, and others in positions of authority, and regulatory proposals concerning derivative and structured product transactions. It is not intended as a substitute for legal advice concerning specific management oversight issues, transactions, regulatory, tax, risk management, or operational matters.

KEY RISKS IN DERIVATIVES AND STRUCTURED FINANCIAL PRODUCTS

The following broad categories of risk are involved in derivatives and structured products for issuers, dealers, and end users. While not unlike risks present in most financial instruments, the management of these risks presents unique challenges due principally to the customized nature of many derivative and structured financial products. It is these risks that boards of directors and senior managers must control in order to maintain effective derivatives and structured product programs.

Credit Risk.   The risk of loss should a counterparty fail to perform pursuant to the terms of an agreement. The loss is the cost of replacement, which is usually equal to the present value of expected cash flows at the time of default or the notional value of outstanding positions.

Legal Risk.   The risk of loss if an agreement is not enforceable due to insufficient documentation, lack of capacity, or unenforceability in bankruptcy or insolvency.

Liquidity Risk.   The risk of loss from either the inability to unwind, offset, or hedge a particular transaction (or the inability to do so without adversely affecting the market price) or the inability to meet payment obligations or collateral requirements.

Market Risk. The risk of loss from an instrument resulting from adverse price movements or market conditions that should generally be viewed from the net or residual exposure of the entire portfolio.

Operational Risk. The risk of loss from deficient or inadequate systems, internal controls of management oversight, or other failures.

LEGAL OBLIGATIONS OF OFFICERS AND DIRECTORS

Directors and officers are obligated to refrain from using their positions for personal profit at the corporation's expense and to make well-informed decisions. The obligations of officers and directors can only be met through the exercise of personal judgment on a daily basis. These legal obligations of officers and directors fall into two broad categories: duty of care and duty of loyalty.

Duty of Care

- Officers and directors have a duty to make informed decisions.

- Officers and directors must discharge their duties in good faith and with that degree of care and skill that an ordinary prudent person would exercise under similar circumstances.

- Officers and directors must act in good faith and on the basis of adequate information.

- Directors must oversee the activities of the corporation by:

    attending directors' meetings,

    requiring that the company provide adequate information upon which to make decisions,

    carefully reviewing the documentation provided, and

    monitoring the activities delegated to corporate officers.

- Business Judgment Rule: There is a presumption that decisions made by directors and officers are in good faith and well informed.

The presumption may be rebutted, however, by evidence that the directors did not have available, or did not seek, the information necessary to make an informed decision. However, officers and directors do not have the benefit of this presumption if a conflict of interest or breach of the duty of loyalty is present (i.e., the officer or director has a personal financial interest in the transaction).

Duty of Loyalty

- An officer or director must act in good faith and with the conscientiousness and honesty that the law requires of fiduciaries.

KEY QUESTIONS OF BOARDS OF DIRECTORS ABOUT DERIVATIVES

The following basic questions should assist directors in focusing on the appropriate issues concerning the management of derivatives:

1. Have clear and internally consistent goals and objectives concerning derivatives been plainly stated and communicated?

2. Are derivatives being used to mitigate risk or for speculative purposes?

3. Is the Board's authorization being properly carried out by management?

4. Are adequate controls in place and carefully monitored to ensure that only authorized transactions occur and unauthorized transactions are detected promptly?

5. Are trading responsibilities segregated from other duties, especially accounting, audit, and risk management functions?

6. Is the risk inherent in the firm's derivative positions consistent with the Board's stated objectives?

7. How do the risks of derivatives affect the ability of the firm to achieve its overall objectives?

8. Do the employees involved in the trading or monitoring of derivatives have the appropriate level of expertise?

9. Is information communicated to the proper parties to ensure effective decision making?

• An officer or director has a duty of fairness and must avoid con- flicts of interest; he or she may only enter into a transaction with his or her corporation if the transaction is fair to the corporation and has the hallmarks of an arm's-length bargain.

• An officer or director may not usurp a corporate opportunity, in- cluding:

> Whether the opportunity falls within the corporation's line of business,
>
> Whether the corporation has a tangible expectancy in the op- portunity, and
>
> Whether based on the facts, the fiduciary's taking of the oppor- tunity was fair.

RECOMMENDATIONS FOR USE

Selected Recommendations from the Group of Thirty's Report: *Derivatives: Practices and Principles* [1]

The report prepared by the Global Derivatives Study Group of the Group of Thirty in July 1993, entitled *Derivatives: Practices and Principles,* is one of the early studies concerning derivatives and is considered one of the most comprehensive about the derivatives market. The report provides guidance to assist in the management of the derivative and structured product activities by derivatives issuers, dealers, and end users. The re- port should be reviewed in detail by managers involved in derivatives ac- tivities. The following list summarizes many, but not all, of the Group's recommendations.

---

[1]The *Group of Thirty* is composed of an international group of government finance and regu- latory officials, senior representatives from worldwide financial institutions, and distin- guished academicians from the United States, the United Kingdom, Mexico, Australia, Germany, Israel, Argentina, Italy, Switzerland, Japan, Denmark, Spain, France, and Canada. A copy of the report may be obtained from Group of Thirty, 1990 M. Street, N.W., Washington, D.C. 20036 or by E-Mail: Info@Group30.Org. The material in this section has been used with permission.

- The role of senior management. Dealers and end users should use derivatives in a manner consistent with the overall risk management and capital policies approved by their boards of directors. Policies governing derivatives should be clearly defined, including the purposes for which these transactions are to be undertaken. Senior management should approve procedures and controls to implement these policies, and management at all levels should enforce them.

- For risk management purposes, derivative positions should be marked-to-market at least daily.

- The market risk of derivative positions should be measured on a consistent basis and regularly compared against market risk limits previously established by senior management.

- The funding requirements arising from derivative portfolios should be periodically forecast to assess cash needs.

- Independent market risk management. Dealers and end users should have an independent market risk management function with clear authority to ensure that risk limit policies are implemented and properly monitored.

- Credit risk exposure arising from derivative activities should be regularly assessed against established credit limits based on frequent measures of current exposure (replacement cost) and potential exposure (future replacement cost).

- Credit exposure of derivatives should be aggregated with all other credit exposures to a particular counterparty when considering enforceable netting arrangements and other risk-reducing agreements.

- Dealers and end users should have an independent credit risk management function with clear authority as well as the necessary analytical capabilities to assess derivative exposure.

- Dealers and end users should assess both the benefits and costs of credit enhancement and related risk reduction arrangements, especially in connection with early termination or collateral requirements and the capacity to meet potentially substantial funding needs.

- Only professionals with the appropriate level of skill and experience should be authorized to enter derivative transactions, manage the risks associated with such positions, and process, report, control, and audit derivatives activities.

- Adequate information systems must be established to ensure the proper measure of the risks associated with derivatives and the reporting of such risks in a timely manner.

- The designation of individuals with the authority to commit their firm to derivative transactions must be clearly communicated by senior management.

- Financial statements should contain sufficient information about their use of derivatives to provide an understanding of the purposes for which transactions are undertaken, the degree of risks involved, and the way in which the transactions have been accounted for.

Framework for Voluntary Oversight, Derivatives Policy Group (Group of Six Report)[2]

The Derivatives Policy Group (DPG or Group of Six) was formed at the suggestion of Chairman Arthur Levitt of the U.S. Securities and Exchange Commission (SEC) in August 1994. The group published its *Framework for Voluntary Oversight (A Framework for Voluntary Oversight of the Over-the-Counter Derivatives Activities of Securities Firm Affiliates to Promote Confidence and Stability in Financial Markets)* in March 1995. The 50-page report provides substantial proposals concerning derivative practices, policies, controls, procedures, and reporting methodology. Mary L. Schapiro, then chairwoman of the Commodity Futures Trading Commission (CFTC), also joined Chairman Levitt shortly after the group's formation as an official regulatory contact.

---

[2]Extracts from the *Framework for Voluntary Oversight* report of the DPG, March 1995, used with permission. The Group of Six comprises senior representatives from CS First Boston, Goldman Sachs, Morgan Stanley, Merrill Lynch, Salomon Brothers, and Lehman Brothers. A copy of the report can be found in *Commodity Futures Law Reports,* paragraph 26,312, pages 42543 to 42564, Commerce Clearing House, Inc., March 1995.

Policy concerns raised by the U.S. Congress, various U.S. government agencies, and others about the over-the-counter (OTC) derivative securities activities of unregulated affiliates of SEC-registered broker–dealers and CFTC-registered futures commission merchants gave impetus to the formation of the group. The regulatory and supervisory community in the United States and abroad has for some time been seeking to find an acceptable method to assess the market risks associated with OTC derivative products. The DPG's objective has been to formulate a voluntary oversight framework intended to address the public policy issues related to derivatives, but recognizes that its efforts in this area are evolutionary and expects further refinement and adaptation of the framework it is advocating. Recommendations include:

- *Management Controls.* This component of the framework consists of the implementation of internal management controls for monitoring and measuring the various risks to which a firm may be exposed as a result of dealings in OTC derivative products and the inclusion of an external audit and verification process. These controls, many of which are already in place, will be implemented individually by each firm and are designed to effectuate prudent risk management practices which, in combination with the other initiatives of the DPG, will enhance the risk management practices of the firms and the marketplace in general.

- *Enhanced Reporting.* This component consists of the periodic submission to the SEC and the CFTC of a series of new quantitative reports covering credit risk exposures arising from OTC derivatives activities and related information.

- *Evaluation of Risk in Relation to Capital.* A framework will be developed for estimating market and credit risk exposures arising from OTC derivatives activities with a view toward facilitating the evaluation of those risks and other relevant factors in relation to capital.

- *Counterparty Relationships.* This part of the framework deals with guidelines for professional intermediaries with respect to their relationships with nonprofessional counterparties in connection with OTC derivatives transactions.

The DPG contemplates that the proposed framework would apply to any affiliate of an SEC registered broker–dealer that is not subject to supervisory oversight with respect to capital; that is primarily engaged in the business of holding itself out to unaffiliated counterparties as a professional intermediary willing to structure and enter either side of an OTC derivative transaction as principal; and whose OTC derivatives activities are likely to have a material impact, directly or indirectly, on its SEC-registered broker–dealer affiliate. For these purposes, OTC derivative products would include:

- Interest rate, currency, equity, and commodity swap contracts
- OTC options (including caps, floors, and collars)
- Currency forward contracts

Given the competitive realities of the marketplace, the DPG seeks to stimulate a more consistent, workable approach to the oversight of these activities and markets that will apply across the international spectrum of participants. The group recognizes that until greater consistency and harmony is achieved, there is a clear danger of a drift toward a climate that encourages market participants to seek out the most benign legal and regulatory regime—an outcome that can only work in the direction of increasing risk for all, an outcome that would be contrary to the interests of the Group of Six members, their official sponsors, and, presumably, the international financial community as a whole.

OVERVIEW OF PROPOSED, PENDING, AND EXISTING DERIVATIVE SECURITIES STUDIES, RECOMMENDATIONS, AND REGULATIONS

The entire area of derivative securities is being studied by various self-regulatory organizations and is the subject of inquiry by several international and U.S. federal regulatory organizations, the results of which among the latter groups have led to U.S. Congressional hearings and proposals to change the existing regulatory structure for derivative-based financial products and, eventually, form new regulatory authorities. The following is a summary of just some of the major derivative reports that have been published or regulatory initiatives that are effective or pending:

> *Developments in International Interbank Relations*, Bank for International Settlements, October 1992.
>
> *Derivative Product Activities of Commercial Banks,* Federal Reserve, January 27, 1993.
>
> *Listing Standards for Index Warrants* (Hybrid Release), NASD, February 4, 1993.
>
> *Report on Derivative Products,* The Bank of England, April 1993.
>
> *Net Capital Rule Concept Release,* SEC, May 4, 1993.
>
> *Derivatives: Practices and Principles,* Global Derivatives Study Group of the Group of Thirty, July 21, 1993.
>
> *Derivative Financial Markets,* a report prepared by the Congressional Research Service for the use of the Subcommittee on Telecommunications and Finance of the Committee on Energy and Commerce, U.S. House of Representatives, John Dingell (Michigan), Chairman, August 1993 (includes responses by the Federal Reserve, the FDIC, and the Office of the Comptroller of the Currency, among others).
>
> *OTC Derivative Markets and Their Regulation,* CFTC, October 1993.
>
> A 900-page study of the financial derivatives marketplace organized by Congressman Jim Leach (Iowa), House Committee on Banking, Finance and Urban Affairs; a series of 30 recommendations for regulatory and legislative guidance of the derivative markets, November 22, 1993 press release.

Following the publication of a 900-page study of the financial derivatives marketplace in November 1993, Congressman Jim Leach of Iowa (then Ranking Minority Member of the House Committee on Banking, Finance and Urban Affairs) introduced a bill in Congress on January 26, 1994, proposing to establish the Federal Derivatives Commission pursuant to the proposed Derivatives Supervision Act of 1994. The terms of the Act seek to provide an "enhanced framework for Federal financial institution regulation of derivative activities." (Legislation was reintroduced on January 5, 1996, by Congressman Leach, then

Chairman of the House Committee on Banking and Financial Services, as the Risk Management Improvement and Derivatives Oversight Act of 1995.)

Financial Derivatives: Actions Needed to Protect the Financial System, U.S. General Accounting Office, May 19, 1994.

Public Disclosure of Market and Credit Risks by Financial Intermediaries (G-10 Central Banks), September 1994 (the Fisher Report).

Report of the Secretary of the Treasury, Chair, President's Working Group on Financial Markets, on financial market coordination and regulatory activities to reduce risks in the financial system in 1993 and 1994, October 1994.

SEC Release No. 34-35135, broker–dealer exemptive order with respect to certain OTC derivative activities, December 1994.

Framework for Voluntary Oversight. A framework for voluntary oversight of the OTC derivatives activities of securities firm affiliates to promote confidence and stability in financial markets. (Derivatives Policy Group of Six Report, March 1995).

Framework for Supervisory Information about the Derivatives Activities of Banks and Securities Firms, Joint report by the Basle Committee on Banking Supervision and the Technical Committee of the International Organization for Securities Commissions (IOSCO), May 1995.

Notice of Proposed Rulemaking (Reg.T Release), U.S. Federal Reserve, June 29, 1995, 60 *FR* 33763 (1995).

The Principles and Practices for Wholesale Financial Market Transactions, International Swap Dealers Association (ISDA) and other trade groups, August 1995.

SEC rule change to establish listing and trading guidelines for stock index, currency, and currency indexed warrants on the AMEX, CBOE, NYSE, PSE, and PHLX, September 7, 1995.

Rule filing concerning multiple currency warrants, AMEX, October 2, 1995.

Disclosure about Derivative Financial Instruments and Fair Value of Financial Instruments, FASB Statement 119, 1995.

NASD proposed interpretation of suitability rule in context of institutional client relationships, published for comment by the SEC, October 1995, 60 *FR* 54530, 1995.

Trading Activities of Commercial Banks, OCC, FRB, and FDIC, December 1995.

Over the Counter Equity Derivatives, a paper prepared by Federation Internationale des Bourses de Valeurs (FIBV) with the assistance of Accountants and Association's Section on Business Law, International Capital Markets Group, 1995.

Position and exercise limit increases for exchanges and expanded equity hedge exemption policy approved by the SEC, October 1995.

SEC proposal on the reporting of derivatives (risk disclosure requirements), 61 *FR* 578, January 8, 1996.

Other general derivative market studies, regulations, and accounting standards that are pending include:

- U.S. General Accounting Office reports
- Public Securities Association studies
- Option (as opposed to equity) margin requirements
- Revised issuer listing standards
- Net capital requirements
- Financial Accounting Standards Board financial disclosure rules

Recent actions by international securities and derivative exchanges, and regulatory and governmental authorities appear to indicate that, although thorough studies have taken place, derivative regulations have been modified and the present framework for regulating derivatives may need additional fine-tuning, a major overhaul of global securities laws does not appear to be in the offing.

Whether or not any substantial changes occur regarding the regulation of derivatives and structured financial products, broker–dealers and others involved in the creation of new derivative instruments may wish to consider developing an internal "white paper" analyzing regulatory proposals including the preparation of appropriate business positions. Where necessary, a consensus should be developed among other broker–dealers and financial institutions and a coherent industry strategy should be initiated. Also, a strategy of commenting on regulatory proposals should be designed and implemented with the primary goal being the adoption of workable positions concerning the regulation of derivative securities and structured financial products.

CONCLUSION

The complexity and proliferation of derivatives and structured financial instruments have increased at a faster pace than the controversies surrounding their use and alleged abuse. Inevitably the responsibilities of senior managers and directors of organizations engaged in the origination and risk management of structured financial instruments have increased. Their oversight is also the subject of a great deal of scrutiny by regulators, shareholders, and courts of law.

Chapter 3 turns the discussion toward the activities involved in structured product creation, development, and marketing. It includes a review of how to identify investor demand for new structured products; the idea generation and structuring process; and the legal and regulatory review and registration procedures that are necessary when engaging in the underwriting, syndicating, and marketing of structured products.

3

THE STRUCTURED PRODUCT CREATION, DEVELOPMENT, AND OFFERING PROCESS

This chapter provides an inside look at what financial engineers must do as they engage in the structured product creation, development, and offering process. Much of the discussion entails an overview of traditional investment banking activities, such as those related to underwriting, syndicating, and marketing initial public offerings of new securities. However, most of the discussion focuses on the rapidly evolving and distinct new area of finance dubbed by industry professionals as *financial engineering*.

Financial engineering as a discrete profession has evolved very quickly. In the late 1980s, ad hoc groups of traders, investment bankers, attorneys, quantitative research analysts, accounting, and operations professionals worked together periodically to produce new financial structures or solve specific corporate financing problems. It soon became evident that derivative-based financial problem solving for corporations produced a variety of capital market, trading, investment banking, and risk management opportunities. By the mid-1990s, firms engaged in the creation of structured derivative products recognized the need to properly support such activities and fused trading, investment banking, legal, research, accounting, and computer professionals into new departments described, for example, as global derivatives, structured products, equity derivatives, or fixed-income derivative groups. As with the types of financial products being developed, the financial engineering profession is evolving as investor needs are identified and matched with professional skills.

The creation and development of structured derivative products involves simultaneous steps that financial engineers (i.e., those who engage in designing and producing new derivative-based investment products) must take in bringing new products to market. Many investment opportunities involve fast-moving markets that can render potential transactions uneconomical in a very short time. Investor perceptions of and interest in potential investment opportunities are highly transient and can evaporate with almost any movement in the underlying market, such as price volatility, interest rate changes, or exchange rate moves. An active or static market can have varied meanings to different groups of investors. Therefore, success in launching structured product transactions is a function of preparation and timing.

Many structured product transactions are unique and, as a result of various legal, regulatory, marketing, and new product development issues and costs, often generate many questions and concerns among managers in charge of derivative trading and structured product groups. Such products often require modification of established administrative or operational procedures. As agents of change within an organization, structured products are often perceived as disruptive to established marketing, syndication, legal and compliance procedures, computer systems capabilities, and back office protocols. Therefore, it is usually necessary to properly address internal concerns in order for a financial engineer to advance his or her business goals.

Within investment banking and securities brokerage firms, like almost all organizations, there are those who run established business franchises and control many aspects of the everyday flow of business. Structuring new financial products represents a relatively new line of business within many financial firms and can be disruptive to routine business procedures. Financial engineers must compete for finite resources, such as management attention, access to capital, distribution channels, syndicate, technical, and research support. To be successful in an area of finance new to many people, financial engineers must constantly build and maintain internal organizational support and an infrastructure of managers, peers, and technicians who understand structured products, who share in the successes of such products, and who are willing to help advance structured product transactions.

The structured product offering process requires an integrated approach to organizational consensus building, process coordination, technical skill, and marketing insight. As mentioned, the financial engineer must communicate effectively in a nontechnical way with a varied constituency (e.g., senior managers, traders, investors, sales personnel, regulators, attorneys, middle managers, etc.). He or she must engage in a new product creation and development process that includes:

1. Identifying investor demand
2. The idea generation and structuring process
3. Legal and regulatory review and registration
4. Underwriting, syndicating, and marketing
5. Pricing, valuing, trading, and hedging

Topics 1–4 are discussed in this chapter. Topic 5 is discussed in Chapter 4.

IDENTIFYING INVESTOR DEMAND

It is important to establish a regular dialogue with those in charge of channels of distribution—that is, the institutional, retail, and private client sales forces. By holding regular new product meetings with marketing and syndicate personnel (preferably including lunch to boost attendance), an agenda of product ideas can be advanced and prioritized according to market opportunities. Through new product meetings, opinions can be assessed, reactions can be gauged to new product proposals, and resources can be allocated to viable structures.

For over-the-counter (OTC) products sold to institutional buyers, morning trader meetings provide a good daily source of ideas. OTC trades can be structured, priced, marketed, and sold on a day-to-day or week-to-week basis. A single or limited number of institutional buyers can provide the economic impetus to pursue an OTC transaction. There are usually relatively few offering costs or regulatory constraints associated with OTC trades. Usually the only effort involved is the time required for structuring a deal, pricing it, and preparing a term sheet (see the sample term sheets in the Resource Guide).

Publicly offered deals, however, require more lead time and consensus building to launch. They require many more buyers, access to larger distribution channels, and months of effort, and are expensive to structure and launch. As a result of the expense, time, and risk of bringing them to market, public deals typically justify greater profit margins than OTC transactions.

The driving force behind any offering is investor demand. With public offerings, soundings of the marketplace are made by financial engineers and retail marketing professionals at various steps in the product development process. Potential investor demand can be assessed using broker surveys that are faxed throughout worldwide retail and institutional distribution networks. The data collected from such market soundings can be studied in new product meetings to determine whether additional steps should be taken and resources committed to an offering. During the new product research and development process, brokers frequently ask questions about product pricing, research, investor suitability requirements, tax issues, and theoretical secondary trading characteristics of the product. This dialogue can provide clues to needed changes in product structures and provide marketing insights for further meetings, marketing presentations, conference calls, and branch office "road show" visits.

The category of product offered must be matched to the appropriate broker and his or her group of investors. Specialized niche products, such as currency warrants, are often marketed to specific groups of brokers and speculative investors familiar with related exchange rate volatility and trading characteristics. Products based on well-known, broad-based equity indices (e.g., the Nikkei 225 or S&P 500), those with enhanced yields (e.g., ELNs, discussed later), or those providing principal protection (e.g., index- or other asset-linked notes, also discussed later) are often marketed to wider investor audiences.

Also, it is important for the financial engineer to monitor in-house research on various markets and asset classes. Although many ideas originate from the front page of *The Wall Street Journal*, internally published research reports usually provide the most compelling incentives for allocating resources to the development of particular ideas.

EXAMPLE: The yen/dollar exchange rate reached a low of 79 yen to the dollar in April of 1995 and was the topic of national media reports. Many investors called their brokers looking for a way to benefit from a potential rally in the dollar. The conditions appeared to exist for launching an initial public offering of currency warrants.

- News articles were appearing daily focusing on Japan/U.S. trade relations and exchange rates.
- Published research forecast a weakening yen.
- With an SEC "shelf" registration in place that allowed for a quick "takedown" of currency warrants, investor demand, attractive pricing, and an established track record, an originator of such products launched a currency warrant offering. Offering costs were approximately $250,000 for legal, printing, and other services.
- Within two weeks, a new currency warrant offering was listed and began trading on the New York Stock Exchange.
- Within two months, investors enjoyed a 300 percent return on investment as the dollar rallied above 100 yen per dollar and each warrant appreciated from $5.00 to $20.00 in secondary trading.

Once structured products are sold, follow-on research reports should be provided to brokers on a regular basis so that they have ready access to information to discuss with clients. Since structured products are often based on transient market opportunities, investors must often lock-in profits or minimize losses in a timely fashion. Profits are well received, losses obviously are not. A broker with poor responses to inquiries can lose credibility with clients, damage relationships, and, as a result, wait years before considering another structured product offering. Therefore, financial engineers should notify brokers of follow-on research that supports existing structured products. Research and concise, one-page trading reports often provide sales personnel with value-added information for discussions with investors.

THE IDEA GENERATION AND
STRUCTURING PROCESS

In pursuit of new ideas, financial engineers must regularly analyze world financial markets. As ideas take shape, basic product structures are usually
outlined on term sheets that can be used for potential new offerings. In the
case of publicly listed transactions, stock exchanges should be consulted
periodically to determine the listing eligibility, regulatory requirements,
and availability of listing rules for new products. Stock exchange officials,
in seeking new listings for their exchanges, are often a helpful source for
new product ideas.

New ideas flow from the structuring process itself and through en-
gagement in developing financial solutions to investor problems. As daily
problems arise, research into legal, regulatory, and tax issues often exposes
new structures. With further analysis, the duration, payoff pattern, type of
registration, customers, and pricing of a proposed structure can be adjusted
until viable solutions emerge. Through an iterative process involving continuous discussions with brokers, branch managers, investors, colleagues,
and regulators, ideas coalesce and gain viability, and new products emerge.
Ideas can also be distilled out of the hundreds of telephone conversations
each week with brokers asking questions about new or existing instruments.

Often, world events, natural disasters, or civil unrest trigger new product ideas. For example, the U.S. Congressional passage of the North American
Free Trade Agreement (NAFTA) generated heightened interest in Mexican
equity-linked notes. A hurricane in Florida produced demand for call warrants on a basket of lumber stocks in anticipation of a rise in construction activity. Also, public filings and registrations by competitors provide a source
of new or reconfigured permutations of existing financial structures.

Financial engineers in charge of new product development must oversee the overall structuring, registration, and marketing process. They engage in regulatory reviews, pricing research, and assessment of hedging
capabilities. When bringing new transactions to market, financial engineers
help assemble underwriting syndicates, negotiate license agreements with
warrant and calculation agents, and enter service contracts with commercial banks, trustees, banknote companies, and financial printers. Directing
the work of attorneys and controlling product development costs are critical responsibilities as well. (See the sample offering expense spreadsheet
and the working group checklist in the Resource Guide.)

The financial engineer also gives in-house presentations to retail and institutional sales, research, syndicate, and support personnel in order to explain new offerings. Once the formal marketing period on a live deal starts, the financial engineer often participates in retail and institutional conference call presentations, branch office visits (called "road shows"), and discussions with investors. As will be discussed, financial engineers must also support the syndicate desk in answering questions from potential underwriting participants and in coordinating the timing and commencement of trading. They must also monitor and trigger the start of related hedging and trading activities.

LEGAL AND REGULATORY REVIEW AND REGISTRATION

Structured product originators usually have a working knowledge of regulatory requirements in order to minimize legal costs and time delays in developing new types of transactions. In global OTC markets, where privately negotiated contractual arrangements among institutions and sophisticated individual investors are largely unregulated, the counterparties can consummate transactions in a matter of hours or days. The OTC structuring process has fewer steps than publicly traded instruments offered to retail investors. A financial engineer should be familiar with various asset classes and markets around the world and possess a general understanding of the relevant regulatory framework that governs the sale and trading of new financial instruments in those markets of focus. When work on a specific product is begun, and in conjunction with the other aspects of product development (e.g., review of published research, structuring, pricing, management presentations, marketing strategy, etc.), a comprehensive study of legal and regulatory issues influencing the particular market and product under development must be initiated by the financial engineer, using in-house and outside legal counsel retained to represent the issuer and underwriters.

In the United States one of the first steps taken when considering the development of any new structured product is to determine whether the instrument will come under the jurisdiction of the Commodity Futures Trading Commission (CFTC) or the Securities and Exchange Commission

(SEC). Under the Commodity Exchange Act (CEA), the CFTC has regulatory jurisdiction over all futures and commodity option transactions. In 1982, Congress amended the CEA and the federal securities laws dividing jurisdiction over options and futures contracts on financial instruments between the CFTC and the SEC. Pursuant to these amendments, the CFTC was granted exclusive jurisdiction over all futures on stock indexes and options on futures contracts, leaving jurisdiction over individual stock options and stock options on stock indexes to the SEC. Adding to the convolution of the U.S. regulatory regime, both the CFTC and SEC retain regulatory authority over currency options, with the CFTC having jurisdiction over currency options, futures, and options on futures, and the SEC having jurisdiction over currency options traded on a national securities exchange. In public offerings, where an effort is made to attract as many individual investors as possible, the CFTC regulatory environment is usually avoided unless the security has an embedded commodity future or option, in which case an exemption to the CEA is required to sell the offering. Only a small percentage of securities brokers and retail investors are qualified to engage in outright futures transactions, such as those involving physical commodities like oil and gold or financial "commodities," such as bond and currency futures. This provides a unique opportunity to create securities that have certain commodity components embedded within their structures.

Most publicly offered structured products in the United States are designed to fall under the jurisdiction of the SEC. Therefore, a basic understanding of the U.S. federal securities laws is essential for working in this area. If a new financial instrument is deemed to be a "security" under the federal securities laws,[1] its offer and sale must comply with federal securities laws, which are enforced by the SEC. Therefore, with regard to such laws, issuers and underwriters of structured derivative instruments are in the same regulatory position as any issuer and underwriter of new public securities offerings.

---

[1]The term *security* is defined in Section 2(1) of the Securities Act of 1933 and Section 3(a)(10) of the Securities Exchange Act of 1934 and generally refers to any "note, stock, treasury stock, bond, debenture, certificate of interest or participation in any profit-sharing agreement . . . put, call straddle, option or privilege on any security . . . or any put, call or straddle option or privilege entered into on a national securities exchange relating to foreign currency . . . ."

SEC Guidelines for Developing New Structured Products

As mentioned, privately negotiated OTC institutional investment contracts have fewer regulatory constraints than publicly issued securities. Regulatory oversight is generally less stringent with regard to nonpublic transactions sold to professional investors, but U.S. securities regulators go to great lengths to protect small investors and maintain confidence in the public markets. At any time the SEC may be reviewing dozens of rules filings on proposed new products submitted by various U.S. securities exchanges and other self-regulatory organizations (SROs) charged by the SEC with monitoring and regulating the markets where such new products are proposed to trade. Because of all the possible permutations and interpretations, a literal reading of existing stock exchange rules may not always provide a clear answer to questions about a new product's qualification for listing. As a result, the SROs engage in ongoing discussions and negotiations with the SEC. The SROs engage in this process in order to have innovative new rules that attract new listings for their organization while ensuring a marketplace that is safe and equitable for all investors. New listings attract investors, who generate transactions revenues for the exchange and its members. New rule filings are the often the feedstock for new listings (see the sample SEC rule filing comment letter in the Resource Guide).

Before an issuer files a registration statement with the SEC, an effort is made to ensure that the SEC believes that the listing of the new product is consistent with existing listing rules. Many SROs maintain informal channels of communication with the SEC's market regulation staff and can usually determine whether a new structure requires a formal rule amendment, which can frequently take months to obtain. The SEC has broad authority to approve or deny proposed securities exchange rule changes based on the principal that the rules of the exchange are designed to prevent fraudulent and manipulative acts and to promote just and equitable principles of trade. For example, as a result of the creation of warrants on a number of popular international equity indices (e.g., the Japanese Nikkei 225, French CAC-40, British FT-SE 100, and Hong Kong 30), the SEC established guidelines regarding the creation and listing of new index warrants:

- The index must be broad-based in the sense that it is composed principally of only the most actively traded and well capitalized stocks.

- The procedures for calculating the index must be clearly defined and understandable.

- The financial instruments related to the index are not likely to adversely impact U.S. securities markets or those in the country or countries where the constituent securities are traded.

- The index value must be widely disseminated and available to the public.

- Relevant customer suitability, disclosure, and compliance requirements must be established and followed.

- An exchange-to-exchange and/or government-to-government information sharing agreement for market surveillance purposes should be in effect between the exchange on which the new financial instrument is traded and the principal exchange or other market on which the constituent stocks comprising the index are traded.

Registration

Once the decision is made to launch an initial public offering of a structured product and a preliminary legal and regulatory review is completed, the drafting of a registration statement can be commenced by the issuer and underwriter's counsel in consultation with the financial engineer. Many investment banks who issue structured products maintain "shelf" registration statements, a type of filing under the Securities Act of 1933[2] that describes the basic elements of a specific category of security. They allow frequent issuers of a securities to preposition their offerings for immediate use when market conditions are optimal, without SEC registration delays.

---

[2]The Securities Act of 1933 specifies the types of disclosure that must be made in registrations with the SEC for the benefit of investors. Issuers of securities and their advisors are liable for any material misstatements or omissions of material facts in such disclosure documents, producing a significant legal and economic incentive to exercise great care in their preparation. In contrast, the Securities Exchange Act of 1934 regulates, in general, the periodic reporting requirements of companies with SEC registered securities and the formation, operation, and listing requirements of securities exchanges and other self-regulatory organizations where securities are publicly traded as well as the activities of broker–dealers.

In the United States corporations are the most frequent users of shelf registrations for periodic debt offerings under medium-term note programs. They are also very useful for publicly offered structured products. Such registrations provide a mechanism for issuers to launch multiple offerings as "takedowns" off the shelf without re-registering each issue. Each takedown must conform to the provisions of the base prospectus in the shelf registration. A takedown is effectuated through the use of a printed prospectus supplement that incorporates the terms of a specific offering and is "wrapped" around (i.e., included along with) a copy of the base prospectus.

The preliminary prospectus supplement (also called a "red herring," so named, in part, because of the red disclosure language printed on its side) is used in marketing the offering to potential investors. It is mailed to the branch offices of each underwriter participating in the offering syndicate. If it involves an instrument familiar to the SEC, a takedown involving a structured product can be effectuated relatively quickly (i.e., in a few days or a week, depending on the SEC's workload). For offerings involving "novel or unique" structures, a takedown can still be used, but it is very important to solicit comments from the SEC's market regulation and corporation finance staffs.

The SEC is usually sensitive to market conditions on which publicly offered structured derivative products are based and has proven to be proficient at providing timely comments on shelf takedowns. Financial engineers and their legal advisors work closely with the SEC to ensure that initial public offerings run smoothly. If the SEC provides significant unanticipated comments after a red herring is mailed to investors, marketing delays can occur while a revised document is reprinted and recirculated. See the Resource Guide for a sample working group checklist that details assignments of responsibility for many of the steps that must be taken and in launching public offerings.

Without a preregistered shelf registration statement, the SEC registration, review, and comment process generally takes between 30 and 90 days or more, depending on the novelty of the structure and the area of the SEC where the registration is reviewed (e.g., registrations for trust structures can often take more time than routine equity and debt-based securities registrations). Certain OTC transactions involving professional and institutional investors may be exempt from SEC registration (e.g., private placements) but are still subject to certain SEC disclosure requirements and antifraud requirements, thus requiring the use of a disclosure document, much like prospectuses used for publicly offered transactions.

Securities Exchange Listing Requirements for Structured Products

Each of the U.S. national securities exchanges has similar listing requirements for structured products, the following of which relate to index warrants:

- Minimum size and distribution requirements (e.g., a minimum of 1,000,000 warrants must be sold to at least 400 public investors)
- Minimum financial standards for the issuer (e.g., $100,000,000 net worth and operating profitability)
- Minimum issue price of $3.00 per warrant

Listing standards are designed to ensure that issuers are capable of meeting their financial obligations to investors and that there is sufficient public distribution and trading liquidity to ensure a "fair and orderly market." Structured products are viewed by regulators as being inherently speculative and complex and are frequently restricted to investors with option-approved accounts. In other instances, regulatory concerns over the possible impact of a derivative security on the underlying cash market may result in some limit being placed on the number of securities that can be created.[3] For example, in approving the rule filing for equity-linked notes (ELNs are described in Chapter 8), the SEC required a minimum market capitalization of $3 billion and certain minimum equity trading volume requirements for companies on which ELNs are based; ELN issues are limited in size to not more than 5 percent of the total outstanding shares of the company on which the ELN is based. See the Resource Guide for a sample comment letter on an SEC rule filing from a hypothetical industry working group relating to SEC proposals for a new category of index warrants.

---

[3]For example, there is an SEC-mandated limit to the number of warrants based on domestic U.S. equity indexes that can be outstanding at any one time.

UNDERWRITING, SYNDICATING, AND MARKETING STRUCTURED PRODUCTS

Underwriting

Securities underwriters are typically brokerage firms that organize offerings of financial products and engage in the economic, legal, quantitative, and marketing process involved with offering such products to investors. In the case of structured products, much like corporate transactions involving traditional common stock and bond offerings, the firm with the principal role in originating a transaction is often the lead manager, who is said to "manage the books" (i.e., perform the various administrative duties required of a lead manager). As will be discussed in further detail, the underwriting process for structured products also encompasses the active solicitation of indications of interest in the proposed offering from other broker–dealers participating as underwriting syndicate and selling group members. Although nonpublic institutional offerings are similar, the following discussion relates to public structured product offerings in the United States.

Structured products, although growing in popularity, are usually sold through a core cadre of brokers to investors who meet certain specific investment suitability criteria mandated by regulators and internal legal and compliance departments. Sometimes there is enough demand within a firm's distribution networks (retail and institutional) to launch an economically viable transaction and, if publicly offered and listed on an exchange, to meet their minimum listing requirements (e.g., 1,000,000 warrants sold to at least 400 investors for at least $3.00 per unit of investment). Many times, however, it is necessary to boost the size of a structured transaction by building interest through underwriting syndicates.

Syndicating

Assembling a group of underwriters interested in forming an underwriting syndicate for an offering is typically the purview of the syndicate department, particularly with routine corporate transactions. However, because of their unique nature, derivative transactions require a specialized marketing effort that is often shared between the syndicate department and structured products group. Financial engineers are usually involved in making presentations and discussing the terms of a particular structured product offering with syndicate personnel at many large Wall Street and regional U.S. brokerage firms. In-house syndicate personnel therefore tend to work closely with financial engineers when responding to inquiries from potential syndicate and selling-group participants about structured product offerings.

Prior to an offering, discussions are held with numerous other investment banks to assess potential demand for a new offering and to determine who is to be included as syndicate or selling-group members (see the Resource Guide for a sample underwriting syndicate invitation). Firms that do not join the underwriting syndicate often participate as selling-group members. Selling-group members, individually, do not usually distribute a large amount of securities, but their combined efforts are often critical to the success of an offering. Selling-group members earn sales credits (discussed later) based on the pro rata amount of securities they sell. They do not, however, share the underwriter's fee. Selling-group members do, however, share the underwriter's liability.[4]

Underwriting and selling-group discussions take place for several weeks prior to pricing an offering, as internal broker surveys are conducted in each firm that expresses an interest in participating in the offering. Terms of the structure and preliminary pricing information are shared with potential comanagers, underwriting syndicate members, and the selling group, who then go back to their respective marketing and syndicate departments to assess potential investor demand.

Once syndicate invitations are accepted and comanagers are determined, a "shadow book" is built from indications of interest received from each participant in the offering. The shadow book provides information on potential demand that allows for a decision on whether to proceed with the offering. The business terms of an underwritten transaction usually start with an indication to sell the product to investors on a "best efforts" basis (i.e., sales will be made if possible, but no guarantee is made to sell or "place" a specific quantity of the new product).

---

[4]*Underwriter's liability* refers to the obligations incumbent upon comanagers of securities offerings to share in any potential damages claimed by and awarded (through arbitration or legal action) to investors, resulting from possible material omissions from or misrepresentations made about the security described in an offering document (i.e., the red herring or prospectus supplement, if a shelf takedown is involved).

Profits from a structured product offering arise principally from three sources:

1. Gross spread
2. Hedge profits
3. Trading profits

The gross spread is traditionally the amount added to the price of an offering to cover offering costs (e.g., legal, printing, etc.) and to compensate the brokers and, in traditional industrial deals, the investment bankers[5] involved in originating an offering. The gross spread can range from 1 percent to 7 or 8 percent, depending on the type of offering (notes, common stock, index warrants, etc.); 2 to 3 percent is typical for index- and asset-linked note offerings. Five percent is the norm for most index warrant offerings or 5 cents for every dollar raised in the offering.

The 5 percent gross spread, for example, is usually divided as follows: 60 percent for the sales credit (3 percentage points), 40 percent for the underwriting fee (1 percentage point), 40 percent for the management fee (1 percentage point). The sales credit goes to the retail brokerage or institutional sales sides of each firm involved in the offering, on a pro rata basis (i.e., based on the amount of securities sold by each firm). The broker at each firm involved in the underwriting usually receives 25–50 percent of the sales credit relating to his or her sales of the structured product being offered to investors, the balance of which is retained by the broker's firm. The higher a broker's production level (i.e., the level of his or her annual sales revenues) the higher "grid" or percent payout he or she earns. Sales credits are usually paid to brokers monthly. The underwriting fee is allocated to the lead manager's costs in bringing the deal, such as legal, printing, road show, and other offering costs. Any amount available after the allocation of such costs is split among the comanagers. Any unallocated underwriting fees, as well as the management fee, are split among the comanagers on a negotiated basis, often equally or, in some cases, with a

---

[5]In structured product transactions, financial engineers usually assume a role similar to that an investment banker fulfills in a traditional corporate finance transaction. Although there are overlapping capabilities, financial engineers usually focus their efforts on capital market and securities trading activities, whereas bankers concentrate on more traditional corporate finance activities.

higher portion of the split going to one firm or another, depending on placement capability or as a "sweetener" to encourage participation in the underwriting at the outset. The amount of management and underwriting fees earned by each syndicate member often forms the basis for determining annual bonus compensation for those individuals at each firm involved in bringing a transaction to market. On a $30 million offering the 1 percent management fee would be $300,000, split evenly, for example, among three firms or $100,000 credited to each firm and some portion of that amount allocated to the annual bonus pool for the individuals and groups involved in the offering.

Unique to structured products, unlike traditional investment banking transactions, are the potential postoffering hedge and trading profits that may accrue to the firm that structures, hedges, and engages in secondary trading of the offering. If the risk management activities are successful over the life of a structured product, such profits can be significantly greater than those resulting from the gross spread. The firm responsible for setting the hedge must manage the position-risk associated with such structured product obligations for the life of the product. If a loss occurs in managing the hedge, the issuing firm must still fund any obligations to investors. Hedge profits, if they are realized, are usually amortized over the life of an instrument, based on the ongoing results of the risk management activities, and represent a risk-adjusted return on investment.

Marketing

Once all of the foregoing premarketing activities are finalized (i.e., idea generation, structuring, legal, and syndicating), senior and middle management executives of the lead managing firm, who would have already given the preliminary go-ahead to initiate the offering, are advised and consulted by the financial engineer of his or her recommendation to proceed with the offering. Once the final go-ahead is given, the legal documentation work for the offering commences. The financial engineer, in-house derivative legal counsel, and underwriter's and issuer's counsel begin the documentation process, summarized as follows:

- A draft of red herring is prepared and provided to the lead manager with copies provided to comanagers for comments.

- A final draft is provided to the SEC for comments; discussions are held among the SEC staff, financial engineer, in-house counsel, and underwriter's counsel.
- SEC comments, if any, are incorporated into the final draft of the red herring and then provided on computer disk to the printer.
- Printed red herrings are distributed to worldwide offices of syndicate and selling-group members.
- Broker marketing memos are prepared by each firm involved in the underwriting and distributed separately within each firm (see the Resource Guide for sample marketing memos).
- Preliminary pricing of the instrument is determined by the firm responsible for hedging and risk management, and "price talk" (i.e., a range of offering prices) is provided to sales personnel.
- Formal marketing activities commence.
- Legal counsel continues with the preparation of the stock exchange listing application, underwriting, warrant or trust agreements, SEC filings and document submissions, NASD notices, opinion of qualified independent underwriter[6] (QIU), due diligence, and other legal matters.

As the documentation process proceeds, the financial engineer coordinates all internal marketing activities with retail and institutional sales managers and brokers. A road show schedule is developed and a team of financial engineers divides up responsibilities for branch visits (see the Resource Guide for a sample road show schedule). Conference calls are arranged with division managers in worldwide offices followed by conference call presentations to brokers. Facsimile notices of the offering are provided to retail and institutional sales personnel. The deal status, basic terms, and timing information are often provided to brokers through mar-

---

[6]A written fairness opinion from a QIU is, under certain circumstances, required pursuant to NASD (National Association of Securities Dealers) Schedule E requirements relating to the fairness to the investor of the pricing of the structured product to be issued where potential conflicts of interest could arise where the issuer and the lead underwriter are affiliated entities. A QIU provides comfort to investors that the pricing of the instrument being offered is fair relative to other publicly traded instruments and market conditions affecting the asset upon which the structured product is based.

keting memos and on an electronic syndicate offering calendar through computerized broker workstations. Internal radio announcements are made by financial engineers about the structure and timing of the offering. (See the Resource Guide for sample marketing memos.) Research analysts also discuss published reports about the market or asset class on which the structured product being offered is based.

As interest in the offering builds, a pricing date is set and the sales effort intensifies as the pricing date approaches. As "tickets are dropped" (i.e., as customer orders are collected from brokers by branch order rooms and conveyed electronically or by telephone to the lead manager's syndicate desk), the book of orders builds and the marketing effort reaches a crescendo. Customer suitability is monitored by internal compliance departments to ensure adherence to internal procedures and stock exchange requirements (see the Resource Guide for sample information relating to customer suitability and compliance matters). Final due diligence meetings are held among comanagers to review and confirm the acceptability of all legal and financial matters relating to the issuer. During the last few days prior to the pricing date, the size of the deal often increases dramatically as brokers call customers and drop tickets once they feel certain that the deal is coming. During this critical time, time delays in bringing the offering can "spook" the book (i.e., cause brokers and investors to withdraw or hold tickets). Time delays in any type of public or private offering can cause brokers and investors to question the investment thesis or pricing and they may back away from the deal. Therefore, in structured product transactions, as in traditional corporate finance transactions, it is critical for the financial engineer to hold to the pricing deadline if at all possible, even if the deal is not fully sold, in order to bolster confidence and prompt smooth ticketing.

Once the requisite number of customer orders is collected, the deal is "sized" (i.e., the final number of instruments to be sold or "printed" is agreed upon) and the product is "priced" (i.e., a price is determined by the financial engineer in conjunction with risk managers and traders). In the case of instruments based on foreign markets, the sizing may be done, but the pricing may occur overnight so that risk managers and traders can set the hedge and price the product off the closing prices of the foreign market. For example, warrants on the Nikkei 225 Index must be priced early in the morning in New York on the day after the ticketing deadline and sizing but after the Tokyo Stock Exchange closes for trading in Japan). Once pricing occurs and the terms of the deal are set (e.g., the strike, expiration or maturity date, size of the deal, price, etc.), underwriting agreements are ex-ecuted, the qualified independent underwriter provides the lead under-writer with a fairness opinion, if necessary, attesting to the equitable pricing of the instrument to the investors, and then the lead manager "breaks syndicate" (i.e., all orders that have been placed by syndicate and selling-group members are considered final and the syndicate group is legally disbanded for that particular offering.) Press releases are then pro-vided to the news media to announce the terms and pricing of the offering and final prospectus supplements are printed and distributed to investors. Stock exchange trading commences for the new structured product and risk managers, traders, the stock exchange specialist, floor brokers, in-vestment executives, investors, senior managers, and the investment com-munity at large monitor the commencement of secondary trading activity.

Approximately three days after the pricing date a closing occurs where all documents relating to the offering are executed and all funds from the offering, net of sales credits, are paid to the appropriate parties (e.g., the issuer, hedge counterparty, structurer). An accounting of syndi-cate expenses usually occurs over the following 90 days, and a distribution is made of pro rata underwriting and management fees to the comanagers.

CONCLUSION

Less than 10 years ago, ad hoc groups of traders, investment bankers, at-torneys, and other professionals came together periodically to solve spe-cific financial problems involving a loose conglomeration of instruments and strategies referred to collectively as derivatives. As new types of trans-actions occurred, evidence emerged from early successes and failures that a great deal of opportunity lay in a new and highly profitable area of fi-nance now referred to by industry professionals as financial engineering. As a profession, financial engineering appears to be solidifying. New prod-uct development processes are being created, the identification and culti-vation of investor demand are being refined, legal and regulatory issues are being clarified, and pre- and postoffering marketing skills are being per-fected. Chapter 4 provides a summary of the constituent concepts of pric-ing, valuing, trading, and hedging new structured financial instruments.

4

OVERVIEW OF PRICING, VALUING, TRADING, AND HEDGING STRUCTURED PRODUCTS

This chapter provides an overview of basic option terminology and some fundamentals regarding pricing, valuing, trading, and hedging structured financial products. This overview illuminates certain very general and basic quantitative concepts of financial engineering and provides continuity as the discussion moves into specific structured product descriptions and examples in the chapters ahead.

BASIC OPTION TERMINOLOGY

Option contracts provide the buyer (*holder*) with the right but not the obligation to buy from (*calls*) or to sell to (*puts*) the seller (*writer*) the underlying asset (e.g., stocks, bonds, currencies, commodities) at a specified price or starting point (the *strike price* or *exercise price*) for determining the intrinsic value of an option at a point in time or during a specific period of time (the *term*). Prior to (*American style*) or at the end of (*European style*) the term (the *expiration date*) the holder can exercise the option if it has any cash value (*intrinsic value*) or let it expire if it is worthless. The holder pays and the writer receives cash for an option (the *premium*).

When puts decrease in value, the asset price on which they are based moves above the strike price, whereupon the puts are said to be trading *out-of-the-money*. When the underlying asset price moves below the strike price, the puts increase in value and are said to be trading *in-the-money*. When puts or calls trade at the strike, they are said to be trading *at-the-money* and have no cash intrinsic value. Calls increase in value as the underlying asset price moves above the strike price. They are then said to be in-the-money. As the asset price decreases below the strike, the calls are said to be trading out-of-the-money. If not exercised by the end of their terms (or automatically exercised by operation of rule or contract), both put and call options expire.

The market value of an option consists of two main parts: intrinsic value and time value. *Intrinsic value* is the dollar amount by which an option trades in-the-money (above the strike price if a call and below the strike price if a put). *Time value* is the amount by which an option price exceeds any intrinsic value and represents that part of the value of an option relating to the amount of time left until the instrument expires. Time value declines over the life of the instrument but also represents the option's potential to acquire more intrinsic value before it expires.[1]

VALUING STRUCTURED PRODUCTS

As mentioned in the Introduction, derivative securities and contracts are the elemental building blocks of structured products and include forward contracts and option contracts. Because of their flexibility (e.g., the ability to adjust the life span of "term," the strike price, and other components), options are an integral part of and form the basis for creating and valuing many structured derivative products.

Options are often used for speculating on stock price movements. They are also used by investors for risk management purposes, helping to

---

[1]John F. Marshall and Vipul K. Bansal, *Financial Engineering: A Complete Guide to Financial Innovation* (New York, NYIF, 1992), 337–362.

preserve the benefit of favorable stock price movements and minimizing losses from price declines. Option theory provides a convenient and adaptable base from which to address risk and construct solutions to financial problems. Therefore, because of their integral role in many structured financial products, options must be properly valued in order to accurately manage risk and capture profits. In evaluating structured derivative products, it is necessary to deconstruct them into their component parts. Much of the work conducted in developing structured products relates to pricing their various components. Debt and equity components are valued using traditional yield to maturity, net present value, book value, earnings ratios, and other established financial ratios and financial statement analysis. The option component embedded in many structured instruments must also be valued to determine if it is over-, under-, or "fairly" priced.

Options are valued by analyzing the following data:

- The strike of the underlying asset
- The underlying stock, bond, or other asset price(s)
- Time until expiration of the option
- Dividend rate (stocks) or yield (bonds)
- Interest rate assumptions
- The price volatility of the underlying asset

Such data is input into computerized option pricing models to generate valuations needed for accurate pricing, hedging, and trading strategies. Entire portfolios can be studied to determine their behavior under a variety of market conditions. Portfolios can also be compared against each other to determine how they behave against a range of values for one or more constituent securities and to structure desired payoff patterns. It may be necessary to construct a portfolio of securities that provides a specific range of payoffs at certain points in time in order to hedge market exposure or to implement strategies reflecting particular market views. Computerized pricing models provide structured product and derivative trading teams with a powerful tool for valuing, pricing, and managing the market risk associated with a wide variety of financially engineered products.

Most option pricing parameters just discussed are readily determinable (i.e., strike, asset price, expiration, and dividend rate or yield). The financial engineer can also select a future interest rate for input into computerized pricing models based on economic forecasts or other assumptions, but the direction and magnitude of price volatility are among the most difficult option pricing parameters to quantify.

Volatility is a measure of the frequency and intensity of price changes of the asset on which an option is based. Of the problems in managing market price risk, volatility is perhaps the most critical determinant because of its pronounced effect on option valuations and overall profitability of a structured instrument. The more volatile the price of an asset, the greater the price risk exposure and the greater the expense in buying put and call options to hedge such exposure. Volatility and its effects on option pricing are evaluated by using various proprietary mathematical "black box" models run on computers. Most broker–dealers engaging in derivative trading have computerized option valuation programs refined from the original Black–Scholes option pricing model.[2] Volatility measures the percentage deviation of the price of an asset from its expected value and is a function of market conditions.

Historical volatility is measurable by computing the historic price changes of the underlying asset. Implied or future volatility is unknowable and must be estimated from calculations by using the option model pricing parameters previously discussed (i.e., strike, price, term, etc.). Implied volatility can be solved for when all the other option pricing variables are given. In conducting pricing research, for example, option price quotations are solicited from competing dealers and help form computer model inputs for reverse engineering solutions for implied volatility. Such solutions represent attempts to predict future volatility.

HEDGING AND TRADING STRUCTURED PRODUCTS

Protecting or *hedging* investments requires the ability to quantify and manage risk over time. *Delta hedging* refers to a risk management strategy whereby an offsetting option position is established in an underlying se-

---

[2]The Black–Scholes options pricing model was introduced by Fischer Black and Myron Scholes at the University of Chicago in 1973, concurrently with the development of standardized, exchange-traded options at that time and based on the needs of investors to determine the fair value of options.

curity equal to the option position multiplied by the value of its delta (to be defined). *Dynamic hedging* includes changing the structure of a risk management strategy employed in response to or in anticipation of market events. An example is selling stock index futures in order to collect premium dollars, to protect stock portfolios from adverse price movements and thus eliminate market risk without incurring stock transaction fees. (Note: Stock transaction fees are higher than the fees associated with using futures instruments; in this case, futures also allow investors to protect their stock portfolios without losing dividend cash flows from the stocks themselves.)

At times, trading positions may be "naked," that is unhedged or at risk for a period of time and as to a portion or possibly all of their notional[3] value. In the case of "unmatched" positions where the term of a hedge is different from that of the related instrument, a loss is possible if the actual volatility at each roll point[4] over the term of the instrument is greater than the implied volatility assumed when the hedge position was first established (i.e., "roll risk"). Firms may hedge a portion of the risk associated with a market position by using listed options, futures, and options on futures, as well as replicating the index with securities in the underlying cash market. On occasion, a hedge may consist entirely of OTC options purchased from creditworthy counterparties.

The management of risk associated with option price changes are quantifiable using the following mathematical constructs:

> ***Delta (index or stock risk).***   The percentage amount an option's price changes in response to a change in the price of the underlying asset. It is also generally an approximate measure of the probability

---

[3]*Notional* refers to the aggregate dollar amount of underlying assets that are controlled by a derivative instrument: the amount of "leverage" that serves as the basis for calculating the potential payoff to the counterparties to the instrument and the amount that is at risk and must be hedged by the issuing party. When a derivative instrument controls a multiple of the underlying asset, the issue price of each unit times the number of units sold times the multiplier equals the notional amount. For example, if a derivative is priced at $50 but it sells better if priced to investors in $5 units, the multiplier is $10 ($10 × $5 = $50). If 5,000,000 units are sold, the notional amount of the offering is $250,000,000 ($5 × 5,000,000 × $10 = $250,000,000).

[4]A *roll point* in time occurs when some or all of a hedge position is reestablished because of the expiration of one of its component securities (i.e., a listed option or future). The price risk associated with reestablishing such hedge is called *roll risk*.

that an option will finish its life in-the-money. This is simply the risk of having a net long or short position in the market. The net delta position is managed by setting limits per index, country, and the firm's derivative business as a whole.

Gamma (actual volatility).   The percentage amount by which an option's delta will change in price in relation to the price of the underlying security. Gamma is a function of the time remaining until expiration of the option. It is the risk due to changes in the net delta position resulting from changes in the level of the market, index, or stock.

Vega (traded volatility, also known as kappa).   The dollar amount of change of an option price with a 1-point change in the volatility of the underlying security. Most option transactions are long dated and highly sensitive to changes in the level of volatility implied by the market. Vega risk can be built up very quickly on a trading desk. It does not take too many institutional-sized transactions to build a big vega position, and if the market flow is one way for an extended period of time, vega risk can grow very quickly. Fortunately, long-term volatility levels are more stable than short-term levels. It is important from a risk management perspective to prevent traders from covering long-term over-the-counter (OTC) vega by buying short-term vega because of the high probability of a volatility curve divergence. Volatility curves move just as much as yield curves. Vega risk can be managed by setting vega limits on each asset class, index, country, stock, and so on. Sublimits can be placed on individual structured products or other positions and monitored on a real-time basis by management via electronic links to trading floor computer systems and pricing models.

Theta (option time decay).   The dollar amount by which an option price changes due to changes in time to expiration, often thought of as the amount of *time value decay* that occurs in the price of an option as it approaches expiration. (Note: time value decay is the amount of decline of an option price as it approaches expiration; it is also called *erosion* or *evaporation* of time premium.) Theta is the profit or loss in an option book due to the passage of time and therefore the decay of an option's premium. Both theta and gamma risk can be managed together by setting exposure limits based on worst-case one-day price swings given, for example, either a 3 percent up move, a 3 percent down move, or no change for a day.

Rho (interest rate risk).   The dollar amount of change in an option price due to changes in interest rates. Interest rate risk is very large for long-term options. A change in market rates of interest changes the forward index price even if the spot index is unchanged. Rho risk is managed by placing currency-adjusted limits on trading positions and hedging such risk using interest rate futures, options, or swaps.

Other risks that must be managed with regard to structured product, derivative, or stock and bond positions include the following:

Currency Exchange Rate Risk.   Currency exchange rate risk arises through long or short positions held on a broker–dealer's global derivative trading desk. Such positions include index options, foreign margin and bank balances, foreign index and interest rate futures contracts, foreign currency interest rate swaps, and index forwards. Exchange rate risk in U.S. dollar terms is managed by establishing a dollar equivalent limit for each currency, using such instruments as foreign exchange forward and futures contracts, currency options, and spot market cash currencies,

Yield Curve Risk.   Risk due to shift in the slope of yield curves; monitored using a "slope matrix" report, extremely complex to limit and difficult to hedge.

Basis Risk.   Cash market or other position risk exposure versus futures or other derivative markets.

Liquidity Risk.   Level of trading volume and float (a lack of liquidity can make it difficult in setting and unwinding hedge positions).

Changes in Dividend Yields.   Difficult to hedge but usually a marginal risk that is smaller than interest rate risk; in creating a two-way flow of business, dividend assumptions usually net out, otherwise the risk is hedged using OTC forward contracts.

Timing and Exercise Risk.   Option contracts should expire on days (accounting for foreign holidays) and at times of day (adjusted for time zone differences) that allow traders to set or unwind hedges.

Credit Risk.   Relating to counterparty creditworthiness.

Market Disruption Events.   Usually covered in contract documentation that provides certain limits or cancellation of exercise rights if liquidity in certain cash and futures markets fails to exist.

Discontinuance of Index Calculation.   Contract document provision that provides for an alternative method of index calculation if the primary calculator fails to update the index values or the cash securities underlying the index cease to trade.

Legal Risks.   Risks associated with customer suitability for or authorization to purchase or trade certain types of investments, compliance with securities regulations, disclosure materials, copyrights, and so on.

New Product Risks.   Risks arising from incorrect assumptions, computerized pricing models, or errors made in structuring a new product or about the underlying asset or market; can be partially mitigated by deferring profit realization or amortizing profits over the life of the instrument until more experience is gained.

Once a new structured product is launched and hedged, it is often necessary for the broker–dealer to create or support a secondary trading market for the product. With exchange-listed products, trading-floor specialists provide some of the secondary trading price support and liquidity. Even so, a portion of the expected profits realized by an issuer of structured products may be used by its derivative trading desk to support the market price of recent offerings in order to prevent price discontinuities caused by the deduction of the gross spread from the offering proceeds. In other words, once the gross spread (i.e., the broker sales credit, underwriting fee, and management fee) has been deducted from the offering proceeds, the value of the instrument is theoretically worth proportionately less. To prevent an immediate decline of the price of the instrument in the secondary market, the derivative trading desk of the broker–dealer involved in hedging a particular structured product may support the trading price of such instruments at their theoretical fair market value. Such secondary trading activity by broker–dealers is often referred to as an "upstairs" market. As the price of the underlying asset on which the structured product is based fluctuates over time, upstairs market makers and the securities exchange specialist buy and sell the related structured product. When the structured product eventually moves into a new trading range, secondary market support can gradually be reduced. Sometimes the visibility of an exchange listing draws in new buyers that were not involved in the initial public offering underwriting syndicate. A surplus of buyers can cause the price to increase as a scarcity value is attached to the instrument.

With regard to OTC products sold to institutions or individual investors, broker–dealers usually make upstairs markets in such instruments, which is managed in much the same way as public offerings, only with the participation of fewer investors. Often, due to the tight profit margins associated with issuing some OTC derivative products, secondary market support is less aggressive. Derivative trading desks often pay less when repurchasing OTC products by widening the bid-ask spread or just lowering their assessment of the fair market value of such instruments.

With either public or privately placed structured products, active market making by derivative trading desks can be the source of significant profitability over the life of such instruments. Firms that originate specific structured products are usually the best equipped to benefit from misvaluations. They typically have the valuation models, hedging, and trading expertise necessary to identify instruments that trade above (selling opportunities) or below (buying opportunities) their theoretical fair market value in the secondary market.

For further information about option valuation, see the Resource Guide for a spreadsheet of sample pricing information. The item entitled "Options as Sport" is an illuminating comparison of option valuation theory to a basketball game. The Guide also provides a collection of sample structured product term sheets.

CONCLUSION

Subsequent chapters are dedicated to reviewing the basic characteristics of a number of structured financial products presently available to individual investors, professional investment managers, and corporate clients around the world. While the product categories presented herein are extensive, they do not encompass every type of derivative product in use and available. Such a compendium is more practically the purview of a more encyclopedic financial text or series.

PART TWO

The Specifics of Structured Financial Products

5

WARRANTS

This chapter briefly describes warrants and how they are structured, issued, and valued. Warrants based on currency exchange rates were first offered publicly in the United States in the late 1980s. They were initially included in corporate debt offerings as sweeteners to entice investors into offerings; an investment in the bonds would also include a publicly listed currency warrant that could be held or traded whenever the investor desired to do so. Unfortunately, the early currency warrants did not perform very well. They were issued during a period of time when the dollar was getting weaker around the world. Most of them expired worthless after several years, although they continued to be popular because of their ease of use and similarity to trading stocks on securities exchanges. In early 1990, the American Stock Exchange gained approval to trade warrants based on the Japanese Nikkei Stock Average. Over a dozen offerings of Nikkei warrants were launched and proved to be extremely popular among investors. The Japanese market declined dramatically in the early 1990s, and the put warrants based on the Nikkei Stock Average increased in value, some as much as 900 percent. Soon after, warrants based on the British, French, Hong Kong, and U.S. stock market indices and on the bond yields and baskets of currencies discussed in this chapter were also offered.

Economically, warrants are very similar to long dated options (i.e., options that have terms equal to or longer than one year). They are sold in private and public transactions. Public offerings are underwritten and often listed for secondary trading on securities exchanges around the world. Whereas the settlement of standardized listed options is guaranteed by an exchange or clearinghouse, warrants are backed by the creditworthiness of a corporate or governmental issuer.

Warrants can be based on U.S. and foreign equity indices, stock baskets on industry sectors, currency exchange rates, interest rates, and other assets or indices. They are often similar to long-term option contracts (one to five years) and can be linked to major international stock indices, such as those based on stocks trading in Hong Kong, Japan, Britain, France, Europe, and so on. Warrants can be issued in the United States as Securities and Exchange Commission (SEC) registered, underwritten initial public offerings, or in private transactions.

As with many other types of option-based or option-linked structured products, the potential profitability associated with originating warrants is achieved through the ability of product originators to capture *volatility spreads* (i.e., the difference between the price a product can be sold for and the price at which a hedge can be purchased, in terms of price volatility), through fees associated with underwriting and selling such instruments (e.g., sales credits, management fees, and underwriting fees), and as a re-

---

EXAMPLE: An investor wants equity exposure to the growth potential of Taiwan but cannot do so without incurring significant transaction expenses in the Taiwanese cash market and does not want to pay the management fees associated with mutual fund investments:

The investor, who is experienced with and understands the risks of buying options and warrants, therefore buys U.S. exchange-listed call warrants on the Taiwan Index for $5.00 per warrant at the strike index level of 825.

In six months the Index moves up 60 percent to 1320 and each warrant trades for $12.50, a 150-percent gain.

Nine months after the issue date the index falls precipitously to 700 due to trade disagreements with China and the call warrants decline 80 percent to $2.50 per warrant.

---

sult of secondary trading (i.e., upstairs market making), whereby deal originators can try to leverage the learning curve advantage they obtained in
structuring, valuing, and pricing a product by trading such products during
periods of misvaluation (i.e., buying low and selling high).

Warrants can be issued by corporations, governments, or sovereign
entities as publicly offered or privately placed transactions. They are useful to investors in capturing, for example, long-term returns, hedging, speculating, securing U.S. dollar-denominated returns from non-U.S. assets, and
limiting downside price risk to cash market holdings. Warrants also provide a means for gaining investment exposure in other countries without
engaging in direct cash market transactions in other countries involving
commissions, costs, and currency translations that often make such transactions relatively more expensive.

An important point to emphasize is that, unlike a number of derivative instruments discussed in the news media that have unlimited risk
and can sometimes produce disastrous results, the risk to a warrant investor is limited to the dollar amount or premium paid for the instrument.
Such a premium, often between $3.00 and $10.00 per warrant in public
deals, provides an investor with exposure to a particular market or type of
asset for a specified period of time. If the investment does not work out,
the investor loses the dollar premium amount paid, no more. There are no
margin calls or unlimited financial risks associated with warrant investments. Just the amount invested is at risk, plus any transaction costs.
Also, since the types of warrants discussed in this chapter are often listed
for secondary trading on U.S. securities exchanges, they provide investors
with a convenient way to access international markets during U.S. trading
hours without having to conduct transactions in markets located in far
away time zones (e.g., U.S. investors can trade Nikkei warrants listed in
the United States during U.S. trading hours as opposed to trading in Japan
during Japanese trading hours).

Warrants are popular among financial engineers because of their flexibility. Like options, warrants can be shaped to suit desired goals. Their
terms, strike price, and overall pricing can be adjusted to suit investor
needs and, for example, to take advantage of the magnitude and time period over which a market is expected to move, as discussed in research reports providing the impetus for launching a new product (e.g., an offering
of warrants based on a weaker yen and a stronger U.S. dollar is based on a

research report indicating that the yen is expected to weaken against the dollar by 25 percent over a two-year period).

Once a warrant offering has been designed for a particular market opportunity, the price that is to be charged investors for each warrant must be determined. Certainly the issuer of such instruments wants to get the best possible price it can, but, in order for both issuers and investors to determine what the "fair" price is for a certain type of warrant offering, it must be compared to the prices charged for similar instruments that currently trade or have traded in the past.

Warrants can be valued by using off-the-shelf computer programs and standard option pricing parameters. Certain electronic information ven-

---

EXAMPLE: A U.S. retail investor seeks protection for Asian mutual fund holdings from exchange rate fluctuations because the fund is not currency protected by the investment manager:

Investor with an options-approved account purchases U.S. dollar put warrants on Japanese yen for $5.00 per warrant.

The warrants expire in 18 months and are listed for secondary trading on a U.S. stock exchange.

Each warrant "controls" the equivalent of $100 worth of yen and gains approximately $1.00 of cash value for every 1-yen move above the strike exchange rate, therefore working to offset a portion of losses in the mutual fund caused by adverse currency moves.

Conversely, each warrant loses $1.00 of cash value for every 1-yen move below the strike, offsetting any gains in net asset value caused by beneficial currency moves.

The strike exchange rate for the warrants is set at 79.00 yen per dollar.

Six months from the offering date, the exchange rate moves to 105 yen per dollar, and the trading price of the warrants increases to $20, a 300-percent increase in value.

Over the next month, the exchange rate moves to 100 yen per dollar and the warrants decline to $16, a 20-percent drop in price from the previous market high.

---

dors (e.g., Bloomberg) provide on-screen option pricing models for valuing all types of optionlike instruments, such as warrants. Such pricing models are simple to use. An investor wishing to determine whether a particular instrument is fairly valued would input the following information into one of many readily available electronic pricing models:

Strike.   The index level or asset price that determines the future value of the warrant in-the-money, at-the-money, or out-of-the-money.

Index Level or Asset Price.   The current level, spot, or cash market price of the underlying index or asset on which the warrant is based.

Interest Rate.   Based on fixed-income instruments of the same duration as the warrant, such as those of one-year or five-year U.S. Treasury bonds, LIBOR, and the like. Note: Since the credit backing a warrant obligation is of a specific issuer and not an exchange or clearinghouse, which is usually considered to be a risk-free rate, the borrowing rate of the issuing or guaranteeing corporation must be added as an input in computerized valuation models.

Dividend or Coupon Rate.   Based on the stock, index of stocks, or bonds on which a warrant is based.

Term.   The number of months or years the warrant is in effect.

Volatility.   A measure of the frequency and the intensity of price changes of the asset on which the warrant is based.

SPECIFIC EQUITY INDEX, CURRENCY, AND YIELD WARRANTS

As global market opportunities continue to be identified, structured products created for institutional clients in over-the-counter (OTC) transactions often evolve into instruments of interest to investors (both institutional and individual retail client) who prefer publicly offered products that trade on securities exchanges. The following are examples of structures approved by the SEC for public trading in the United States:

Amex Hong Kong 30 Index Warrants.   In June 1993 the American Stock Exchange created and began calculating a capitalization-weighted index (share price times shares outstanding) comprising 30 common stocks traded on the Hong Kong Stock Exchange. Warrants on the Index began trading in October 1993.

Japanese Nikkei Index Warrants.   Warrants on the Nikkei 225 Stock Average were introduced in the United States in early 1990. The Nikkei 225 Index is a price-weighted index comprising 225 of the leading Japanese common stocks traded on the First Section of the Tokyo Stock Exchange. The index was first published in 1949 and is owned and published by Nihon Keizai Shimbun (NKS), a Japanese news service.

British FT-SE 100 ("Footsie") Index Warrants.   Warrants on the *Financial Times*–Stock Exchange 100 share index started trading in the United States in 1990. First published in 1984 by the London Stock Exchange and *The Financial Times,* the broad based FT-SE 100 Index represents 100 industrial companies throughout the United Kingdom. As a capital-weighted index (as opposed to the price-weighted Nikkei 225 Index), the FT-SE 100 is affected by price changes for shares of companies with a large number of shares outstanding as opposed to those for smaller capitalized companies.

French CAC 40 Index Warrants.   The French-based CAC-40 Index (Cotation Assistee en Continu, or Continuous Calculation and Quotation) was first published by Societe des Bourse Francaises in 1988 and reflects the movements of the top 40 common stocks trading on the Paris Bourse.

Eurotrack 200 Index Warrants.   Index warrants on the Eurotrack 200 Index began trading in the United States in 1994. The index is compiled and calculated by the London Stock Exchange and is intended to measure the market performance of the common stocks of 200 major European corporations. The Eurotrack 200 is a combination of the *Financial Times*–Stock Exchange (FT-SE) 100 Share Index and the FT-SE Eurotrack 100 Index. The Eurotrack 200 Index, first published on February 25, 1991, and denominated in European currency units (ECU), is designed with a weighting restraint factor that maintains the U.K. weighting in the index of approximately 41 percent, while stocks of Germany and France each comprise approximately 14 percent of the index. As a capital-weighted index, the Eurotrack 200 will be more affected by price changes for shares of larger market value companies than those for shares of smaller capitalization companies.

Currency Warrants.   Currency warrants reflect changes in the value of the U.S. dollar relative to another single currency, such as the Japanese yen, Deutsche mark, or British pound. Currency warrants have been publicly traded in the United States since 1987. Many of the original currency warrant offerings in the late 1980s were issued in conjunction with debt offerings. The additional premium raised through the sale of the warrants effectively lowered the cost of such financings to the corporate and U.S. agency issuers.

Cross Currency Warrants.   Cross currency warrants are similar to the currency warrants mentioned previously except that their value relates to the exchange rate differentials between two non-U.S. currencies (e.g., yen/D-mark, D-mark/F-franc, etc.). U.S. traded currency, cross currency, and currency index warrants are traded and cash settled in U.S. dollars.

Currency Index Warrants.   Warrants on a three-currency index were first issued in the United States in 1993 and were based on an equal-weighted currency index calculated and published once per day based on noon buying rates provided by the Federal Reserve. The index measured day-to-day percentage price movements in the value of the U.S. dollar relative to the British pound, deutsche mark, and Japanese yen.

Bond Yield Warrants.   Warrants based on bond yields began trading in the United States in 1991 and allow investors to speculate on the direction of interest rates without being fully invested in the cash instruments. The interest rate benchmark for these instruments can be the 30-year U.S. Treasury bond (i.e., the "long bond") or any other widely used measure of interest rates throughout the world.

U.S. Domestic Equity Index Warrants.   Warrants based on U.S. benchmark equity indexes such as the S&P 500, S&P 400, or the Russell 2000 and future indexes based on volatile sectors of the U.S. economy such as takeover candidates or research-backed groups of stocks that are undergoing cyclical price changes.

INVESTMENT CONSIDERATIONS

Investors should be aware that investments in warrants involve a high degree of price risk, including the risk of expiring worthless if the market on which the warrant relates does not move in the investor's favor. They can lose value over time, as the expiration date approaches (i.e., the loss of time value). Many structured warrant transactions (as opposed to traditional warrants relating to a single common stock) may only be sold to investors (both retail and institutional) who meet the following requirements prior to entering into primary and secondary market transactions in such instruments (specific requirements may vary from firm to firm):

- Must have option-approved accounts
- Must have prior option transaction experience
- Must be considered a suitable investment given each investor's experience, goals, and objectives

Furthermore, in private, over-the-counter warrant transactions, investors should be aware that secondary trading liquidity may be limited. Only upstairs markets may be available (i.e., perhaps only the issuer of the warrant makes a secondary market in the security), and any bid-ask quotation spreads may be significantly wider than for warrants traded on stock exchanges. Also, the offering materials provided in connection with public or private warrant offerings should be reviewed by investors for other risks, tax issues, and customer suitability requirements.

CONCLUSION

This chapter dealt with warrants, optionlike instruments that can be linked to the performance of many different kinds of underlying assets in publicly underwritten offerings or privately placed OTC transactions. Chapters 6–8 move the discussion into the area of coupling optionlike structures, such as warrants, to debt securities to address the needs of yield- and income-oriented investors. As mentioned in Chapter 1, one way of conveying complex concepts is by linking them to concepts with which one is familiar. Since many investors are familiar with bonds, the following chapters describe how bonds can be used to preserve an investor's principal investment while providing exposure to equity markets around the world. Index- and other asset-linked notes, convertible securities, and equity-linked notes have been described as "common stocks with training wheels." They allow clients to invest conservatively yet put their toes in the water regarding speculative worldwide investments they read about but hesitate to participate in.

6

INDEX- AND OTHER
ASSET-LINKED NOTES

Index- and asset-linked notes are debt securities that offer investors principal preservation (i.e., return of the principal investment at maturity) and potential capital appreciation as a function of the price changes of an index or other asset (sometimes referred to as an equity, debt, commodity, or exchange rate "kicker"). They are referred to by financial engineers as *hybrid securities* or instruments comprising two or more asset classes fused together, such as equity and debt. There are usually no periodic coupon payments with index- and asset-linked notes, although some structures include limited interim cash distributions. Interest is typically paid at maturity based on price movements of the underlying asset (e.g., price movements of the S&P 500 Index, oil prices, or U.S. long bond yields, etc.).

Proceeds from the sale of asset-linked notes are typically used by the issuer for general corporate funding purposes and hedging their risk exposure to market price fluctuations under the notes. The principal amount is repaid by the issuer to investors at maturity. The debt portion of index- and asset-linked notes is the economic equivalent of a zero-coupon bond, and the equity component is the economic equivalent of a long-term option. Many investors are confused by the construction of such instruments when they hear of the inclusion of a zero-coupon bond and an option. The words "economic equivalent" are therefore used to convey the fact that no specific zero-coupon bonds and options are taken out of the marketplace to build such instruments. Since asset-linked notes are created around specific market opportunities, their components are tailor-made to the instrument itself; they are created contractually or "synthetically."

Index- and other asset-linked notes are designed to be the economic equivalent of a zero-coupon bond tied to the price movements of an underlying asset, usually represented by either a put or call option. Both the zero-coupon bond and the related option are interwoven into the note. The offering proceeds from such instruments that are not apportioned to the zero-coupon debt component are used to finance the creation of an option relating to the underlying "linked" asset. The option is then designed and embedded into the note to provide an enhanced payout potential to the investor at maturity. The potential value of underlying asset price movements is captured by the investor through the option. The portion of the proceeds not treated as a zero-coupon bond is used by the issuer during the life of the note to hedge its exposure to potential payment obligations to investors arising from future price movements of the underlying asset or index. Such hedging activities involve the purchase of stock options, index options, futures, options on futures, cash securities, over-the-counter contracts, or a variety of the foregoing.

Index- and asset-linked notes allow investors to speculate in worldwide markets while preserving their principal investments, subject to the creditworthiness of the issuer and obligor of the note. An investor receives enhanced interest income from the notes while sharing in the risk and possible reward of stock or other asset price fluctuations. They are issued in the United States by corporations or governmental agencies as Securities and Exchange Commission (SEC) registered and exchange-listed instruments or in private transactions. Also, under certain circumstances, notes on foreign issues can be designed to be currency neutral, that is, hedged against exchange rate movements.

EXAMPLE: An investor believes the U.S. stock market is going to be volatile in the near term but wishes to establish a long-term position in U.S. blue-chip stocks without risk to his principal investment:

Investor buys $100,000 worth of S&P 500 Index–linked notes.

The notes are sold in $1000 denominations and have five-year durations; they are sold in both publicly offered and privately placed transactions.

The starting or strike S&P 500 Index level when the instrument is sold is, for example, 650.

Notes offered to the public in underwritten transactions are typically listed on a stock exchange; in private transactions, they are typically traded upstairs by the dealer that structured the original offering.

Under the terms of the notes, investors earn 100 percent (the index participation rate, which can also be above or below 100 percent) of any future appreciation of the index above the strike index level during the life of the notes.

Assuming the S&P 500 Index increases by 65 percent to 1073 over the five-year duration of the notes, investors would receive $1650 per note held, composed of repayment of their $1000 principal investment and an additional, contingent payment (based on the appreciation of the index) of $650 ($1000 × 65%).

Investors should be aware, however, that if at maturity of the note the S&P 500 Index is below the 650 strike, only the $1000 principal amount of the note will be returned.

The value of an index-linked note at maturity that is returned to the investor is often determined as *principal return* plus *the final coupon payment,* if the notes carry any coupon obligation, plus *the contingent payment based on the appreciation,* if any, of the underlying asset to which the note is linked (e.g., the principal amount multiplied by the index participation rate).

EXAMPLE: An investor seeks exposure to U.S. growth stocks over five years with principal protection of the initial investment:

Investor buys five-year, $10 principal amount, S&P MidCap 400 Index–linked notes.

The index level is 180, the strike index level.

The notes can be acquired in a public offering or in a private over-the-counter transaction.

The investor has the right to earn 110 percent of any future appreciation in the index during the term of the notes.

At maturity in five years, the S&P MidCap 400 increases 150 percent to 450 (a 14-percent annualized growth rate) and the investor receives $26.50 per note, composed of repayment of the $10 principal amount plus a contingent payment of $16.50 per note ($10 × 150% × 110%).

However, if at maturity of the note the index is at or below the 180 strike index level, the investor receives only the principal amount invested and no contingent payment.

INVESTMENT CONSIDERATIONS

Index- and other asset-linked notes are usually less speculative than warrants, options, and other more leveraged instruments, but investors must still satisfy relevant customer suitability requirements. Investors should be aware that at maturity most asset-linked notes return only the principal amount invested if the underlying index does not appreciate above the starting index level, resulting in a loss of whatever return of value the investor might have received from alternative investments in interest-bearing or other securities.

Secondary trading of asset-linked notes is affected by the creditworthiness of the issuer, the ranking of the debt by the issuer (e.g., senior, subordinated, or unsecured obligations), interest rate movements during the life of the notes, the amount of time remaining to maturity, trading liquidity and fluctuations of the index level, among other factors. Due to the deep discount, zero-coupon bond nature of index- and asset-linked notes, interest rate fluctuations can significantly influence secondary trading prices, irrespective of the movement of the underlying index or asset price to which the note is linked. An increase in interest rates early in the life of such an instrument will cause greater discounting in the remaining net present time value of the instrument, causing its market value to decline; conversely, an early decline in interest rates will tend to increase the price of the instrument. Also, since the imbedded option in such notes is often European style (i.e., it cannot be exercised until maturity) it is usually not until the notes approach maturity that the index level becomes a significant factor in the trading value of the notes. As maturity approaches, interest rates are less a factor than the expected payout associated with movements of the underlying index or asset.

In private, over-the-counter index- and asset-linked note transactions, investors should be aware that secondary trading liquidity may be limited. Only upstairs markets may be available (i.e., perhaps only the issuer of the notes makes a secondary market in the security), and any bid-ask quotation spreads may be significantly wider than for such notes traded on stock exchanges. Investors should also be aware that offering materials provided in connection with public or private index- and asset-linked note offerings should be reviewed for other risks, tax issues, and customer suitability requirements.

7

CONVERTIBLE SECURITIES

A convertible security, although based on equity, is usually categorized by financial engineers as a fixed-income instrument that allows investors to convert their debt positions into common stock, cash, or other types of assets at any time prior to maturity or redemption. Convertibles offer investors a means of obtaining equity appreciation at lower risk than owning stock outright. They offer issuers the possibility of securing funds at a lower cost relative to other capital funding sources, and enable corporations to reduce the need to issue additional equity. Although typically viewed as traditional corporate finance products, the issuance and trading of convertible securities often require the involvement of derivative trading and structured product professionals for properly valuing the embedded option or convertible component of such instruments. Convertibles are examples of hybrid and synthetic instruments.[1] A convertible is less risky than common stock due to the price support provided by its fixed coupon or dividend payment and, in the case of bonds, the return of principal at maturity. A convertible's appreciation potential comes from its

[1]In this case, a convertible is considered a *hybrid* because it combines elements of two different asset categories, such as debt and equity. Convertibles can also be considered *synthetic* equity because they replicate the characteristics of another instrument, in this case the dividend and appreciation characteristics of common stock.

conversion feature; a convertible can be converted at any time into a fixed number of shares of common stock, cash, or other asset to which it may be linked. However, equitylike returns from convertibles come at a price as they pay lower yields than nonconvertible securities with similar credit risk.

Convertibles are most actively traded in the U.S. listed market, but are also sold privately in over-the-counter transactions or in Eurobond transactions. In addition, a convertible can be structured as debt or as preferred stock.

The principal benefits of a convertible security include the following:

- Higher income than common stock; income from convertibles is more "secure" as it is a more senior obligation of the issuer than common stock dividends.

- Equity appreciation potential via the conversion feature.

- Less risk than common stock, resulting from the convertible's higher-yielding price support.

- Favorable leverage, implying that a convertible typically participates more in the common stock's upside appreciation than it does in downward price movements.

Convertibles are attractive to equity investors wanting more yield and less price volatility than the common stock. Fixed-income investors seek investments in convertibles because of the attractive current income and equity return potentials rather than the somewhat greater risk associated with nonconvertible securities. Those attracted to convertibles include so-called defensive investors, whose objectives are income with some downside protection, along with traditional fixed-income buyers seeking substantial current income and equity participation with less volatility than owning the actual common stock on which a convertible is based. Lastly, growth and income fund managers often place convertible instruments into the portfolios they manage because of the convenient combination of yield and participation in price appreciation.

The parameters that determine the value of a convertible security are fixed at the time of issue. In effect, the issuing company sells an out-of-the-money call option with a strike price equal to the conversion price (the embedded call). The issuer then uses the option premium received from the sale of the call to reduce the coupon or dividend it pays on the convertible; that is the reason why convertibles pay lower yields than similar risk nonconvertible debt or preferred stock. Simply put, a convertible issuer sells volatility in order to reduce its borrowing costs. In its simplest form a convertible can be viewed as a package containing a bond and an embedded call option on the underlying common stock. The bond component provides it with price support and makes it less risky than common. The embedded call option gives it appreciation potential. The bond component, as explained earlier, is its investment value and is determined by valuing the convertible's coupons at a discount rate appropriate to its credit quality.

The value of the option embedded in convertible securities depends on the following parameters:

Conversion Prices.   The ratio of the common stock price to the conversion price; as the common stock price rises in relation to the conversion price, the embedded call gains in value.

Volatility.   The common stock's volatility; the more volatile the stock price, the greater the value of the embedded call.

Call Protection.   The greater the length of call protection, the higher the value of the call option.

EXAMPLE: An investor is interested is capital appreciation and prefers a less risky approach to owning common stock. Convertible securities offer such investors the following:

- A low conversion premium convertible allows considerable capital gain potential.

- The convertible's superior income can result in substantial upside participation with the common.

- Call protection need be compared against the convertible's trading price in an effort to estimate the probability of a call. In the event of a call, investors are given about 30 days to either accept the call price or to convert into common.

The level of participation of a convertible in the appreciation of the corresponding equity is determined mainly by the conversion premium; high conversion premiums largely insulate the convertible against common stock price movements. Other considerations that affect participation include the following:

Investment Premium.   A convertible's downside is often limited to its fixed income or investment value; convertibles trading well above investment value are therefore exposed to much of the common stock's downside price risk.

Income Advantage over the Common Stock.   The greater the advantage, the higher the participation level.

Call Protection.   When all else is equal, a convertible has better leverage when it is call protected than is the case when call protection expires.

If at maturity of a convertible security, the common stock closes below the conversion price, the embedded call option expires out-of-the-money and the convertible is worth par value. On the other hand, if the common stock price closes above the conversion price, the embedded call is in-the-money and the convertible is worth its conversion value. Therefore, holders of the convertible security should convert into common stock rather than accept the redemption price. For an entertaining discussion of convertible securities and how they can be understood by reference to baseball, see "Convertibles as Sport" in the Resource Guide.

EXAMPLE: An investor whose primary need is income with minimal downside exposure might consider an investment in a convertible security:

- A high-yielding convertible clearly meets the income requirement.
- A small investment premium protects the convertible against the downside price risk of the underlying common stock.
- Capital gain potential exists; should interest rates fall, the company's credit is enhanced or the equity rises sufficiently to allow upside participation through the conversion feature.

INVESTMENT CONSIDERATIONS

The ability to participate in an equity's appreciation potential while earning a higher yield than common stock makes convertibles suitable for "total return" investors (i.e., investors who focus on yield plus appreciation as opposed to one or the other). Although some investors prefer owning convertible securities as a lower-risk alternative to owning common stock (because they have less price volatility), there are at least two exceptions. The first exception occurs after a substantial rise in common; the convertible then trades essentially like equity and, lacking price support, trades like and is suitable only for equity-oriented investors. The other exception occurs after common falls considerably; as a result, the convertible declines to the point where it trades like a bond and possesses very little equity price sensitivity (usually called a "busted" convertible, which is thereafter usually only found suitable by yield-oriented investors).

8

EQUITY-LINKED NOTES

Equity-linked notes are referred to generically as *ELNs* but are also referred to by specific issuers as ELKS, DECS, CHIPS, PERCS, PERQS, YEELDS, and a growing number of other acronyms. Like index- and other asset-linked notes, ELNs are hybrid debt securities; that is, they include elements of multiple asset classes, for example, both debt and equity combined into one instrument. ELNs generally have two- to five-year maturities and are structured either as convertible into the underlying equity or as nonconvertible. Investors receive an enhanced yield but are subject to limited upside appreciation potential based on movements of a single underlying common stock. At maturity, the value of an ELN is usually determined as the lesser of the closing price of underlying stock and the initial ELN issue price, multiplied by a fixed or (in the case of DECS, which are discussed later) variable participation percentages.

ELNs offer investors enhanced fixed-income yield and equity market exposure. The funds derived from ELN offerings are used by the issuer to structure an instrument that provides investors with the economic equivalent of an enhanced quarterly coupon or dividend yield along with the right, during the life of the note, to participate in a portion of the price appreciation of the stock upon which the ELN is based. ELNs are issued as Securities and Exchange Commission (SEC) registered, exchange-listed instruments or as custom-made products in private transactions. They are typically issued by broker–dealers or by corporations with significant equity stakes in other companies that they seek to "monetize." Corporations

EXAMPLE: A client has certain specific growth and income objectives and, with the help of her investment executive, considers purchasing an exchange-listed equity-linked note:

Investor wants to own one of several growth stocks but needs income, and the stocks targeted for investment do not pay dividends.

ELNs based on a specific growth stock are purchased for $30.00 each with a 35-percent appreciation cap (a maximum value or upside appreciation limit of $40.50 per ELN).

ELNs are issued and sold at the market price of the underlying stock.

Each ELN has, for example, a 6-percent coupon, equal to $0.45 per quarter, $1.80 per year, or a total of $5.40 over the typical three-year life of ELNs

The maturity value of ELNs is based on the then-current market price of the underlying stock ($30.00 in this example), limited by the specified cap price ($40.50 in this example).

If the underlying stock price has moved up to the 35-percent cap by the maturity date of the ELNs, the investor receives, in this example, $45.90 for each ELN; the total return is approximately 15 percent per year ($40.50 cap price + $5.40 of coupon payments = $45.90 over three years).

If the stock is trading higher than the ELN cap price, the maturity value paid to the investor is limited to the cap price plus all coupon payments.

If on the maturity date of the ELNs, the underlying stock price has fallen, for example, to $18.00, the investor receives $23.40 for each ELN ($18.00 maturity value + $5.40 of coupon payments = $23.40 over three years), a 22-percent loss on the $33.00 investment in the ELNs.

ELN prices are generally less volatile than the underlying stock price because the ELN coupon payments partially offset the effect of stock price declines.

For example, a 40-percent loss to a holder of a stock is greater than the 22-percent loss experience by a holder of an ELN on the same stock (i.e., the common stockholder would receive $18.00, whereas ELN holders would receive $23.40 per share, which includes coupon payments).

The last quarterly coupon payment is made to investors on the ELN maturity date.

often seek to monetize common stock investments in other companies by issuing ELNs and deferring tax on the sale of such holdings.

GENERAL INVESTMENT CONSIDERATIONS

ELN trading prices may be less volatile than the underlying common stock on which they are based (due to the price stabilizing effect of the income stream from the ELN coupon payments), and a number of factors that are difficult to predict influence ELN trading prices, including interest rate movements and the price of the underlying common stock, among others. The value of ELNs during their lives and at maturity is based on the trading price of an underlying common stock; as a result, investors should be aware that, like owning the stock itself, they can lose their investments if the underlying stock becomes worthless or receive less than their principal investments at maturity, notwithstanding any coupon payments.

In private, over-the-counter equity-linked note transactions, investors should be aware that secondary trading liquidity may be limited. Only upstairs markets may be available, and any bid-ask quotation spreads may be significantly wider than for ELNs traded on stock exchanges. Investors should consult their tax advisors to review specific tax issues pertaining to investments in ELNs, such as taxation of coupon payments as ordinary income and any long-term appreciation as capital gains. Offering materials provided in connection with public or private equity-linked note offerings should also be reviewed by investors for other risks and customer suitability requirements.

PERCS AND ELKS

PERCS (also a similar security referred to as PERQS) and ELKS[1] are hybrid equity-linked notes that, in exchange for a cap on equity upside, pay a substantially higher dividend yield than the underlying common stock. In

---

[1]PERCS and Preferred Equity Redemption Cumulative Stock, and PERQS and Performance Equity-linked Redemption Quarterly-Pay Securities are trademarks of Morgan Stanley & Co. ELKS and Equity Linked Securities are trademarks of Salomon Brothers Inc.

structure and valuation, both PERCS and ELKS are similar to holding covered calls on the underlying common stock (i.e., long a share of common stock and short a call option), except that instead of receiving the option premium up front, the holder receives the premium in the form of incremental dividends over the life of the instruments (often referred to as a "buy/write" strategy). In other words, both PERCS and ELKS convert a portion of the potential equity appreciation of the underlying stock into current income for investors.

High yield and an upside cap usually make PERCS and ELKS less volatile than the underlying common stock to which they relate. On the downside, common stock declines are partially mitigated by the receipt of interest or dividend income. On the upside, a fixed cap limits gains when the common rises.

The main characteristics of PERCS are that:

- They pay a cumulative preferred dividend.
- They typically have a life of two to three years, after which holders must convert them into the underlying common stock or cash equivalent, at the issuer's option.
- They are usually issued by corporations based on their own common stock at the then-current market price of their underlying stock.
- The issuer of the PERCS can call them and replace them with the underlying common stock or cash equivalent.
- The call price of PERCS typically declines over their lives.
- The final call price is typically 35 to 40 percent above the PERCS issue price.
- If the underlying stock price exceeds the call price, the company who issued the PERCS may call them and give the holder the underlying common stock or cash equivalent at the call price (i.e., the company who issued the PERCS will return to the investor a specified cash amount relating to one share of common stock per PERCS if the common stock exceeds the call price, resulting in the PERCS holder having limited participation in any upside appreciation of the stock).

PERCS are usually issued by corporations[2] as an alternative to traditional equity or debt sources of capital funding, whereas ELKS are usually
debt securities issued and underwritten by broker–dealers. Although usually
issued at the same market price as the underlying common stock, PERCS
usually have a higher dividend payment rate than that paid by the company
on its own common stock. In return for the higher dividend rate, investors
accept a limit of 35 to 40 percent on the future potential appreciation of the
stock until the expiration of the PERCS two to three years from the date of
issue. As "preferred" securities, any unpaid PERC dividends are generally re-
garded as more secure than common stock in the event of bankruptcy of the
issuer. However, PERC investors still have market risk and could suffer a loss
on their investments if the market price of the underlying common stock is
less than the initial PERC cost. Each PERC automatically converts into as
much as one share of common stock at expiration and can be redeemed by
the issuer before the conversion date at predetermined prices.

Reasons to Consider PERCS or ELKS Investments

PERCS and ELKS-like equity-linked notes are often very popular with investors, sometimes more so than the common stock to which they relate.
During periods of increased market volatility, where relatively conservative investors may become hesitant, these types of structures offer a degree
of price stability that many investors find appealing. The most compelling
reasons to consider PERCS and ELKS-like investments include the following:

- Participation in an equity's upside appreciation while earning a
  higher yield provides investors with an attractive total return (i.e.,
  the combined return from dividend income plus potential capital
  appreciation).

- Less price volatility than common stock offers a lower risk alternative to stock; however, investors with an extremely positive outlook on an equity should avoid these securities due to their limited
  equity upside.

---

[2]PERCS, although usually issued by corporations, have also been issued by broker–dealers;
for example, Morgan Stanley & Co. Inc. issued PERCS on TELMEX stock off its own balance
sheet.

- Yield investors looking for price support should only consider PERCS or ELKS after the common has risen substantially above the call price.

Differences Between PERCS and ELKS

PERCS and ELKS-like structures are constantly being modified and adapted for new market conditions and investment objectives. The basic differences between these two categories of equity-linked notes are as follows:

Issuer.   PERCS are equity securities issued by companies on their own stock, whereas ELKS are usually debt securities issued and typically underwritten by broker–dealers or their affiliates. Interest payments on ELKS may, therefore, be deductible expense obligations of the issuing broker–dealer. Even though issued under different names, many covered calls originated by broker–dealers are often referred to as ELKS. ELKS issuers include:

ELKS (equity-linked securities; Salomon Brothers Inc)

YEELDS (yield enhanced equity–linked debt securities; Lehman Brothers Inc.)

CHIPS (common-linked higher income participation debt securities; Bear Stearns & Co., Inc.)

PERQS (performance equity-linked redemption quarterly pay securities; Morgan Stanley & Co. Inc.)

Call Protection.   PERCS are callable at any time with the call price declining in a straight line from the highest to the lowest specified call price just prior to maturity; ELKS are not callable prior to maturity.

Redemption Value.   PERCS can be redeemed in cash or common stock, at the issuer's option; ELKS can be redeemed only for cash.

Maturity Value of PERCS or ELKS

At maturity if the common trades below the call price, PERCS will not be called for redemption and will convert into one share of common stock; ELKS holders receive the value of common in cash. If the common stock trades above the call price, a PERCS will be called for redemption with the call price paid in cash or stock at the issuer's option; ELKS holders receive the call price in cash, but if the stock trades above the call price, a PERCS can be called prior to maturity.

Price Support of PERCS and ELKS

PERCS are sensitive to equity movements and do not possess price support when the common stock trades below the call price; however, declines with common stock are partially mitigated by the receipt of income. The price support of a PERCS or ELKS improves as the common rises above the call price; once the common stock price rises well above the call price, PERCS and ELKS become less sensitive to movements in common due to the increased certainty that the call price will be paid at maturity.

Investment Considerations of PERCS and ELKS

In pure economic terms the payoff profiles of PERCS and ELKS can be replicated effectively but less conveniently by an investor through the sale of a covered call on his or her holdings of the underlying common stock (thereby giving up a portion of the upside appreciation potential of the stock); the proceeds from the sale of the covered call can then be used to produce a PERCS or ELKS-like cash flow by purchasing, for example, U.S. Treasury strips. Investors should be aware that with PERCS and ELKS, an owner of the underlying common stock in effect sells an out-of-the money call option. The premium from the sale of the call option is then paid back to the investor in the form of quarterly coupon or dividend payments; the net present value of the income pickup (i.e., the amount by which the PERCS or ELKS yield exceeds the common yield) equals the value of the embedded call option and represents the PERCS or ELKS holder's payment for accepting a limit on the potential price appreciation of the common stock.

Although the secondary trading prices of PERCS and ELKS are usually less volatile than the underlying common stock (due to the price stabilizing effect of the income stream from coupon payments), a number of factors that are difficult to predict influence PERCS and ELKS trading prices, including interest rate movements and the price of the underlying common stock, among others. The value of PERCS and ELKS during their lives and at maturity are based on the trading price of an underlying common stock, so investors should be aware that, like owning the stock itself, they can lose their investments if the underlying stock becomes worthless or receive back less than their principal investments at maturity. For private, over-the-counter transactions in PERCS and ELKS, investors should be aware that secondary trading liquidity may be limited, only an upstairs market may be available for such instruments, and any bid-ask quotation spreads may be significantly wider than for PERCS and ELKS traded on stock exchanges.

Investors should consult their tax advisors to review specific tax issues pertaining to investments in PERCS and ELKS, such as taxation of coupon payments as ordinary income and any long-term appreciation as capital gains. Offering materials provided in connection with public or private PERCS and ELKS offerings should also be reviewed by investors for other risks and customer suitability requirements.

DECS

DECS,[3] like other equity-linked notes, pay a higher yield than the underlying common stock from which they derive their value but have the same exposure to downside risk as the underlying stock. The downside price risk of DECS is partially mitigated by the income they provide to investors, therefore they experience less secondary price volatility than the underlying common stock. Unlike PERCS or ELKS, DECS do not have an absolute cap on upside appreciation potential. Because DECS are convertible, investors share in some potential appreciation of the underlying stock, but at less than a one-to-one rate of conversion. A less than one-to-one conversion rate causes DECS prices in the secondary market to lag upward price movements of the underlying common stock.

Reasons to Consider DECS Investments

The value of a DECS is determined as follows:

- The value of one share of common
- Less the value of the short call (with a strike price equal to the issue price), if any

---

[3]DECS, Dividend Enhanced Convertible Stock, and Debt Exchangeable for Common Stock are trademarks of Salomon Brothers Inc.

- Plus the value of the long call (with a strike price equal to the conversion price), if any
- Plus the present value of the income pickup

The ability to participate in an equity's upside while earning a higher yield than common stock may make DECS suitable for investors looking for total return. Less price volatility than common stock also makes DECS suitable for investors looking for a lower risk alternative to common; however, the lack of price support makes DECS less attractive for conservative yield investors.

Differences Between DECS and Other Similar Structures

Other equity-linked notes have the same structure as DECS, such as PRIDES,[4] ACES,[5] and SAILS.[6] The only differences are the terms to maturity, the length of call protection, and whether they are issued as debt or preferred stock. A typical DECS matures in four years, is callable after three years, and is issued by a company on its own common stock. In a few instances, companies that own common stock of another entity have used the DECS-type structure as a means of monetizing such positions. The first DECS was issued by Mascotech Inc. and underwritten in a public offering lead-managed by Salomon Brothers Inc. Since then a large number of similar securities have been issued by other corporations and underwritten by broker–dealers under a variety of names, although there is no reason why investment banks cannot also act as issuers.

DECS are priced off the most recent closing price of the underlying common stock. The difference between the DECS issue price and the conversion price (the strike price of the long call) is referred to as the conversion premium. The conversion ratio, or the fraction of one share into which a DECS converts, is computed by taking the reciprocal of one plus the conversion premium.

---

[4]PRIDES and Preferred Redeemable Increased Dividend Equity Securities are trademarks of Merrill Lynch & Co., Inc.

[5]ACES and Automatically Convertible Equity Securities are trademarks of Goldman Sachs & Co.

[6]SAILS and Stock Appreciation Income Linked Securities are trademarks of CS First Boston Corporation.

EXAMPLE: A DECS issued at $20 with a $24 conversion price has a 20 percent conversion premium and a 0.833 conversion ratio. Since the conversion ratio is less than 1, the value of the long call is the value of one call option with a strike price equal to the conversion price times the conversion ratio.

Determining the Number of Common Shares a DECS Converts Into

The number of shares of common stock received by a DECS holder depends on the trading level of the common stock in relation to the DECS issue price and conversion price.

EXAMPLES

- Common trades below the issue price: At maturity, if the common trades below the issue price, a DECS converts into one share of common.

- Common trades between the issue price and the conversion price: If the common trades between the issue price and the conversion price, the DECS will be called for redemption and the DECS holder will receive the issue price in cash or common, at the issuer's option. Between the issue price and the conversion price, the conversion value of a DECS (the conversion ratio times the common price) equals the issue price and remains unchanged even with a change in common; above the conversion price, however, the conversion value of a DECS rises with common due to its fixed conversion ratio.

- Common trades above the conversion price: If the common trades above the conversion price at maturity, a DECS converts into a fraction of common stock equal to the conversion ratio; of course, if a DECS is callable and the common trades above the issue price, the DECS can be called prior to maturity.

Investment Considerations of DECS

Investors should be aware that DECS are the economic equivalent of owning one share of common stock, a spread option consisting of long and short call options on the underlying common stock, dividend income that is higher than the common and with limited participation in potential equity appreciation. In effect, when an owner of common stock buys DECS, he or she sells an at-the-money call option (the short call) and the option premium income from the sale of the short call is used to purchase a fraction of an out-of-the-money call option (the long call). The balance left over from the purchase of the long call is then stretched out and paid to the investor over the life of the DECS in the form of quarterly coupon or dividend payments. In exchange for relinquishing a portion of potential stock price appreciation, DECS pay the investor a higher yield than the common stock; the net present value of the income pickup equals the net value of the two embedded call options, that is, the premium received from the sale of the short call net of the premium paid for the purchase of the long call is paid to the investor over the life of the DECS in the form of income.

DECS do not offer price support relative to common; at maturity, were the common to decline below the issue price, DECS holders would receive one share of common stock, therefore, DECS, like common stock ownership, possess full equity risk, but common stock price declines are partially mitigated by the receipt of income during the life of each DECS. For private, over-the-counter transactions, investors should be aware that secondary trading liquidity may be limited, only an upstairs market may be available for DECS, and any bid-ask quotation spreads may be significantly wider than for DECS traded on stock exchanges.

Investors should consult their tax advisors to review specific tax issues pertaining to investments in PERCS and ELKS, such as taxation of coupon payments as ordinary income and any long-term appreciation as capital gains. Investors should also review offering materials provided in connection with public or private PERCS and ELKS for other risks and customer suitability requirements.

CONCLUSION

Chapters 6–8 examined the linkage of debt securities to the performance of other types of assets, such as equities. Just as options offer flexibility in designing instruments to suit investor's needs, bonds, too, can provide the basis for creating innovative new financial products. Bonds provide a foundation from which traditional payoff patterns in the form of coupon payments can be modified to provide exposure to different types of assets around the world without undue risk to principal. Index- and other asset-linked notes, convertible securities, and equity-linked notes make intuitive sense; they are like having your cake and eating it too. Through a single instrument, an investor can receive the return of his or her principal investment after a stated period of time and, simultaneously, satisfy any speculative inclinations he or she may possess by obtaining market exposure to higher risk asset categories, like stock, currencies, or commodities.

Index- and other asset-linked notes, convertible securities, and equity-linked notes, however, do not usually appeal to natural stock or bond buyers. Bond buyers usually want yield, stock buyers usually want appreciation, and finding buyers that want both requires careful marketing. Many times account executives would rather spend the few moments they have with their clients talking about products that sell themselves and have easier stories to tell, such as the latest initial public offering of a technology stock or corporate bond offering with an attractive yield. Most index- and other asset-linked notes, however, perform well, with yields that often outstrip those of similarly rated bonds, without the downside price risk associated with investments in equities, currency exchange rates, or commodities.

Specific market conditions often make structured notes (as this class of instruments is generally referred to by financial engineers) very attractive, such as during those periods of time in the advanced stages of a bull market where investors want to continue participating in the appreciation potential of stocks but fear a market correction that could wipe out their gains. Structured notes offer an attractive alternative during such periods of time. An investor can move some of his or her market gains into structured notes that provide for continued participation in a more speculative asset class. If the linked asset continues to move up over the life of the note, the investor still participates in such appreciation. But if the linked asset suffers adverse price moves, the investor's principal investment is protected by the creditworthiness of the issuer, just as for all bonds. Over time, as their performance and trading characteristics are studied by investors, it appears likely that index- and other asset-linked notes will move more into the mainstream of investment alternatives.

The next chapter moves back into the option and warrant arena with the introduction of exotic instruments. Exotics are used primarily by market professionals because they can be used to achieve very specific financial goals. The discussion provides an entertaining glimpse at some of the products and investment strategies that are often relegated to the realm of "rocket science." It is like traveling to a new country and tasting the local foods. At first strange, they are soon found to be appealing. Exotic options and warrants are no more complicated than the various types of structured products discussed previously; they just target more specific investment goals. Exotics can still be broken down into their basic component parts and valued and priced in the same ways that stocks, bonds, and standardized options are studied for their investment characteristics.

9

EXOTIC OPTIONS
AND WARRANTS

BASKET OPTIONS, SECTOR OPTIONS, AND WARRANTS

As mentioned in previous chapters, options provide investors and financial engineers with flexible tools for achieving specific investment goals. Exotic options are nonstandardized instruments, tailor-made in private, over-the-counter (OTC) transactions and designed to capture specific market opportunities. They are often referred to as *exotics* because of their unique structure and relative complexity compared to standardized options. Despite the lack of standardization, however, they are not difficult to understand. They are valued and priced in the same way as standardized options are (e.g., using the strike price, the current index level or asset price, interest rate, dividend or coupon rate of the underlying asset, term over which the option or warrant is in effect, and the implied price volatility of the underling asset). A variety of exotic securities, such as flex options and reset warrants, are presently available to the public and traded on national securities exchanges in the United States.

Basket options, sector options, and related warrants are based on specific, custom-made portfolios of equities, currencies, commodities, and bonds that are bundled, usually to exploit fast-moving market events. For example, because of falling oil prices, an investor might want to purchase a call warrant that increases in value based on a basket of 10 of the largest international airline stocks. The hope is that airline stock prices will rise in anticipation of a decrease in variable fuel costs and result in higher profits.

Incidentally, there is a legal distinction between options and warrants. Warrants are often referred to as long-term options. Options traditionally cover time periods of less than a year, warrants usually over a year. Standardized, exchange-listed options in the United States are issued by, and settlement is guaranteed by, the Options Clearing Corp., a clearinghouse owned by a group of broker–dealers and other financial institutions. Investor participation in standardized options (i.e., open interest) builds over time. Alternatively, warrants and OTC options are issued by and subject to the creditworthiness of corporate issuers. They are usually sold via underwritten transactions to a large number of investors (which creates the equivalent of an immediate "open interest") or through private placements to individuals or small groups of investors.

Stock baskets on which basket options, sector options and warrants are based usually include a relatively small number of constituent stocks (e.g., 5 to 50 stocks) that may be in the same industry or part of a central investment theme (e.g., "takeover" stocks). On the other hand, broad-based indices (on which the equity index warrants discussed in Chapter 5 are based) usually represent an entire market and usually include a greater number of stocks (e.g., as few as 20 and up to thousands of stocks, such as the S&P 500 Index or the Russell 2000 Index). Basket and sector options and warrants often combine U.S., international, or custom-made combinations of assets or stocks (e.g., airlines, oil companies, international government bonds, etc.). The periodic movement of price levels of stock baskets can be based on continuous index calculations using real-time price information or once-per-day calculations using closing prices at the end of daily trading.

Like other option and warrant structures, exotic options and warrants based on stock baskets can be custom-made for investors with strikes in, at, or out-of-the-money: puts, calls, spreads, strangles, or straddles. They offer investors a way to capture leveraged returns (i.e., the ability to receive investment returns that are many times greater than the underlying cash market) based on their particular economic or market views or specific research reports. Structured products based on stock baskets offer investors a convenient way to gain exposure to a desired industry group or segment without having to engage in individual stock picking and without the transaction costs associated with assembling a portfolio of equities.

Refer to the Resource Guide for examples of term sheets for a variety of warrants, notes, and other structured products.

EXAMPLE: A professional trader believes that small capitalization stocks will outperform the market as a whole during the next year and consults with his account executive for available investment products:

The account executive's structured products group creates a new basket of 50 small cap stocks and provides him with a price quote on a two-year, at-the-money call warrant.

The investor pays $12.00 of premium (i.e., 12 percent) for each $100 of value represented by the stocks in the basket.

Using the offering proceeds from the sale of the warrant, the warrant issuer hedges its obligations under the position and retains a "spread" as compensation for structuring the trade.

The stocks in the basket move up 10 percent during the month following the offering and each call warrant, as a result of its financial "leverage," increases in value by 50 percent to $18.00 (in contrast to the value of the stocks in the basket, which may have increased by only 5 percent).

The investor may choose to realize a gain on his warrants by selling half of the appreciated position back to the issuer–market maker, less a selling spread paid to the issuer–market maker.

The issuer funds the payoff to the investor by "unwinding" its hedge in small cap stocks (i.e., selling a portion of the position(s) it holds as a hedge for the warrant).

The investor decides to hold the remaining position and three months later it decreases by approximately 40 percent to $7.80 after the index falls 22 percent.

Investment Considerations of Basket Options, Sector Options, and Warrants

Basket and sector option and warrant transactions are usually sold to institutional or sophisticated individual investors as private over-the-counter transactions. Investors should be aware that instruments such as basket options and warrants can expire worthless and are speculative investments.

There is no established exchange-based market for secondary trading of OTC options and warrants; therefore investors should be aware that trading liquidity may be limited. Only upstairs markets may be available for such instruments (i.e., perhaps only the issuer of the OTC instrument makes a secondary market in the security), and any bid-ask quotation spreads may be significantly wider for OTC instruments than for instruments traded on stock exchanges.

Depending on the terms governing such financial products, the ability to exercise (e.g., European style options can only be exercised at expiration versus American style, which are continuously exercisable) as well as the times of exercise may be limited. Over-the-counter investment products are often supported only by a term sheet and an OTC investment contract; therefore, investment risks and the terms should be thoroughly reviewed with investment advisors and the issuer of such products.

RELATIVE PERFORMANCE OPTIONS (SPREAD OR OUTPERFORMANCE OPTIONS)

Another example of exotic structures includes relative performance options. They give investors the right to receive the price return of one asset or index of assets over and above the return of another index. In consideration of paying the cost of the option, an investor receives the greater of zero and the difference between the returns (i.e., the relative performance) of one asset versus another (e.g., the better of or outperformance of the S&P 500 Index versus the S&P MidCap 400 Index).

EXAMPLE: Market research highlights the possibility that growth stocks are expected to outperform large capitalization stocks over the next two years. Financial engineers structure a relative performance option for institutional investors that gains value if the S&P Midcap 400 Index outperforms the S&P 500 Index:

> Over the two-year life of the option the MidCap Index appreciates 40 percent while the S&P 500 Index appreciates only 18 percent.
>
> Payoff upon exercise or at maturity is 22 percent (40% − 18% = 22%) times the notional* amount of the option.
>
> If at expiration of the relative performance option the S&P 500 Index has outperformed the MidCap Index, the option expires worthless and the investor loses the cash premium paid in establishing the position.

Relative Performance options are structured for investors who believe that one class of asset will outperform another and who seek a strategy that risks a finite dollar amount (i.e., the option premium) in order to obtain the potential for leveraged returns. Relative performance options can be structured to compare individual stock returns or single stock versus equity index returns (e.g., IBM outperformance relative to the S&P 500 Index), the possible outperformance of index returns (e.g., S&P 500 versus S&P 400), the possible outperformance of the assets in one country versus another (e.g., Japan versus German equities), one asset class against another (e.g., bonds versus stock indexes), and a particular industry or country sector performance versus another (e.g., the better of airline versus auto stocks or Pacific Rim stocks versus Emerging Market stocks).

Notional, in this case, relates to the aggregate dollar amount of underlying assets that are controlled by a derivative instrument. For example, one option costing $6.00 of premium controls 100 shares of stock costing $25 per share; each $6.00 option controls $2500 of notional value of stock (100 shares × $25 per share = $2500).

Investment Considerations of Relative Performance Options

Relative performance option transactions are usually sold to institutional or sophisticated individual investors as private OTC transactions. Investors should be aware that instruments such as relative performance options can expire worthless and are speculative investments. There is no established exchange-based market for secondary trading of relative performance options; therefore investors should be aware that trading liquidity may be limited. Only upstairs markets may be available for such instruments (i.e., perhaps only the issuer of the OTC instrument makes a secondary market in the security), and any bid-ask quotation spreads may be significantly wider for OTC instruments than for instruments traded on stock exchanges.

Depending on the terms governing such financial products, the ability to exercise (e.g., European style options can only be exercised at expiration versus American style, which are continuously exercisable) as well as the times of exercise may be limited. Investors should also note that OTC investment products are often supported only by a term sheet and an OTC investment contract; therefore, investment risks and the terms should be thoroughly reviewed with investment advisors and the issuer of such products.

BARRIER OPTIONS (KNOCK-IN AND KNOCK-OUT OPTIONS)

Barrier options are triggered when an underlying asset price moves to a given price level. *Knock-in* options are *activated* when a specified price level is reached; *knock-out* options are *canceled* when a specified price level is reached.

Usually a barrier option will start out-of-the-money or at-the-money, and the underlying asset or index level will be on the other side of the barrier option strike price. Barrier options are path dependent and can be canceled or "brought back to life" when the underlying asset or index crosses a specified level before the option expires. Their payoffs depend not only on the value of the underlying asset but also on the path or course of movement the underlying asset took to get there. This path dependency makes barrier options less valuable and therefore less expensive than standard options. Their cheapness relative to standard options is often why they are attractive to investors who believe an asset or index will move in a specific manner and who wish to speculate or hedge their portfolios based on their perception of such potential movements. Barrier options are valued just like standard options. The barrier level must be input into computerized option model calculations along with other pricing variables.

The following are general descriptions of the characteristics of various types of barrier options:

- Barrier option prices are usually lower than standard options with otherwise identical features due to the triggering features.

- Up & out put knock-out options are canceled if the underlying asset price rises above a specified level prior to expiration.

- Up & in put knock-in options do not commence until the underlying asset price rises above a certain stated barrier level, whereupon it is brought to life (the underlying asset must fall and remain below the strike price for this put to have intrinsic value).

  Note: An up & out put plus an up & in put is the economic equivalent of a standard put option.

- Down & out call knock-out options are canceled if the underlying asset price falls below a certain price level prior to expiration.

- Down & in call knock-in options do not commence until the underlying asset price falls below a certain barrier level, whereupon it is brought to life (the underlying asset must rise and remain above the strike price for this call to have intrinsic value at expiration).

  Note: A down & out call plus a down & in call is the economic equivalent of a standard call option.

- Barrier options are attractive to purchasers seeking to pay lowest possible dollar premium for an option.

- Although there is a greater risk of loss, barrier options are less expensive than standard options but provide similar potential investment returns.

EXAMPLES: Institutional investors can use barrier options in the following scenarios:

- Knock-out calls to capture upside stock price movements under the assumption that the underlying asset price will not decline and remain below the barrier level.

- Knock-out puts to lock-in profits if upside price moves appear to have peaked.

- Knock-in call options as an inexpensive strategy to participate in the potential for volatile stock price movements.

- Knock-in puts as "insurance" for bondholders fearing inflation and lower bond prices.

Investment Considerations of Barrier Options

Barrier options are usually sold to institutional or sophisticated individual investors in private OTC transactions. Holders of barrier options should be aware that such instruments can expire worthless and may be canceled under certain circumstances. As with all options, the less time remaining until expiration the greater the risk that the value of the option will decline or "evaporate." Investors should also be aware that there is no established exchange-based market for secondary trading of OTC options, so trading liquidity may be limited. Only upstairs markets may be available for such instruments (i.e., typically, only the firm that issues an OTC instrument makes a secondary market in the security), and any bid-ask quotation spreads may be significantly wider for OTC instruments than for instruments traded on securities exchanges.

Depending on the terms governing such financial products, the ability to exercise may be limited (e.g., European style options versus American style) as well as the times of exercise. Over-the-counter investment products are often supported only by a term sheet and an OTC investment contract; therefore, investment risks and the terms should be thoroughly reviewed with investment advisors and the issuer of such products.

LOOKBACK OPTIONS AND WARRANTS

Lookback options and warrants provide investors with tremendous investment flexibility. Lookbacks offer a reset feature whereby the starting strike price of an option can be changed to a more favorable level during a specified period of time after the option is sold. If during the life of a lookback option the underlying asset or index moves against the investor, the lookback feature protects the position by changing or resetting the strike to an at-the-money level (i.e., so it is no longer out-of-the-money).

EXAMPLE: An institutional investor thinks the U.S. economy will falter in the next several quarters due to resurgent inflation and higher interest rates. As a result, the investor thinks the stock market will suffer a severe correction during the next six months. The investor consults the structured products group at one of the broker–dealers she does business with for a product that will allow her to take full advantage of any short-term price appreciation in the U.S. stock market yet provide portfolio protection in case of a sudden market decline. The structured products group provides terms and pricing for a two-year S&P 500 Index warrant with a six-month "lookback" feature included that will allow the client to maximize potential returns given the market conditions she anticipates, as follows:

The client buys the warrants and, as she expected, the S&P 500 Index continues to appreciate, but after three months begins to decline as negative government economic statistics are published.

After the end of six months, the lookback period ends and the strike of the warrant is automatically reset to the highest level the S&P 500 Index reached during the first six-month period of the warrant.

During the remaining 18 months of the warrant term the S&P 500 Index continues to decline and the value of the put warrant increases, offsetting losses the client is sustaining in her stock portfolio.

The warrant fluctuates in value relative to index value changes by reference to the strike level set at the end of the initial six-month lookback period.

Lookback premiums cost significantly more than a standard option with otherwise identical features. They are essentially the economic equivalent of two or more options (i.e., the reset feature is like another option with a shorter duration) combined with a longer-term option into one instrument. The lookback feature provides for a reset of the strike price during the first portion of an option's life, for example, for the first two to six months of a one- or two-year term, respectively. As with options in general, lookback options can have in-, at-, or out-of-the-money strikes. They can be structured as puts or calls on almost any type of financial asset or category (e.g., stocks, bonds, currencies, and commodities or other assets and indices). Lookbacks allow investors to lock in the best achievable strike price during the lookback period so that for the remaining term of the instrument a maximum intrinsic value may be achieved. With lookback options and warrants, the investor expects the "best" price level of an underlying security to occur during a specific future period of time.

Investment Considerations of Lookback Options and Warrants

Lookback options and warrants are usually sold to institutional or sophisticated individual investors in private OTC transactions. Holders of lookback options should be aware that such instruments can expire worthless and may be canceled under certain circumstances, and are speculative investments. As with all options, the less time remaining until expiration the greater the risk that the value of lookback options will decline or evaporate. Because of the reset feature whereby the starting strike price of an option can be changed to a more favorable level during a specified period of time after the option is sold, lookbacks are significantly more expensive than standardized options with otherwise identical features. Furthermore, investors should be aware that there is no established exchange-based market for secondary trading of OTC options like lookback options; therefore, investors should be aware that trading liquidity may be limited. Only upstairs markets may available for such instruments (i.e., typically, only the firm that issues an OTC instrument makes a secondary market in the security), and any bid-ask quotation spreads may be significantly wider than for exchanges-traded instruments. Furthermore, depending on the terms governing such financial products, the ability to exercise may be limited (e.g., European style versus

American style) as well as the times of exercise. Also, OTC investment contracts are often supported only by a term sheet; therefore, investment risks and the terms of such transactions should be thoroughly reviewed with investment professionals and the issuer of such products.

OTHER EXOTIC OPTIONS AND WARRANTS

Reset Options, Warrants, and Notes.   A provision in an option-, warrant-, or index-linked note that allows for the strike price to be moved or reset at a specific point in time to the then-current asset or index level to which the instrument is linked; in contrast to a lookback option where the "best" strike may be obtained, the reset feature in a reset instrument is often triggered at predetermined time(s) or asset levels during the life of the instrument, whereupon certain payments may be made to or by holders. Because of their relative cheapness compared to standard options, the reset feature is usually designed as one-way, meaning the strike is moved in only one direction (down if a put or up if a call) over the life of the contract.

"You Choose" Options and Warrants.   For investors waiting for certain events to occur between the present time and a specific date in the future before deciding what direction to play. For a single payment today, investors hold the right to decide at a specific future date whether to hold a European style call or a put on the underlying asset or index. Most "you choose" options and warrants have the same strike for the put and the call (although different strikes can be provided) and are attractive to investors who believe volatility in the marketplace will increase in the future and who seek to lock in correspondingly lower option premiums at the present time. Traditional strategies for investors who envision increased future volatility but cannot decide which direction the market is headed include straddles (long at-the-money puts and calls) and strangles (long out-of-the-money puts and calls), both of which involve paying for two full-priced options and one of which may be nearly worthless by the choice date in the "you choose" options. "You choose" options allow investors to discard that option with the least likely chance of success prior to expiration. They give holder the most "bang for the buck," that is, the most leverage or control over volatility for the money.

Digital Options.   Options that pay a predetermined amount at such time as a certain specified trigger point is reached relating to the underlying asset.

Options on Futures.   Exchange-listed options that give the holder the right to acquire or sell a specified exchange-listed futures contract at a predetermined price. (Note: OTC options on futures are illegal in the United States and are subject to exclusive jurisdiction of the Commodity Exchange Act.)

GENERAL INVESTMENT CONSIDERATIONS

Over-the-counter option and warrant products are often supported only by a term sheet and an OTC investment contract; therefore, investment risks and the terms should be thoroughly reviewed with the issuer of such products. Investors should also note that certain exotic option and warrant structures (e.g., lookbacks, resets, "you choose," etc.) are more expensive than others; therefore, investors should be aware that undesirable market movements can produce potential losses that are greater than single period standardized options. Furthermore, exotic option and warrants are usually structured in private OTC transactions with institutional clients or sophisticated, high-net-worth investors meeting appropriate customer suitability requirements.

CONCLUSION

The exotic options and warrants discussed in this chapter are tailor-made for transactions designed to capture specific market opportunities. They are usually used by specific types of investment professionals that are familiar with option strategies and transactions. Exotic structures are sometimes built into structured notes, for example, whereby certain reset features allow an index level to be reset at some future point in time. By and large, however, they remain outside the mainstream of investment products, but a familiarity with their characteristics is useful in gaining an understanding of structured products.

A very general discussion of swaps contracts is introduced in Chapter 10. Swaps are private agreements among counterparties and, like exotic options and warrants, are used predominantly by institutional clients and high net-worth investors in private transactions. Usually, one party wants to minimize or fix its exposure to price fluctuations of an underlying asset, and a counterparty is willing to accept exposure to floating price movements. Swaps agreements allow such parties to, in essence, exchange cash flows relating to the market price movements of an underlying asset or assets to achieve desired investment objectives, be they speculative or rigidly conservative in nature. They are highly flexible instruments that are designed to satisfy the specific needs of the parties involved.

Due to their private nature, it is difficult to measure the size of the international swap market, which is one reason for concern by some regulators. The notional amount of assets controlled by swap agreements is estimated to be in the hundreds of billions of dollars worldwide. The international swap market is also known to be extremely efficient, highly intolerant of excessive credit risk, and brutally punitive with regard to parties that default in their obligations under swap contracts.

10

SWAPS

Swaps are private over-the-counter (OTC) contractual agreements negotiated between two or more counterparties who agree to exchange periodic cash payments on an agreed-upon dollar or notional amount based on changes in the price of an underlying asset or assets, such as interest rates, equity prices, currency exchange rates, or commodity prices changes. Swaps agreements are highly flexible and are designed to satisfy the specific needs of the parties involved. Usually, one party wants to minimize or fix its exposure to price fluctuations of the underlying market (e.g., interest rates), and the other party is willing to accept exposure to floating price movements (e.g., variable interest rates). Alternatively, in order to avoid the large cash outlay for a portfolio of common stocks and incurring significant transaction and custodial expenses, a client may enter into a swap transaction based on an equity basket or index of stocks and simply exchanges payments as the equities fluctuate in value. The investor's hope is, of course, that the portfolio will appreciate and payments will be received during the life of the swap. Also, investors in one country can participate in equity or fixed-income markets in other countries by using swaps whereby one investor nets the return (appreciation) of one index against the return of another.

Typically, at the time the counterparties enter into a swap agreement, the cash flows to be exchanged are equal in value. As time passes and the cash flows relating to the underlying asset fluctuate in value, the counterparties make payments back and forth to one another at prearranged periods of time (e.g., quarterly or semiannually). The terms of swap agreements usually dictate how often the value of an underlying asset is reset on the variable side of the swap. With the exception of foreign currency swaps, most swaps do not result in the exchange of principal, but some swaps are structured to require different interest payment dates. The counterparties settle their obligation on a net basis (i.e., at the end of each payment period they add and subtract price movements of the underlying assets during that particular period to determine which counterparty to the agreement makes a payment).

Often, one counterparty to a swap agreement will receive the total return (price return plus dividends) on a stock or other asset class and pay

---

EXAMPLE OF SWAP FINANCING STRUCTURE

Institutional client wants to hedge the market price risk associated with an equity position but wants to retain long-term appreciation potential.

Client "swaps" the future profit and loss on the stock position with a counterparty based on an "initial swap price" (i.e., depending on how the swap is structured; generally speaking, if the value of the stock declines below the initial swap price the counterparty pays the client the cash value of such decline at predetermined time intervals, and the client pays the counterparty if the position increases above the initial swap price).

As compensation to the counterparty for entering the swap, the client negotiates an adjustment to the initial swap price in favor of the counterparty.

Client is now "long" a swap with the counterparty to the agreement and is still holding the stock position.

Because the swap offsets price fluctuations of the common stock held by the client, the position is hedged or "immunized" against price risk to the client.

When the swap expires, the counterparties to the swap agreement make final payment to one another relative to the current market price of the stock.

Note, once the position is hedged, the client may choose to monetize the position by using it as collateral for a loan.

---

to the other counterparty a floating rate of interest (U.S. dollar or LIBOR-based) on the value of the underlying stock or other asset.

One or more counterparties (i.e., usually institutional investors) agree with a swap intermediary (e.g., a swap dealer) to exchange periodic cash flows until the maturity date. The intermediary then structures the transaction, values and prices the cash flows, documents the transaction, and collects fees from one or more counterparties involved in the trade. The swap value equals, for example, the number of shares of stock specified in the agreement multiplied by the daily (or other time period) closing stock or asset price.

Swaps provide investors with controllable exposure to the market or asset class of particular interest. They can be based on the outperformance of one asset over another (e.g., two stocks, stock versus index, index versus index, basket versus index, or other combinations). Swaps based on the outperformance of a single stock versus an index provide diversification without requiring the sale and loss of control (e.g., voting rights and dividends) of the stock position. In order for a counterparty to hedge its risk associated with establishing an equity swap position, the underlying stock must be "borrowable" (i.e., freely tradable and in sufficient quantity in the open market to obtain through stock loan activities). Any restricted stock (i.e., stock subject to Rule 144 or 145; see Chapter 13 for a further discussion of restricted stock) subject to a swap agreement must

---

EXAMPLE OF AN INTEREST RATE AND EXCHANGE RATE SWAP APPLICATION

An international investor wants to fix the interest rate and currency exposure on his investment portfolio.

A swap intermediary finds a counterparty for the transaction and structures a LIBOR-based interest rate swap

Under the swap agreement, any payments made during the life of the swap will be converted from dollars into yen at a fixed or floating exchange rate.

At maturity of the swap, the investor converts his principal investment in the swap back into dollars at the spot exchange rate in order to close the position.

---

be "clean" (i.e., it must be subject to an effective registration statement filed with the SEC).

Other types of swap transactions include:

Forward Start Swaps.   Swaps whose start date and subsequent exchange of interest payments are deferred to some time in the future.

Basis Swaps.   Contracts to exchange interest payments based on different interest rates, such as the exchange of LIBOR-based (i.e., London Inter Bank Offer Rate) cash flows for U.S. Treasury rates.

Commodity Swaps.   The exchange of cash flows linked to a specific commodity price or index of prices (e.g., U.S. Dollar Index, Natural Gas Index, etc.).

Currency Swaps.   The counterparties to the swap contract agree to swap principal and interest payments denominated in different currencies based on an agreed-upon currency exchange rate with specified interest at fixed or floating rates.

Diversification Swaps.   Investor holding unsalable stock enters into equity swap with counterparty whereby counterparty pays the investor the total return of a specified market index and the investor pays the counterparty the total return of the unsalable stock; flexible as to maturity, size, and type of underlying asset; investor diversifies out of single stock, into another desired index, stock or asset class, including income-producing assets, such as debt instrument (see Chapter 13 for further discussion of monetization and hedging strategies).

Index Amortizing Swaps.   The economic equivalent of a swap with an embedded option; for a certain specified lock-out period of time they function as regular swap contracts, after which, however, payment of the principal amount is delayed, extended, or payable according to a predetermined schedule linked to a benchmark interest rate or price fluctuations of some other asset or index.

Leveraged Swaps.   Many different permutations but generally involve a series of variable rate interest payments that adjust at some specified multiple of actual interest rate movements.

Swaptions.   An option contract on an interest rate swap with the swap having some future commencement date; a type of option contract used to manage interest rate risk.

INVESTMENT CONSIDERATIONS

Swap agreements are typically entered into by institutional clients, high-net-worth investors, and investment professionals. Investors must satisfy credit and suitability requirements prior to engaging in swap transactions; creditworthiness is critical to swap counterparties in assessing the possibility of default or nonperformance of a party to the contract. Investors must be aware that when entering into a swap transaction, and depending on the terms of each specific agreement, they are exposed to the economic risk of price movements in the assets underlying agreement, such as those arising from adverse market movements, interest rate fluctuations, foreign exchange rate changes, credit risk, and other factors. Also, investors should note that there is no formal secondary market for trading swap contracts. Swaps are usually "unwound" or liquidated by entering into offsetting swaps whose terms reflect the market conditions and other prevailing market conditions at the time of liquidation. Investors should be aware that should they decide to unwind a particular swap agreement prior to termination, the cost of doing so may be significantly higher if the assets or interest rates on which the swap is based suffer price movements that are adverse to the investor's position in the existing swap.

CONCLUSION

The chapters on warrants, structured notes, convertibles, exotic options, and swaps dealt with instruments that fuse the economic characteristics of one or more cash instruments or markets into a new structured derivative product. The next type of structured product, investment trusts, discussed in Chapter 11, can be distinguished from others by its ability to mix actual cash instruments and securities (such as stocks, bonds, forward commodity contracts, currencies, equities, options, treasury strips, swap agreements, etc.) in one legal "container" called an investment trust, and then reissue smaller units of investment to investors. Such units of investment offer new payoff patterns that provide yet another means for investors to achieve their particular investment goals using structured financial products.

11

INVESTMENT TRUSTS

Investment or "grantor" trusts provide a legal container into which a variety
of assets can be deposited and resold in smaller economic units or denom-
inations than are normally available to investors that might not otherwise
be able to participate in certain types of financial markets (e.g., the crude oil
market, other commodities or currencies, etc.). Trust investments provide
investors with a means to acquire direct ownership in a specific asset or
combination of assets (e.g., equity, debt, currencies, or commodities) for a
nominal investment (e.g., for the same price as a share of common stock or
an option).

In order to make trust units appealing to investors, combinations of
other securities are often deposited into the trust (e.g., stocks, bonds, treasury securities, forward contracts, options, etc.) in order to modify the
payoff pattern of the trust units and provide investors with income combined with potential price appreciation or other investment characteristics. Assets are deposited in the trust and managed by a trustee on behalf
of the beneficiary investors. When trusts are terminated, the assets or cash
proceeds from the sale of such assets are distributed to investors, net of
transaction costs and fees. Trusts may also be used in certain structured
transactions for investors seeking to monetize large equity holdings (Chapter 13 further discusses monetization strategies).

EXAMPLE: An individual investor is concerned about inflation eroding the value of her personal assets. Research available through her investment advisor indicates that ownership of crude oil is a good inflation hedge. But she is hesitant to invest in oil through the futures market. Her broker provides her with a prospectus describing exchange-traded oil trust units:

The structured products group in her investment advisor's firm has originated an oil trust that is registered with the SEC.

Units in the trust cost $12.00, each of which controls the cash equivalent of one barrel of oil, deliverable to the trust five years in the future.

The oil trust units are listed on a national U.S. security exchange for secondary trading where investors can trade their units at any time during the five-year life of the trust.

The proceeds from the public offering are used by the trustee to purchase a five-year forward contract specifying that a certain quantity of oil must be purchased by the trustee at a specified date in the future.

The forward oil contract is obtained and deposited into the trust by the trustee.

Investors, through their ownership of oil trust units, are effectively owners of crude oil.

The forward contract is the economic equivalent of owning a prepaid, cash-settled call option on a specified quantity of oil.

Payoff to investors at termination of the trust is determined by the price received by the trustee for the quantity of oil sold by the trustee multiplied by the number of units each investor holds.

Trusts can hold more than one prepaid forward contract on almost any type of asset. Such contracts can be written with staggered expiration dates in order to provide cash flows to investors at predetermined dates through commodity auctions (in the case of oil) or sales at specified locations and markets at their prevailing market prices. At expiration of a forward contract, the asset it controls is sold by the trustee. The cash proceeds are then distributed to trust unit investors.

Agreements that govern the operation of the trust provide that the trustee will liquidate the forward contract upon expiration of the trust and distribute the cash proceeds to trust unit investors.

The forward contract expires in five-years and the oil is sold by the trustee at the spot oil price of $23 per barrel, a 92-percent increase above the initial public offering (IPO) price of the units.

If the price of oil has fallen to $10 per barrel on the maturity date, unit holders will suffer a 17-percent loss on their investments.

In this example, when the trust terminates, the proceeds from the sale of the oil, net of expenses (trustees management fee, administrative expenses, etc.), are distributed to unitholders in cash.

INVESTMENT CONSIDERATIONS

Grantor trust units are sold to both retail and institutional investors in registered public offerings and to institutional and high-net-worth individuals in unregistered, private transactions. Public trust unit offerings are regulated under the Investment Company Act of 1940 and are required to be registered. However, private trusts involving fewer than 100 investors are generally unregulated but are still subject to applicable contract law and state or federal laws and antifraud statutes.

Investors in trust units should be aware that, at termination of the trust, the assets backing the trust may have declined in value or become worthless and that distributions of trust assets, upon termination of the trust, could be entirely absorbed by trust expenses and fees. Also, investors should note that trusts are not usually subject to a separate federal income tax as long as there is only one type of ownership interest held by the trust, and the trustees cannot legally alter the investment objectives of the trust.

Investors should be aware that trading liquidity may be limited. Only upstairs markets may be available for such instruments, and any bid-ask quotation spreads may be significantly wider than for exchanges-traded instruments. Furthermore, offering materials provided in connection with trust unit offerings should be reviewed for other risks, tax issues, and customer suitability requirements.

CONCLUSION

This chapter provided insight into how a long-established legal structure, a grantor trust, can be used in creative new ways to provide new means for issuers and investors to achieve their financial goals. Trusts offer the ability to mix actual cash instruments and securities for reissue as smaller units of investment. One of the drawbacks of using trust structures is the expense involved in creating them. Since trustees must be hired by the trust, and such trustees must engage in a certain amount of oversight activity, a level of expense is incurred by trusts, compared to the relatively few ongoing expenses regarding warrant, option, and note offerings. Regardless, trust structures, beyond their use in equity-based unit investment trusts and real estate trusts, among others, are useful to financial engineers.

Chapter 12 deals with OTC private placements, which is a type of offering that can be used for structured products as an intermediate step between publicly offered warrants and structured notes, for example, and larger private transactions among institutions. OTC private placements, although not typically offered to retail investors, can be structured and issued in units of investment that are attractive to individual and institutional clients, usually in the tens of thousands to hundreds of thousands of dollars. They are also attractive because of the speed with which they can be brought to market.

12

OTC PRIVATE PLACEMENTS FOR INSTITUTIONAL AND INDIVIDUAL CLIENTS

Because of their flexibility and ease of issuance and sale to qualified groups of investors, private placements of custom-made structured products provide an attractive means to exploit rapidly changing market events. In contrast to publicly offered transactions, even those that can be issued off of shelf registration statements that are designed for rapid use, which can take several weeks to a month or more to launch, private placements can be launched in hours or days to discrete categories of suitable endusers. Over-the-counter (OTC) private placements offer custom-made private transactions for institutional clients and individuals or groups of accredited investors.

Issuers of privately placed instruments must satisfy applicable credit standards established by regulatory authorities. Such offerings are usually exempt from registration under the Securities Act of 1933, as amended (e.g., as Section 4(2) or Regulation D transactions), and provide unique opportunities to quickly and efficiently invest in various sectors of the U.S. and world financial markets. Private placement exemptions eliminate registration delays associated with exchange-traded products (e.g., such delays can involve from 30 days to a year or more, depending on how novel

---

EXAMPLE OF A PRIVATELY PLACED WARRANT STRUCTURE

A research analysis forecasts steel prices doubling within 18 months and that the stock of various steel supply companies will benefit:

Broker–dealer originating a transaction for a group of institutional and accredited individual clients compiles a price-weighted index of 20 steel suppliers and sets the starting or strike index level at 512 (the sum of the stock prices of the 20 stocks).

Broker–dealer arranges for the issuance of an 18-month at-the-money call warrant on the steel index for $5.00 per warrant.

A total of 30 investors joins the offering; the average investment is $75,000 per investor and the total size of the offering is $7 million.

If the index rises to 665 by the expiration date, a 30-percent increase, the call warrants may trade for approximately $15.00, a 200-percent increase from the issue price.

If the index is below the strike level at the end of the 18-month term of the warrants, they expire worthless.

---

the offering is). As soon as economic opportunities are identified (i.e., an increasing, decreasing, or even a "flat" market), private transactions can be structured and issued quickly to exploit such opportunities. Private placement equity products can include warrants, equity-linked notes (whose maturities match an economic outlook), and other structures.

INVESTMENT CONSIDERATIONS

OTC private placements of structured products are sold to institutional clients and accredited individual investors. Although interpretations of individual customer suitability requirements may vary among issuing firms, private placements are usually only offered to accredited investors who, among other criteria, satisfy the following:

1. Individual net worth (or joint net worth, if married) must exceed $1,000,000 (excluding the value of the investor's principal residence).

2. Individual income must be in excess of $200,000 in each of the two most recent years with a reasonable expectation of receiving the same level of income in the current year.

Investors should be aware that warrants are subject to a high degree of price risk, including the risk of expiring worthless if the particular market on which the warrant relates does not move in the investors' favor. Warrants can also lose value over time, as the expiration date approaches (i.e., loss of time value). OTC private placements of structured warrants are usually only sold to investors who have option-approved accounts and have prior option transaction experience. In private OTC warrant transactions, investors should note that trading liquidity may be limited. Only upstairs markets may be available (i.e., perhaps only the issuer of the warrant makes a secondary market in the security), and any bid-ask quotation spreads may be significantly wider than for warrants traded on stock exchanges.

Index- and other asset-linked notes are less speculative than warrants, options, and other more leveraged instruments. Therefore, such notes usually do not require that customers have option-approved accounts. However, investors should be advised that at maturity most asset-linked notes return only the principal amount invested if the underlying index does not appreciate above the starting index level, resulting in a loss of whatever returns the investor may have received from alternative investments in interest-bearing securities. Any secondary trading of index- and other asset-linked notes is also affected by the creditworthiness of the issuer, the ranking of the debt (e.g., senior, unsecured, or subordinated obligations), interest rate movements during the life of the notes, the amount of time remaining to maturity, trading liquidity, and fluctuations of the index level or asset price, among other factors. Due to the deep discount, zero-coupon-bond nature of index- and asset-linked notes, interest rate fluctuations can significantly influence the value of such instruments.

Documentation of OTC transactions for institutional clients usually involves only a term sheet, whereas with individual clients a private placement memorandum is usually used that includes the terms of each transaction and extensive risk disclosure materials. Investors and their financial representatives are also often required to make certain written representations about the suitability of the investment for the investor. Offering materials provided in connection with private warrant offerings should be reviewed for other risks, tax issues, and customer suitability requirements.

EXAMPLE OF A PRIVATELY PLACED INDEX-LINKED NOTE STRUCTURE

Research forecasts steel prices doubling within 18 months and that the stock of various steel supply companies will benefit:

Broker–dealer arranges for the issuance of an 18-month index-linked note based on the steel index; the issue price is $100 per note and the strike index level is 512.

A total of 25 investors joins the offering; the average investment is $250,000 per investor and the total size of the offering is $18 million.

At maturity each investor receives $100 plus a coupon equal to any percent increase in the index.

If the index rises to 665 by the maturity date of the note (a 30-percent increase), investors receive $100 plus a coupon payment of $30.

If the index is unchanged or below the strike index level on the maturity date, the investor receives $100 return of principal but no coupon payment.

CONCLUSION

Chapters 5 through 12 dealt with structured financial products that are by and large designed to exploit certain market conditions or to modify the payoff patterns of more traditional stock and bond investments. Some structures, such as warrants and exotic options, are designed to speculate on market events. Others, such as various structured notes, convertible securities, swaps, and investment trusts, generally are used for some form of financial risk management or hedging activity. OTC private placements can be used to achieve speculative and risk management investment goals, and can be brought to market very quickly while appealing to the levels of investment of institutional and individual accredited investors.

Chapters 13–15 deal with trading and capital-raising strategies for individuals holding restricted stock, low-cost-basis, or other concentrated equity positions, and corporations seeking to raise capital by using structured product strategies involving various new registration mechanisms and trading procedures that tend to fall naturally into the financial engineering arena. Chapter 13 provides an overview of trading strategies that are based on well-established option or swap structures. The monetization and hedging strategies for restricted stock and other concentrated equity positions constitute an exciting area of financial engineering that is as legally complex and difficult to maneuver as it is challenging from trading and hedging perspectives. It is of intense interest to those who have a significant portion of their net worths locked up in the common stock of a company they may have founded and later sold. Usually owners of unsalable securities have only two choices: sell under restricted conditions or hold. Holding often means risking one's assets to the stock market, where adverse price moves can wipe out one's life savings. Conversely, selling often translates into heavy tax payments and the loss of voting rights and dividend income.

PART THREE

Trading Strategies and Capital-Raising Approaches

13

MONETIZATION AND HEDGING STRATEGIES FOR RESTRICTED STOCK AND OTHER CONCENTRATED EQUITY POSITIONS

Individual or institutional investors frequently have significant equity positions in publicly traded companies involving restricted or low-cost-basis stock. Wealth preservation and enhancement of those assets are of paramount concern to these types of investors.

Owners of Rule 144 or Rule 145 stock,[1] unregistered stock,[2] or other

---

[1]Rule 144, among other things, imposes holding period and trading volume limitations for affiliates and other holders of restricted stock, as proscribed under the Securities Act. There are two categories of stock subject to selling restrictions: *control stock,* which is any stock of an issuer (including registered and unregistered shares) owned by an affiliate of the issuer (i.e., an officer, director or other person who, through stock ownership or otherwise, controls the management policies of the issuer); and *restricted stock,* which is unregistered stock owned by an affiliate or nonaffiliate that was sold by the issuer or an affiliate in a private transaction. Rule 145 pertains to stock received in connection with a merger, consolidation, or other reorganization by a person who was an affiliate of the disappearing company (and who

unsalable stock positions[3] often seek liquidity, diversification, and tax minimization in preserving their wealth. Such holdings are often acquired in connection with the founding of a new company, from venture capital partnership distributions, as consideration in connection with mergers, acquisitions, buyouts, and compensation to executives. Tax or regulatory constraints may make it difficult to diversify such concentrated or restricted equity positions. Traditional methods of locking in gains or diversification may also be unavailable. Usually owners of these securities have only two choices: sell under restricted conditions or hold.

Restricted stock positions are difficult to liquidate by traditional means and often represent a significant portion of an individual's net worth. But a number of structured product strategies that have become popular among certain groups of investors are available that offer holders of concentrated equity positions ways to protect their assets:

- Monetization (i.e., maximize the price when selling large blocks of restricted stock or enhance the yield of low-tax-basis holdings)
- Diversification
- Hedging
- Maintaining price appreciation potential
- Cash generation
- Deferral of taxes
- Participation in stocks, markets, or other asset classes unavailable in existing listed securities

---

does not become an affiliate of the surviving company), or stock acquired from such a person by a nonaffiliate of the issuer in a private transaction. Rule 145 stock is subject to some of the same selling restrictions of Rule 144 stock.

[2]Unregistered stock may not be sold to the public until it is registered with the Securities and Exchange Commission or the sale is otherwise exempt from registration.

[3]Other unsalable stock positions include stock subject to contractual restrictions (including underwriting lock-ups and special shareholder agreements), *low-cost-basis stock* (securities that are unsalable without realizing a taxable event), securities acquired under and subject to a *pooling of interest* (i.e., securities relating to the merger or acquisition that are subject to the public release of financial accounting statements on the new combined entity), and *qualified replacement securities* (securities acquired pursuant to a business owner's sale of company stock to an employee stock ownership plan (ESOP) are unsalable without triggering the gain deferred on the original sale).

- Customization of portfolios

- Maintenance of voting and dividend rights

The monetization and hedging strategies available to investors depend on whether they meet certain levels of suitability.[4] Although certain strategies may be pursued for persons affiliated[5] with the company and whose stock is involved in a proposed transaction (i.e., officers, directors, or other control persons, such as shareholders of greater than 5 percent of the company's outstanding common stock), many of these strategies relate only to nonaffiliates (i.e., individuals who are not officers, directors, or other control persons). The proposed counterparty to each strategy is assumed to be a broker–dealer or other financial organization that legally engages in structuring concentrated equity transactions. Such private transactions usually arise through introductions made by investment executives or other sales personnel to financial engineers. Restricted stock and concentrated equity transactions typically provide higher broker commissions than other, less complex types of securities transactions.

The main types of strategies and transactions available to investors for monetizing restricted stock, other concentrated equity positions, and customizing solutions to meet particular investment needs are summarized as follows:

> ***Discounted Private Equity Sales.***   Discounted private sale by investor of restricted stock to counterparty who holds stock until it is freely tradable or otherwise further monetizes it or sells it pursuant to an exemption from registration; investor loses all control and equity ownership in the stock, receives less than 100 percent of the current market value of the stock, but has no economic risk in the position going forward.

---

[4]Suitability, in this case, refers to an investor's net worth, his or her relationship with the company who issued the underlying common stock, the number of shares proposed for a transaction, the daily trading volume of the stock, the length of time the stock has been held, stock trading price volatility, and other legal and regulatory constraints.

[5]In addition to reporting requirements, under Section 16(b) of the Act, if an insider buys and sells, or sells and buys, any equity security of the issuer (including options or other derivative securities) within any six-month period and realizes any net positive difference between the prices of such buy and sell (or sell and buy) transactions, the issuer may "recover" such net positive difference from the insider. Furthermore, Section 16(c) prohibits an insider from selling short any equity security of the issuer but does not preclude writing (selling) calls or buying puts with respect to securities held by insiders.

Monetizing Equity Swap.   Investor exchanges cash flow obligations with a counterparty relating to investor's restricted stock or concentrated equity position in exchange for the returns of another asset or diversified index; transaction generates temporary cash proceeds to the investor who retains stock ownership and voting rights but is still exposed to market price risk

Sale of Deep-in-the-Money Call Options.   Investor partially monetizes and hedges restricted or clean stock position, retains control of stock and avoids taxation; investor's downside price protection is limited to amount of premium received; no investor participation in upside appreciation beyond value of premium received; at expiration investor must pay counterparty any per-share amount above the strike; investor's upside price exposure mitigated by eventual salability of stock position; moderate risk to investor.

Sale of Out-of-the-Money Call Options.   Costless yield enhancement strategy to investor; investor sells the option, receives cash, retains control of stock, and avoids taxation; price protection to investor up to the strike and downside protection equal only to the value of the premium received; investor suffers loss if the stock price declines below the value of the premium received; investor's upside price exposure mitigated by eventual salability of stock position; investor retains downside stock price risk.

Purchase of Put Options.   Investor obtains downside price protection on equity position by purchasing a put option; investor retains control over stock and all appreciation potential.

Zero-Cost Collar Transactions.   Costless trade to investor seeking hedge protection of equity position without incurring any out-of-pocket costs (e.g., also referred to as "costless" or "cash settled" collars); investor retains control of stock and avoids taxation; investor achieves price protection by selling a call and buying a put, therefore locking in gains between put and call strikes; investor's upside price exposure through the sale of the call option is offset by the ability to sell the actual stock position; minimal risk to investor.

Monetizing Collar.   A zero-cost collar transaction (see above) combined with a margin loan; proceeds to investor are typically greater than a conventional margin loan.

Short against the Box.   Investor fully monetizes restricted or clean stock, locks in price, has use of cash proceeds during the term of the position, and retains control of stock; investor runs the risk of borrowed stock being called away, but risk is mitigated by deliverability of stock held as collateral; presently not a taxable event but currently being reviewed and subject to change by the Internal Revenue Service.

Trust Structures.   Legal "containers" into which restricted stock can be deposited or pledged and resold as units to other investors; investor retains voting rights, partially monetizes a concentrated equity position, hedges price risk, and defers potential tax payments during the life of the trust.

Sale of Stock Through a Structured Equity Program.   Provides public corporations, affiliates, and shareholders with a means to sell large amounts of stock over time in a cost-effective, consistent, and "quiet" manner; outright sale of stock through an SEC shelf registration.

Many of the strategies to be discussed involve a high degree of risk and, as such, the client will be required to have the appropriate sophistication to understand the relevant risks of the transaction and the financial ability to satisfy any payments that might be required to be made. Clients should be advised to conduct an independent review, consult their investment advisors, and reach their own conclusion regarding the legal, tax, and accounting aspects of a proposed transaction as it relates to their asset, liability, or other risk management objectives. Investors should also be aware that, as a private OTC transaction, there is no established secondary trading market for the positions established in most of the strategies to be discussed. Therefore, secondary trading liquidity for the position, if any, will be provided by the counterparty to the transaction, thus creating additional risks for the investor.

DISCOUNTED PRIVATE EQUITY SALES

Frequently individual nonaffiliates of public corporations hold sizable restricted stock positions that they seek to monetize. Because of the two-year holding period and the trading volume requirements of SEC Rule 144, many investors enter into privately negotiated agreements whereby such stock is sold at a discount to a purchaser (who then becomes subject to

---

EXAMPLE: An investor owns 250,000 shares of restricted Tech Corporation stock currently selling for $75.00 per share, which the investor has held for the last 12 months. The investor must hold the stock for another 12 months under Rule 144(k) before it can be sold in the open market. The investor, however, believes the stock price is as high as it is going to be during the current business cycle and wants to sell it at the end of the current fiscal year.

The investor negotiates with counterparty broker–dealer for the confidential private sale of his Tech stock position.

Counterparty purchases the Tech stock from the investor and pays him, for example, 95 percent of the current $75.00 market price or $71.25 per share or $17,812,500 in aggregate ($71.25 per share × 250,000 shares = $17,812,500).

Investor avoids exposure to price movements of the stock.

---

the seller's restrictions) thereby generating immediate proceeds to the investor without running afoul of the holding, volume, or filing requirements of Rule 144. Discounted private equity sales generate immediate cash liquidity to investors. They eliminate an investor's economic exposure to an equity position without resetting the restricted stock holding period. Furthermore, the quantity of shares sold privately by the investor is not limited by Rule 144 provisions.

Structuring Procedures, Risks, and Economics

In almost all cases, like the investor, the counterparty broker–dealer or other financial intermediary to a discounted private equity sale will not want to be subject to the future price movements of the stock because its holding period "tacks" onto the investor's holding period and, therefore, will also be subject to any remaining disposition restriction before resale is permitted. The counterparty will therefore want to lock in its profit vis-à-vis the stock by hedging its position risk. An effective way for the counterparty to hedge, for example, its stock price risk to Tech Corporation stock, mentioned in the preceding example, is by selling the position "short," that is, selling unrestricted clean Tech stock that it does not own and locking in the same price as the private equity sale transaction. Therefore, if the restricted Tech stock position declines in value at the termination of the holding period, the counterparty to the trade can sell the restricted Tech stock position into the open market and use the proceeds to cover the short Tech stock position by then purchasing Tech stock in the open market to replace the clean stock the counterparty previously shorted. Before shorting the position, the counterparty coordinates with its stock loan department to determine whether enough clean Tech stock is available to use to cover its short position on the private equity sale transaction. The stock loan department holds clean stock in the accounts of many investors and maintains written permission from such investors to use their stock, if necessary, for stock loan transactions.

Other general counterparty structuring procedures are as follows:

- Negotiate the discount. In order to induce the counterparty to enter into a concentrated equity transaction, holders of restricted or concentrated stock positions must provide a discount from the existing market value on the sale of their restricted stock to the counterparty; such discount is negotiated among the parties to the transaction.

- Determine the pricing variables. Other variables involved in the pricing analysis include the availability of and ability for the counterparty to borrow the underlying stock, trading volume, price volatility, and the period of time remaining during which the stock is restricted.

- Verify holding period. The counterparty must determine the exact time remaining until the restricted stock can be freely tradable in order to determine the duration of its risk exposure and calculate the economics of the transaction.

- Pursue documentation and due diligence research. The counterparty, in conjunction with legal counsel, engages in due diligence research of the company whose stock is subject to the sale, legal review, and related documentation with the broker and client in order to support a transaction (see the Resource Guide for a sample questionnaire that the originator of a transaction may require from sellers of restricted securities).

- Pay client. Once the terms of the transaction have been agreed upon, the due diligence and legal review have been completed, and all documentation consummated, the client is paid the negotiated amount per share of restricted stock.

- Pay broker. The counterparty negotiates a commission with the introducing broker or salesperson for the transaction; the payment to the broker is made by the counterparty when the transaction is entered into.

- The counterparty unwinds the trade at the end of the two-year holding period.

- Transaction risks to the counterparty:

    Takeover risk[6]

    Short squeeze risk[7]

    Unwind risk[8]

    No dynamic hedging required; stock position locked-in[9]

---

[6]*Takeover risk* occurs when a company is taken over by another company, because any holder of restricted stock who has hedged its position through the short sale of such stock runs the risk of having his short position called away by holders of the takeover stock who seek to monetize their holdings through the tender offer.

[7]*Short squeeze risk* is the risk that stock that has been borrowed is called away by the owner of such stock during a period when the stock price is rising or in situations where the number of shares in the market is so limited that reestablishing the short position becomes very expensive to the short seller; a "squeeze" occurs as short sellers trying to cover their positions create a scarcity of stock and drive the stock price up, compounding the losses suffered by short sellers.

[8]*Unwind risk* relates to the possibility of having to reestablish a hedge at an uneconomic price; in this case, if a hedge that involves the short sale of a stock has to be deconstructed or "unwound" because of a takeover or short squeeze, it will have to be reestablished so that the party obligated to perform under the terms of the transaction that is being hedged is not fully exposed to market risk.

[9]*Dynamic hedging* has a number of meanings; in this case it refers to the active management of a hedge position through continuous trading and risk management activities. When a stock position is locked in, for example, a short position may have been established that virtually offsets the position risk involved in the transaction, notwithstanding takeover, short squeeze, and related unwind risks.

EXAMPLE: Mega Corporation sells one of its subsidiaries to LBO Corporation in exchange for 2 million shares of LBO common stock. The stock has not been registered with the SEC and Mega has to hold it for two years before it can be sold in the open market. After 22 months, Mega wants to sell its LBO stock position, for tax reasons.

Counterparty broker–dealer negotiates to buy the restricted LBO stock position at a 2.75-percent discount from the $25.00 market price of freely tradable LBO shares.

Counterparty then resells Mega's LBO stock at $25.00 and pays Mega $23.50 per share.

In addition to the stock price discount counterparty receives from Mega, counterparty will attempt to realize a hedge profit over the life of the transaction as determined by ongoing trading and transaction costs, bid-offer spreads, the trading liquidity of LBO stock, and possible stock loan short rebate and financing spreads.

Investment Considerations of Discounted Private Equity Sales—Counterparty

The counterparty to a discounted private equity sale must allocate resources based upon the amount of time estimated to set up transactions; concentrated equity trades are labor intensive and require a significant amount of effort to consummate. The investor must meet net worth and financial requirements at least equivalent to or higher than those set forth pursuant to SEC Regulation D requirements. The investor must have held the underlying position for at least three months or more and must have appropriate sophistication to understand the salient risks of the transaction. Furthermore, the investor must have discussed the trade with tax, financial, and legal counsel to seek advice as to the appropriate issues involved with this type of investment.

The counterparty usually will want the equity position to be valued at $2,000,000 or more; otherwise the economics of the transaction may not be favorable. The minimum stock trading price should be at least $5.00 per share in order to avoid thinly traded or stocks with low market capitalizations and liquidity risks associated with counterparty's short selling of the position to hedge its price risk. Also, the minimum daily trading volume of the stock should be 10,000 shares per day or more (i.e., sufficient to sell short the aggregate position over five to ten trading days without adversely affecting the stock price) in order to ensure adequate trading liquidity for counterparty's hedging purposes.

Investment Considerations of Discounted Private Equity Sales—Investor

The private sale of restricted stock provides an investor with immediate cash proceeds and liquidity and eliminates exposure to adverse stock price movements. The investor should be aware that he or she will receive less than 100 percent of current market price of the stock. The sale itself and the quantity of shares sold, in this case, by an investor who is not an affiliate of the company whose stock is involved in the transaction, is not limited by the holding or trading volume requirements of SEC Rule 144.

A private sale of restricted stock is a confidentially negotiated agreement between the investor and the counterparty involved in the transaction. Affiliates (i.e., directors, officers, or control person[10]) of the company on whose stock the transaction is based may not legally engage in discounted private equity sales of restricted stock. Furthermore, investors engaging in this type of trading strategy should be aware that gain on a private equity sale of stock, if any, is taxable in current year of sale.

MONETIZING EQUITY SWAP

Investors who wish to hedge their stock positions and generate cash proceeds (which must be repaid at maturity) without realizing a taxable sale

---

[10]*Reporting Requirements:* Under Section 16(a) of the Securities Exchange Act of 1934 (the "Exchange Act"), every officer or director, and every beneficial owner of more than 10 percent of any class of equity security of an issuer that is registered with the SEC under the Exchange Act, must file reports with the SEC disclosing any equity interest in such issuer (including options and other derivative securities) and any changes in such ownership interest; and all acquisitions, dispositions, and exercises of options and other derivative securities must be reported.

of the underlying stock, might consider a monetizing equity swap. This type of transaction combines elements of an equity swap (consisting of the exchange of a stream of cash flows under an agreed set of contractual terms; see Chapter 10) and a loan. The concentrated equity holder exchanges the total return (price performance and dividend income) of the holdings for the total returns of a specified asset (an index, portfolio of securities, or other asset).

A monetizing equity swap transaction provides investors with a cost-effective and efficient way to diversify their investments into other assets without actually owning the underlying securities. The swap component of the transaction reduces or eliminates the investor's exposure to stock price fluctuations of the original holdings. Swap terms are flexible and negotiable as to maturities, interest payments, settlement, underlying assets, and so on. There are no initial out-of-pocket expenses to the investor. All costs are locked in at trade date, and the investor maintains stock ownership and voting rights. The investor may receive a loan of up to 95 percent of the value of the stock involved at the initiation of the transaction, and may also receive (depending on the type of structure) a negotiated rate of interest on the value of the shares swapped. Up to 100 percent of the cash generated can be further invested in other securities if so desired. There is no margin maintenance, the investor retains the ability to substitute other collateral for the stock pledged at the initiation of the swap, and the transaction can be unwound at any time. At maturity, the investor must assume any depreciation of the price and any dividends paid on the stock that, presumably, may be offset against possible gains realized through diversification and any dividends or interest received on the swap component of the transaction.

Investment Consideration of Monetizing Equity Swaps

Investors should be aware that proposed changes under tax and other laws are pending and, if implemented, may render this strategy inappropriate for many investors from a tax, legal, or investment perspective. At maturity, or as otherwise agreed, the investor must be prepared to pay to the counterparty to the trade any appreciation of the stock that occurred during the life of the transaction. Investors should note that there is a possibility that the asset swapped into will underperform relative to the original investment holdings.

In monetizing equity swap transactions, dividends are usually forfeited by the investor as total price returns of the stock (stock price plus dividends) are used as the basis for determining the amount of cash flows to be periodically exchanged.

SALE OF DEEP-IN-THE-MONEY CALL OPTIONS

An investor holding a block of stock may wish to avoid an outright sale of the stock in order to, for example, maintain voting rights, or dividend income, or possibly avoid or defer incurring taxable gains on the sale of the position. Transactions for such concentrated equity positions can be structured so as to allow an investor to partially monetize and simultaneously hedge the downside price risk exposure on such position through the sale of a deep-in-the-money call option. By selling a deep-in-the-money call option (i.e., the option is priced at a percentage of the current stock price), the investor generates immediate tax-deferred income (equal to the difference between the strike price and the market price of the stock). Any losses incurred on the underlying stock position because of an expiration price that is lower than the strike price may be mitigated by the premium income generated to the investor through the sale of the option. Dividends, voting rights, and other benefits are preserved by the investor, and any gain or loss on the option position is not taxed until the option expires or the position is unwound. The cash settlement feature of the transaction avoids any sale of the shares.

A deep-in-the-money call transaction (so called because it uses a below-market strike price) produces cash for the investor in an amount approximately equal to the in-the-money intrinsic value portion of the option. The position provides price risk protection to the investor from the market price of the stock down to the strike price of the option during the life of the transaction. The terms of the option include cash settlement by the counterparty to the trade at expiration on any in-the-money amount. The following examples provide insights into how deep-in-the-money call options work for investors and counterparties to such transactions.

EXAMPLE: An individual investor meeting appropriate suitability tests (see the Investment Considerations section) owns 250,000 shares of Highflyer Corporation common stock that currently sells for $60.00 per share. The investor wants to hedge his downside price risk in the stock, monetize the position (i.e., generate cash), and avoid a taxable transaction if possible. The position is structured as follows:

Counterparty broker–dealer purchases a deep-in-the-money call option on Highflyer from the investor using a negotiated $40.00 strike price.

Highflyer is trading at $60.00 per share so a $40 strike means that the option has an intrinsic cash value and counterparty pays the investor $20.00 (i.e., the option is in-the-money by $20.00).

The option is European style (i.e., may only be exercised at expiration) and may only be settled in cash.

If the option is in-the-money at expiration (i.e., Highflyer stock is trading above the $40.00 per share strike price), the investor agrees to pay counterparty such in-the-money amount, which is offset by an increase in value of the Highflyer stock the investor still holds and can now sell since the restricted stock holding period has ended.

If the option is out-of-the-money (i.e., Highflyer is trading below $40.00 per share) or at-the-money (i.e., Highflyer is trading at exactly $40.00 per share), then the option position expires worthless and the investor owes nothing to counterparty.

Although Highflyer is trading at $60.00 per share when the position is created, the investor retains price protection down to the $40.00 strike of the call for the duration of the option position.

Incidentally, the investor may be able to generate cash from the transaction through a margin loan (using his Highflyer stock as collateral).

The following list of stock prices and corresponding explanations provide clarification of how deep-in-the-money call option values are influenced at various stock price levels.

Per-Share Price of Highflyer Common Stock at Expiration	Economic Impact on Investor's Position
$20.00	Investor keeps the $20.00 per share premium initially paid by the counterparty and still holds stock worth $20.00 per share. The position value = $40.00 per share and the option expires worthless.
$40.00	Investor keeps the $20.00 per share premium and still holds stock worth $40.00 per share. The position value = $60.00 per share and the option expires worthless.
$60.00	Counterparty exercises the options, investor keeps the $20.00 per share premium but pays counterparty $20.00 per share (the difference between the $40.00 call strike and the $60.00 price of the stock). Investor still owns stock worth $60.00 per share. Therefore, the position value = $60.00 per share ($20.00 − $20.00 + $60.00 = $60.00) and the counterparty to the transaction exercises the option at expiration.
$80.00	Counterparty exercises the option, investor keeps the $20.00 per share premium but pays counterparty $40.00 per share (the difference between the $40.00 call strike and the $80.00 price of the stock). Investor still owns stock worth $80.00 per share. Therefore, the aggregate position value = $60.00 per share ($20.00 − $40.00 + $80.00 = $60.00).

Structuring Procedures, Risks, and Economics for Deep-in-the-Money Call Options

The following list provides an insight into the actions and procedures required of a financial engineer structuring deep-in-the-money call option transactions. Such activities are explained in more detail in the earlier section of this chapter concerning discounted private equity sales.

1. Check with stock loan for borrow.
2. Negotiate discount with investor.
3. Determine pricing variables.
4. Verify holding period of any restricted stock.
5. Pursue documentation, due diligence.
6. Hedge position down to strike.
7. Pay client the per share in-the-money amount.
8. Pay broker.
9. At expiration of the position, collect any call value from the investor (i.e., that per share cash amount or intrinsic value above the strike).
10. Unwind trade and buy back hedge when option expires.
11. Counterparty risk:

    Short squeeze risk

    No unwind risks

    Minimal takeover risk

    Minimal dividend risk[11]

    No dynamic hedging needed

---

[11]*Dividend risk* pertains to the possibility that the company on whose stock the transaction is based decides to stop paying the common stock dividend (due to poor earnings, a shortage of funds, or the need to preserve funds for operating needs, etc.). The loss of the dividend changes the value of any options relating to the stock; for example, calls may become less valuable due to the loss of income accruing to the holder of the stock on which the call options are based, and the puts may become more valuable if the loss of the dividend causes the stock price to decline.

EXAMPLE: Unaffiliated investor holds 35,000 shares of Cyberweb Corporation restricted common stock. Cyberweb stock is trading in the open market at $40 per share. The investor has held the stock for one year, which is less than the two-year holding period required for resales under SEC Rule 144. The investor, wanting to avoid the loss of voting rights and, to the extent possible, a taxable sale of the stock, chooses to partially monetize and hedge her Cyberweb position through the sale of a deep-in-the-money call option. The position is structured as follows:

> Counterparty broker–dealer purchases a deep-in-the-money call option on Cyberweb stock from the investor using a negotiated $20.00 strike price (i.e., the option on Cyberweb is in-the-money by $20.00 since the stock is currently trading at $40.00 per share).
>
> To hedge its exposure to the position, counterparty sells Cyberweb stock short at $40.00 and, as negotiated with the investor (through the broker), sets the strike of the option at $20.00 and pays the investor $18.72 per share ($20.00 less a 3.72-percent discount) or a total of $655,200 (35,000 shares × $18.72 = $655,200).
>
> Counterparty seeks to avoid the possibility of an early exercise by the investor, which could expose counterparty to inordinate risk on its Cyberweb short sale established to hedge the position, and structures the option as European style.
>
> At expiration, if the option is in-the-money (i.e., Cyberweb is trading above the $20.00 strike price), the investor pays counterparty the in-the-money amount. But remember, the investor benefits from a corresponding increase in the value of the Cyberweb stock she still holds and can pay counterparty by selling the now freely tradable stock, if necessary. If the option is at or out-of-the-money (i.e., Cyberweb is trading at or below $20.00 per share), the option expires worthless and the investor owes nothing to counterparty.
>
> Although "clean" Cyberweb stock is trading at $40.00 per share when the position is created, and is expected to trade higher, the investor is nervous about the volatile price movements of her Cyberweb stock. The in-the-money call therefore allows her to monetize a portion of her restricted stock position and retain price protection down to the $20.00 strike for the duration of the call option.

In addition to the stock price discount counterparty receives from the investor, counterparty will attempt to realize a hedge profit over the life of the transaction as determined by ongoing trading and transaction costs, bid-offer spreads, the trading liquidity of Cyberweb stock, and possible stock loan short rebate and financing spreads.

Investment Considerations of Deep-in-the-Money Call Options—Counterparty

The counterparty to a deep-in-the-money call option transaction must ascertain that the investor must have a net worth of at least $1 million (if restricted stock is involved, frequently the amount of total assets must be higher), the investor must be approved for options transactions, the investor must have held the underlying position for at least three months or more, and the investor must be sophisticated,[12] understand the risks of the transaction, and have the financial ability to satisfy any payments required to be made should the stock be trading at a price above the call strike at expiration. The investor's stock may be freely tradable or restricted.

The equity position should be valued at least at $2,000,000 or more; otherwise the economics of the transaction may not be favorable. The minimum stock trading price should be at least $5.00 per share in order to avoid thinly traded or stocks with low market capitalizations and liquidity risks associated with counterparty's hedging activities, and the minimum daily trading volume of the stock involved in the transaction should be 10,000 shares per day or more (i.e., sufficient to sell short the aggregate position over five to ten trading days without adversely affecting the stock price) to ensure adequate trading liquidity for counterparty's hedging purposes. The counterparty to the trade can structure strikes in deep-in-the-money call option trades up to 30 percent in-the-money. (Note: Strikes deeper in the money than 30 percent may cause the transaction to be deemed an illegal sale.)

---

[12]The term *sophisticated* as it pertains to investor suitability for securities investments relates to an SEC and NASD (National Association of Securities Dealers) concept developed when standardized listed options were first introduced in the United States in the 1970s and pertains to the overall financial wherewithal of an investor, his or her ability to sustain a loss in a particular investment, and his or her understanding of the risks and investment considerations of a particular investment or trading strategy; specific net worth, investment experience, and other financial criteria vary depending on the type of transaction.

Investment Considerations of Deep-in-the-Money Call Options—Investor

A sale of a deep-in-the-money call option by an investor should involve no out-of-pocket cost to investor. The investor collects a cash premium from the transaction. Such a trade strategy provides the investor with immediate liquidity and partially mitigates his or her stock price risk exposure.

The sale of deep-in-the-money call options by investors monetizes the difference between the strike price of the option and the market price of the stock. The stock position (or portfolio of stocks, if applicable) is hedged down to the strike price of the call for the term of the option. The quantity of shares monetized is not limited by Rule 144 volume limitations, and the cash settlement feature avoids the sale of shares, avoids the loss of voting control of stock, and avoids capital gains tax treatment. Other benefits to the investor include the continuation of dividend income and voting control over the shares. The transaction is confidentially negotiated between the investor and counterparty with an option strike price and term that can be customized to meet the investor's needs. Also, the investor usually does not have any regulatory reporting or disclosure requirements with regard to establishing a deep in-the-money call option.

The investor should be aware, however, that during the life of the option the investor relinquishes the appreciation potential of the stock (above the strike) and is obligated to pay the counterparty the amount, if any, by which the market price of the stock exceeds the strike price of the option at expiration. The investor's downside price risk below the strike price of the call option still exists. Investors should be cognizant of the fact that if the restricted stock on which a deep in-the-money call option is issued has not been held for more than one year on the date the option position is established, the tax holding period may be completely terminated and may not start again until the option position has expired or is closed out. Investors must post the underlying stock or additional margin as cover for establishing the short call option position. Furthermore, affiliates involved in such transactions may have public reporting and "short swing profits" obligations.

SALE OF OUT-OF-THE-MONEY CALL OPTIONS

Another monetization strategy for investors holding concentrated or restricted equity positions includes the sale by an investor of an out-of-the-money call option. In most cases, without engaging in a taxable sale, an investor can sell an out-of-the-money call option on the underlying stock to a broker–dealer or other counterparty and collect a cash premium. The sale provides the investor with an enhanced yield over and above any dividend income. The investor retains ownership of the stock and the potential benefit of any appreciation of the stock up to the strike of the call for the duration of the option.

EXAMPLE: An investor holding 50,000 shares of Cyclical Corporation stock she inherited thinks the company's stock price will test new lows prior to resuming a growth cycle in the year ahead. Cyclical is currently trading at $53.00 per share, and her holdings are worth approximately $2,650,000. She seeks to generate some cash from her holdings without liquidating the position. Through her broker, she consults counterparty broker dealer for ideas on how to attain her investment goal and to compare ideas and pricing she obtained from other firms. The investor decides to sell an out-of-the-money call option, as follows:

The investor sells a 10-month cash-settled call option with a $60 strike on Cyclical stock to counterparty and collects $350,000 of premium income ($7.00 per share × 50,000 shares).

The option is European style.

If the option is in-the-money on the expiration date, the investor will pay counterparty the difference between the market value of Cyclical stock on the expiration date and the strike price of the option.

If the option is at- or out-of-the-money (i.e., equal to or less than the strike price), the investor owes counterparty nothing and retains the premium counterparty paid her for the option.

Counterparty has no right to call the stock away from the investor for the duration of the option position.

The following list of stock prices and corresponding explanations provide clarification of how out-of-the-money call option values are influenced at various stock price levels.

Per-Share Price of Cyclical Common Stock at Expiration	Economic Impact on Investor's Position
$40.00	Investor keeps the $7.00 per share premium initially paid by counterparty and still holds stock worth $40.00 per share. The position value = $47.00 per share ($40.00 + $7.00 = $47.00) and the option expires worthless.
$53.00	Investor keeps the $7.00 per share premium and still holds stock worth $53.00 per share. The position value = $60.00 per share ($53.00 + $7.00 = $60.00) and the option expires worthless.
$60.00	Upon expiration of the option, the counterparty exercises the position. The investor keeps the $7.00 per share premium, pays counterparty $7.00 per share (the difference between the $60.00 market price of the stock and the $53.00 strike). Investor retains ownership of the stock worth $60.00 per share. Therefore, the position value = $60.00 per share ($7.00 − $7.00 + $60.00 = $60.00).
$70.00	Upon expiration of the option, the counterparty exercises the position. Investor keeps the $7.00 per share premium, pays counterparty $17.00 per share (the difference between the $70.00 market price of the stock and the $53.00 strike), and retains ownership of the Cyclical stock now worth $70.00 per share. Aggregate position value = $60.00 per share ($7.00 − $17.00 + $70.00 = $60.00).

Structuring Procedures, Risks and Economics for Out-of-the-Money Call Options

The following list highlights the actions and procedures required of a financial engineer structuring out-of-the-money call option transactions. Such activities are explained in more detail in the section at the beginning of this chapter concerning discounted private equity sales.

1. Check with stock loan for borrow.
2. Negotiate discount with investor.
3. Determine pricing variables.
4. Verify holding period of any restricted stock.
5. Pursue documentation, due diligence.
6. Hedge position down to strike.
7. Pay client the per share in-the-money amount.
8. Pay broker.
9. At expiration of the position, collect any call value from the investor (i.e., that per-share cash amount or intrinsic value above the strike).
10. Unwind trade and buy back hedge when option expires.
11. Counterparty risk:
    Short squeeze risk
    No unwind risks
    Minimal takeover risk
    Minimal dividend risk
    No dynamic hedging needed

Investment Considerations of Out-of-the-Money Call Options—Counterparty

The counterparty to an out-of-the-money call option transaction should determine that the investor involved in the trade has a net worth of at least $1 million (if restricted stock is involved, frequently the amount of total assets must be higher). The investor's stock may be freely tradable or restricted, and he or she must be have an options-approved account and must have held the underlying position for at least three months or more. The investor must be sophisticated and understand the risks of the transaction, and have the financial ability to satisfy any payments required to be made should the stock be trading at a price above the call option strike price at expiration. The equity position should be valued at least at $2,000,000 or more; otherwise the economics of the transaction may not be favorable to the counterparty. The minimum stock trading price should be at least $5.00 per share in order to avoid thinly traded or stocks with low market capitalizations and liquidity risks associated with counterparty's hedging activities. Also, the minimum daily trading volume should be 10,000 shares or more per day (i.e., sufficient to sell short the aggregate position over five to ten trading days without adversely affecting the stock price) to ensure adequate trading liquidity for counterparty's hedging purposes.

Investment Considerations of Out-of-the-Money Call Options—Investor

Out-of-the-money call option transactions involve no out-of-pocket cost to the investor since the investor collects a cash premium. Such transactions provide the investor with immediate liquidity and partially mitigate stock price risk exposure. If the investor's shares are restricted, the quantity of shares sold is not limited by Rule 144 volume limitations. The cash settlement feature avoids sale of shares and, therefore, no loss of voting control of stock and treatment of sale that incurs a capital gains tax. The investor may continue to receive dividends and vote the shares and benefits in any appreciation in stock up to the strike price of call for the term of the option. The transaction is confidentially negotiated between the investor and the counterparty to the trade. The option strike price and duration may be customized to meet investor's needs. The investor usually does not have any regulatory reporting or disclosure requirements with regard to establishing a deep in-the-money call option. The transaction is confidentially negotiated between the investor and the counterparty.

Investors should be aware, however, that during the life of the option they relinquish the appreciation potential of the stock (above the strike) and are obligated to pay the counterparty the amount, if any, by which the trading price of the stock exceeds the strike price of the option at expiration. There is no secondary or public market for the option, and, as such, secondary trading liquidity will be limited, creating additional risks. The options in such a trade are European style and may only be exercised at maturity. Investors should also be aware that if the restricted stock on which an out-of-the-money call option is issued has not been held for more than one year on the date the option position is established, the tax holding period may be completely terminated and may not start again until the option position has expired or is closed out. As a result, the investor should be aware that certain tax and holding period issues may arise, depending on the investor's financial position.

PURCHASES OF PUT OPTIONS

Investors unwilling to sell their equity positions due to, among other reasons, the belief that their stock is undervalued or adverse tax implications could arise, may wish to reduce their downside risk while preserving their upside appreciation potential. The purchase of a put option provides an investor with the ability to hedge his or her downside price risk exposure to a common stock position because of the ability to lock in a floor price (i.e., the strike price) for the stock position. All upside potential is maintained. Dividends, voting rights, and other benefits are preserved by the investor, and the cash settlement feature of the investment strategy defers the sale of the underlying shares. Investors who purchase put options pay an upfront, out-of-pocket expense in establishing the position.

ZERO-COST COLLARS

A self-financing strategy available to holders of concentrated equity positions is referred to as *zero-cost,* costless, or cash-settled collars. Like deep-in-the-money call options, zero-cost collar trades allow investors to partially monetize their restricted stock holdings as well as hedge downside price risk without relinquishing control of their stock. Investors purchase a put option while simultaneously selling a call option on the same underlying restricted shares of common stock. The result is the establishment of a "floor" and "ceiling" for the stock that creates a hedged "comfort" or "safety" zone for the investor with no up-front cost. The investor has price protection below the strike of the put option and participates in any appreciation up to the strike of the call for the life of the collar position.

Collared option transactions are usually structured as cash settled and with European style settlement. No net out-of-pocket expense is incurred by the investor because the sale of the call position finances the put position. Dividends, voting rights, and other benefits are preserved by the investor. The investor hedges the equity position below the put strike price and participates in stock price appreciation, if any, up to the strike price per share of the call option. The cash settlement feature allows for the sale of the underlying shares to be deferred. Furthermore, a zero-cost collar may be combined with a margin loan to further monetize the position (see the section entitled Monetizing Collar).

The following example provides step by step explanations of how zero-cost collar transactions work.

Structuring Procedures, Risks, and Economics for Zero-Cost Collars—Counterparty

The counterparty to the transaction provides the client with the ability to lock in an established price range with a lower limit (put strike) and a higher limit (call strike). If at expiration the stock price is below the put strike, the counterparty pays such amount to the client and hedges its price risk exposure. If the stock price is above the call strike at expiration of the options, the client pays such amount to the counterparty, financed by client, if necessary, through the sale of the underlying common stock position that the client has maintained for the duration of the collar position. The counterparty's incentive to enter into trade is determined by the potential profitability realizable from the volatility spread that can be captured in the transaction (e.g., the counterparty determines at what volatility the stock is trading, such as a 35-percent volatility). When the customer buys a put from a counterparty, the counterparty prices the put at a higher volatility (such as a 40-percent volatility). When the customer sells a call to a counterparty to pay for the put, the counterparty prices the call at a lower volatility (such as a 30-percent volatility). The counterparty who structures a zero-cost collar transaction attempts to capture a volatility spread in establishing the collar.

Counterparty Risks

- Short squeeze risk
- Must hedge trade continuously
- No unwind risk
- Minimal dividend risk
- Minimal takeover risk

Investment Considerations of Zero-Cost Collars—Counterparty

The counterparty to a zero-cost collar transaction should confirm that the investor has total assets of at least $1 million (if restricted stock is involved, frequently this number is higher and differs from the financial suitability requirements of discount purchases). The investor must be options approved, must have held the underlying position for at least three months or more, and must be sophisticated, understand the risks of the transaction, and have the financial ability to satisfy any payments required to be made should the stock be trading at a price above the call strike at expiration.

The counterparty will wish to make certain that the equity position is valued at least at $2,000,000 or more; otherwise the economics of the transaction may not be favorable. The minimum stock trading price should be at least $5.00 per share in order to avoid thinly traded or stocks with low market capitalizations and liquidity risks associated with counterparty's hedging activities, and the minimum trading volume should be 10,000 shares or more per day (i.e., sufficient to sell short the aggregate position over five to ten trading days without adversely affecting the stock price) to ensure adequate trading liquidity for counterparty's hedging purposes. The strike of options cannot be the same, and the investor's stock may be freely tradable or restricted.

EXAMPLE: A sophisticated investor who is a nonaffiliate owns 100,000 shares of restricted Alphawave Corporation stock, which he acquired for $15.00 per share. One year remains on the two-year holding period before the stock can be sold without violating the holding period and volume restrictions of SEC Rule 144. Alphawave stock is presently trading at a record high of $63.00 per share and the investor's holdings are worth approximately $6,300,000. The investor is nervous about possible technological breakthroughs by industry competitors that would depress the price of Alphawave stock. He would like to lock in as much of his gain in Alphawave as possible without relinquishing all future price appreciation potential. The investor enters into a customized cash-settled collar on Alphawave stock with counterparty broker–dealer, as follows:

> The investor purchases a one-year put option from counterparty with a strike of $56.00 per share when Alphawave is trading at $63.00.

> To finance the purchase of the put option, the investor simultaneously sells a one-year call option to counterparty with a strike of $72.00 per share.

> The option positions established in the collar transaction are both cash settled with European style exercise.

> The put option in the collared trade provides the investor with protection below the strike of $56.00; any cash loss he suffers to his Alphawave stock holdings from price declines below $56.00 is recouped dollar-for-dollar from counterparty.

> The investor also benefits in any upward price movement if Alphawave appreciates up to and including the $72.00 strike price of the call option.

> The investor's exposure to market fluctuations is limited to Alphawave stock prices ranging from $56.00 to $72.00.

The following list provides an insight into the actions and procedures required of a financial engineer structuring zero-cost collar option transactions. Such activities are more fully explained in the earlier section of this chapter concerning discounted private equity sales.

Per-Share Price of Alphawave Common Stock at Expiration	Economic Impact on Investor's Position
$50.00	The put is exercised by the investor at expiration and counterparty pays the investor $6.00 per share (the difference between the $56 put strike and the $50.00 price of the stock at expiration). The investor still holds a cash Alphawave stock position worth $50.00 per share. Therefore, the aggregate collar position value = $56.00 per share.
$60.00	The put ($56.00 strike) and call option ($72.00 strike) positions both expire worthless (i.e., both options are at-the-money). The investor still holds stock worth $60.00 per share, however, and the position value = $60.00 per share.
$75.00	The call is exercised by counterparty at expiration. The investor pays counterparty $3.00 per share (the difference between the $72.00 strike of the call and the $75.00 price of the stock). The investor, however, still holds Alphawave stock worth $75.00 per share that can be sold, if necessary, to fund the payoff to counterparty. Therefore, the position value to the investor = $72.00 per share, which is higher than the $63.00 Alphawave stock price when the collar was established.

Investment Considerations of Zero-Cost Collars—Investor

The cost of a zero-cost collar transaction is built into the pricing of the collar; therefore, the investor has no out-of-pocket expenses in connection with establishing such a position. The investor benefits in any appreciation in stock up to the strike price of call for the term of the option, and the option strike prices and term may be customized to meet the investor's goals. The stock position (or portfolio of stocks, if applicable) is protected below the strike of put for the term of the option. The cash settlement feature at expiration of a zero-cost collar transaction allows the investor to avoid a taxable sale of the shares. The transaction is confidentially negotiated between the investor and the counterparty, and the investor may continue to receive dividends and vote the shares. Also, there are no regulatory reporting requirements of the investor regarding the transaction.

Investors should be aware, however, that at expiration of the collar, they relinquish, and must pay to the counterparty to the transaction, any upside price appreciation of the stock above the strike price of the call, and they must pay the amount per share by which the market price exceeds the strike price of the call option. The investor should also note that he or she receives less than 100 percent of current market price of the stock involved in the collar transaction, and, although cash settled at expiration, the options involved in the trade are European style and may only be exercised at maturity. Furthermore, trading liquidity may be limited. Only upstairs markets may be available, and any bid-ask quotation spreads may be significantly wider than for listed options. Also, options involve a high degree of risk, including the risk of expiring worthless.

MONETIZING COLLARS

An investor wishing to hedge an equity position while simultaneously generating cash may wish to consider a cash-settled monetizing or zero-cost collar transaction combined with a margin loan. Because the put option related to the restricted or control stock involved in the transaction generates and, in effect, locks in a minimum value for the stock position, money can be lent on the position up to 90 percent of the strike price of the put option. The investor participates in any stock price appreciation up to the strike price of the call and simultaneously hedges the equity position below the put strike while retaining ownership, voting rights, and dividends. Monetization through this strategy may be greater than the proceeds obtained through a conventional margin loan, which is typically limited to 50 percent of the market value of the stock. The interest rate on the margin loan component of the transaction is usually LIBOR based. Furthermore, no capital gains are recognized or tax payable until the original stock position of the investor is sold.

Investment Considerations of Monetizing Collars

Investors should be aware that, unlike zero-cost collars, there are costs associated with structuring monetizing collar transactions because of the continuous American style exercise feature. Investors also relinquish potential price appreciation above the call strike price for the life of the option and must pay upon expiration or exercise the amount by which the market price per share exceeds the strike price of the call option. Furthermore, the loan proceeds above 50 percent of current market value of the underlying stock may not be invested in other securities.

SHORT AGAINST THE BOX

In addition to the strategies previously discussed for monetizing and hedging restricted and other concentrated equity holdings, establishing a short against the box position allows an investor to monetize a block of restricted or freely tradable stock without actually selling it. It presently allows investors to avoid adverse tax consequences from an outright sale of stock and lock in a particular market price for the position; however, tax proposals currently pending could significantly curtail or eliminate the favorable tax treatment investors can receive from this strategy.

Investors employing a short against the box strategy deposit their holdings of a particular stock as collateral for borrowing the same stock and then selling such borrowed stock short. The position is "stopped out" or established at the price at which the short position is established. The accompanying example will help clarify the procedures followed in establishing and unwinding a short against the box position.

EXAMPLE: An investor holding 150,000 shares of Halcyon Corporation wants to completely monetize the position at the current $50.00 market price. The aggregate market value of the position is $7,500,000. However, since her cost basis is so low and there may be a legislative reduction in the capital gains tax rate over the next year, the investor wants to hold off incurring a taxable gain on the position. Through her broker, the investor approaches counterparty broker–dealer to engineer a financial solution to her investment goal:

Counterparty recommends establishing a short against the box position that completely monetizes the investor's Halcyon holdings and locks in the price of the stock at $50.00 per share, currently an all-time high.

The investor deposits her 150,000 Halcyon shares with counterparty as collateral for the transaction, counterparty arranges with its stock loan department for her to borrow 150,000 different shares of Halcyon stock, and then executes a short sale of the 150,000 borrowed Halcyon shares at the $50.00 market price.

The 150,000 borrowed Halcyon shares are designated for this specific trade and held by counterparty's stock loan department for use in the event the investor's short position has to be covered.

Counterparty pays the investor $6,750,000 (90% × $50.00 per share × 150,000 shares) less a spread for counterparty and a sales credit for the broker as compensation for structuring and facilitating the trade.

The investor maintains the box position until such time as it is voluntarily closed or until the Halcyon stock is no longer borrowable.

If the Halcyon stock is no longer borrowable (e.g., it is called away by the owner of the borrowed stock in order to sell or take physical possession of the shares), additional shares must be arranged by counterparty to be borrowed to cover the investor's short position.

If additional Halcyon shares can not be borrowed from other investors, the box position must be "unwound" and closed out.

When the box position is unwound, the investor's original 150,000 Halcyon shares held as collateral by counterparty (assuming they are out of the restricted period and freely tradable) are used to cover or replace the 150,000-share short-sale position and the box is then closed out and the investor retains the $45.00 per-share proceeds paid when the box position was established, irrespective of where the price of Halcyon shares has traded during the period of time the box position was maintained. (Note: If the shares are not freely tradable and the box position is unwound, the cash proceeds received by the investor when the position was first established can be used to close out the short position by purchases of unrestricted shares in the market.)

Investment Considerations of Short against the Box—Counterparty

The counterparty to a short against the box transaction provides the client with the ability to lock in a price on a concentrated equity position. The counterparty earns spread on the short sale of the stock, but the borrowed stock for which the short position is covered must be freely tradable. The counterparty must usually determine that the investor is sophisticated, understands the risks of the transaction, and has the financial ability to satisfy any payments required to be made should the stock be trading at a price above the call strike at expiration. The counterparty will also usually wish to confirm that the investor has consulted with one or all of his or her tax, financial, and legal counsels about this type of transaction.

Investment Considerations of Short against the Box—Investor

There is no out-of-pocket cost to investor in a short against the box transaction; the cost is built into pricing of the position. The trading strategy provides the investor with immediate cash liquidity and eliminates stock price risk exposure. In order to leverage the position further, investor may be able to borrow against the hedged position up to 95 percent of the short sale at a low interest rate, and 100 percent of the loan may be reinvested in securities, if desired. The investor receives the current market price of shares involved in the trade but relinquishes any appreciation above the price at which the shares are pledged. Any dividends received are usually forfeited by the investor and used as one of the determinants of counter-party's compensation for the transaction. The investor does, however, retain voting rights on the shares. The transaction is confidentially negotiated between the investor and the counterparty to the trade, and there are usually no regulatory reporting requirements as to the disclosure of the investor.

The investor should be aware that he or she assumes the stock loan risk associated with borrowing the stock to cover the short position in the transaction for the term of the trade (i.e., the stock could be called back by the institution that initially lent the stock for establishing the short position). There is also potential annual mark-to-market interest expense on the position, and an increase in the price of the stock could result in maintenance margin calls. It is also very important for the investor to note that tax authorities may determine that short against the box trading strategies may not be established to avoid taxation on restricted stock holdings.

TRUST STRUCTURES

The number of restricted shares that individual or corporate affiliates can sell is proscribed by Rule 144. Among other ways, a trust structure or a nondiversified, closed-end investment company (i.e., a grantor trust, as discussed in Chapter 11) can provide a legal container into which re-stricted stock can be deposited or pledged and then resold as trust units to other investors. In order to make the trust units more appealing to investors, other securities may also be deposited into the trust (e.g., treasury securities, forward contracts, options, etc.) in order to modify the payoff pattern of the trust units and provide income or other investment characteristics to investors. As a result, an affiliate's concentrated equity position can be monetized, price risk can be hedged, and potential tax payments deferred during the life of the trust.

Investment Considerations of Trust Structures

Corporate clients or other investors engaged in the use of a trust structure for monetizing a restricted stock position retain the stock voting rights and the rights to any dividends, they defer any tax obligations until termination of the trust, they hedge the price risk in the underlying stock, and

EXAMPLE: Anon Corporation (Anon), an investment banking client of Broker–Dealer Inc., owns 6,000,000 shares of Zenon Incorporated (Zenon) common stock. Zenon is rated a "buy" by several top research analysts and currently trades for $40 per share with an average daily trading volume of 200,000 shares. There are a total of 40,000,000 Zenon shares outstanding. Since Anon owns 15 percent of Zenon's outstanding shares, Anon is considered to be an affiliate of Zenon and is subject to the SEC Rule 144 trading restrictions. Anon needs cash for its operating needs and would like to monetize its Zenon stock position. Anon is also concerned that the price of Zenon stock might fall and would like to lock in its gains in the position and, if possible, defer payment of capital gains tax as long as possible.

Broker–Dealer's structured products group proposes structuring a three-year investment trust for the purpose of holding Anon's equity position in Zenon and reselling trust units.

Anon pledges its 6,000,000 Zenon shares to the trust (alternately, Anon could deposit a forward contract on its Zenon shares).

Broker–Dealer then sells 6,000,000 trust units with a 7 percent coupon to institutional investors for $40 per unit.

Broker–Dealer earns a 3-percent gross spread [($40 per unit × 6,000,000 units = $240,000,000 to offering proceeds) × 3% gross spread = $7,200,000 to Broker–Dealer], pays 60 percent of the gross spread (i.e., 1.8 percent) as a sales credit or commission to the brokers who sold the trust units to their clients ($7,200,000 × 60% = $4,320,000), and retains the balance less the offering costs as its compensation for structuring the offering [($7,200,000 gross spread – $4,320,000 sales credit = $2,880,000 management and placement fee) – $250,000 of offering costs = $2,630,000 structuring and placement compensation].

Broker–Dealer provides Anon with approximately 75 percent of the proceeds from the offering as a three-year loan for its Zenon shares for the three-year life of the trust and retains the remaining 25 percent of the proceeds to finance the purchase of quarterly maturing U.S. Treasury strips, which are deposited into the trust in an amount sufficient to produce a 7-percent yield to unit holders; Broker–Dealer also receives its proceeds from the gross spread as compensation for structuring the transaction.

Anon retains voting rights and rights to any dividends paid on its Zenon stock pledged as collateral for the loan received from the trust.

Investors receive a 7-percent annual coupon on their trust units (paid quarterly).

At termination of the trust, investors receive their final coupon payment and a contingent payment (i.e., a "kicker") based on the price performance of Zenon stock, determined as follows:

> If Zenon is trading at or below the $40 offering price of the trust unit, investors receive the market price of Zenon shares for each trust unit they hold, paid in cash or Zenon stock.

> If Zenon is trading from $40 to $50 per share, investors receive $40 for each trust unit they hold or the equivalent amount in Zenon stock.

> If Zenon is trading above $50 per share, investors receive 85 percent of such amount, payable in cash or Zenon stock.

At termination of the trust, Anon delivers the appropriate amount of stock or cash to the trust in order to satisfy the contingent payment provisions outlined above and retains the stock or cash value of Zenon shares that may have appreciated above the contingent payment made to trust holders.

---

they monetize the stock holdings and retain a portion of the upside appreciation potential in the underlying stock. Alternately, clients engaged in the use of a monetizing trust structure receive less than 100 percent of the market value of the underlying stock from the sale of the trust units to other investors.

The use of a trust structure allows holders of restricted stock to receive current income at an attractive yield as well as to share in a portion of the potential upside price appreciation of the underlying stock. However, they remain exposed to downside price risk on the stock position. The broker–dealer counterparty to the trade earns gross spread as compensation for structuring, registering, underwriting, and marketing the trust units for sale to other investors. It also receives a fee for managing the trust during its life.

SALE OF STOCK THROUGH A STRUCTURED EQUITY PROGRAM

Corporations, affiliates, and shareholders may wish to sell large amounts of stock over time in a cost-effective, consistent, quick, and "quiet" manner (see Chapter 15). A structured equity program provides for the sale of equity into the market in a manner that allows corporate issuers, affiliates, and shareholders to raise funds through equity sales in a specially designed program that is less expensive, more quickly implemented, and lower profile than a standard underwritten offering. The program is designed to eliminate any adverse market price impact on the stock. The client is insulated from trading risk through an average pricing mechanism. The client sets threshold price levels for sales and may turn the program on and off each week. Negative market signals associated with overhang of shares under registered shelf or in underwritten transactions are minimized. Control stockholders may be able to register and sell restricted shares without the constraints of Rule 144.

Investment Considerations of Structured Equity Programs

A company availing itself of structured equity programs must have been a reporting entity for at least one year and have a public float capitalization of at least $75,000,000. Selling shareholders must have the cooperation of the issuing corporation and, like the corporation's sale of shares, if any, under the program, will not receive share proceeds in a single payment but over periods of time as shares are sold. Furthermore, the company must undertake to register shares and to keep the registration effective until all shares subject to the program are sold.

CONCLUSION

The strategies discussed in this chapter are divided between monetization and hedging. Private equity sales, the sale of deep-in-the-money and out-of-the-money call options, monetizing collars, monetizing swaps, trust structures, and stock sales from equity shelf programs produce varying amounts of cash proceeds, depending on the investor's circumstances and status vis-à-vis the corporation from which the underlying stock was issued. The purchase of OTC put options, zero-cost collars, and shorting against the box offer investor's price protection from market risk to their restricted or other stock holdings.

A careful marketing strategy must be developed when offering monetization and hedging strategies. A significant number of legal, tax, trading, hedging, and customer suitability issues have to be explored when engineering financial solutions to restricted stock problems. It is important that the sales personnel involved in introducing potential clients to the structuring team that handles these types of transactions be extremely familiar with the basic structures mentioned herein, among others. The experience level of clientele involved in restricted and concentrated stock trades typically includes the most sophisticated of investors who are inclined to use those firms with demonstrated expertise in structuring financial solutions to their particular circumstances. Developing restricted stock strategies is an intensive and time-consuming business. Only a small percentage of transactions that are proposed are usually consummated.

Chapter 14 discusses a number of examples of capital-raising alternatives available to corporations using structured financial products.

14

STRUCTURED PRODUCTS FOR CORPORATIONS

Investment banks often provide a range of structured product origination and distribution capabilities to corporate clients in support of their capital raising needs. Structured derivative product strategies can be used for effecting corporate treasury-type programs such as stock repurchases. Structured transactions can be used in assisting corporations, corporate insiders, and large stockholders (e.g., venture capital and LBO firms) with the monetization, hedging, and diversification of concentrated securities positions (see Chapter 13). Furthermore, some of the structured note, convertible securities, and equity-linked structures discussed in previous chapters can be used by corporations for their capital-raising activities. Many of the original U.S. publicly offered currency warrant transactions in the late 1980s were borne out of corporate debt offerings, where the warrants were attached as sweeteners for investors who would forego a bond yield many basis points higher in exchange for the appreciation potential and secondary trading liquidity represented by the currency warrants. Also, the proceeds from many types of structured notes are used by issuers not only for hedging purposes but also for general corporate funding purposes, much like the funds generated from periodic medium-term note offerings.

Some of the types of capital market transactions corporations have used involving a variety of structured products include:

- Convertible debt
- Convertible preferred stock
- Convertible trusts
- Index- and asset-linked notes
- Enhanced dividend convertible preferred stock [e.g., DECS (Dividend Enhanced Convertible Stock) or PERCS (Preferred Equity Redemption Cumulative Stock)]
- Step-up convertible debt
- Zero-coupon convertible debt [i.e., OID (original issue discount debt obligations)]
- Convertible tax advantaged preferred stock
- Mandatorily exchangeable preferred stock
- Various proprietary structures

Corporations are not strictly limited to traditional equity and debt financing alternatives. Capital costs can often be reduced significantly by using structured derivative products. Corporations can retain significant control over their repurchase, conversion, and exercise of outstanding equity and debt by using derivatives. Financial engineers can identify and design trading strategies and financial structures that exploit, monetize, and leverage off of options or cash flows that may be hidden within a corporation's capital structure (e.g., conversion rights, reset provisions, redemption features, etc.).

Structured products will enter the mainstream of corporate finance activities at such time as general misperceptions about derivatives begin to recede, as senior managers more clearly understand derivatives securities and their applications, as boards of directors develop internal derivative policies and oversight procedures that properly guide the development of structured product businesses, and as the appropriate personnel are retained to manage risk, trading, and investment strategies. Within some investment banking firms, the role of structured derivative instruments when providing advice to corporate clients is often ill defined and poorly

EXAMPLE OF CAPITAL-RAISING STRUCTURE

Tomahawk Corporation seeks $100 million debt financing to pay off bank loans and for general corporate purposes. Tomahawk believes the best terms it can negotiate for an initial public offering of convertible debt include the following:

- Six percent annual coupon
- Twenty percent Conversion Premium on Tomahawk's common stock
- Five-year term

Broker–Dealer Inc.'s structured products group offers Tomahawk dramatically better terms than it would get on a conventional public convertible offering, as follows:

- Five percent annual coupon
- Twenty-eight percent conversion premium on Tomahawk's common stock
- Five-year term

Broker–Dealer's structured products group suggests a structured financing arrangement involving the use of a grantor trust. Essentially, the structure involves deconstructing (i.e., stripping or bifurcating) the convertible securities into their basic economic debt and equity components and selling such components to separate groups of investors in the form of trust units and equity options on Tomahawk's common stock. Tomahawk receives better financing terms than it could through a conventional offering of convertible securities, and investors receive, respectively, income-producing trust units and Tomahawk equity options. The basic process using hypothetical pricing information is as follows:

Formation of a grantor trust by Broker–Dealer.

Tomahawk deposits into the trust, $100 million of senior unsecured, five-year, 4-percent coupon, noncallable convertible notes with a 28-percent conversion premium.

Broker–Dealer, on behalf of trust, sells an American style option that allows the buyer of the option to purchase the convertible notes in the trust at a specified strike price any time during the five-year term of the trust, therefore "deconstructing" the notes into debt and equity pieces, stripping away the convertible feature of the notes and monetizing it in the form of an equity option.

Broker–Dealer, on behalf of the trust, uses a portion of the proceeds received from the sale of the option to buy U.S. Treasury Strip Securities (i.e., government obligations that make coupon payments only) in an amount sufficient to add an additional 1-percent yield to the 4-percent convertible notes in the trust and boost the total yield of the securities in the trust to 5 percent.

Broker–Dealer underwrites a $100 million private placement of the trust units (comprising the convertible notes and Treasury strips) to institutional investors, who then hold callable trust units with voting rights, maturing in five years and yielding 5 percent (paid semiannually).*

At maturity trust unit holders receive the principal amount of the notes from Tomahawk via the trust plus any unpaid interest held by the trust.

Tomahawk receives $100 million from the trust, less applicable underwriting costs and fees payable to Broker–Dealer.

Broker–Dealer recoups underwriting costs and retains any fees paid to it by Tomahawk as well as any proceeds, if any, derived from the difference between the cost of the Treasury strips deposited in the trust and proceeds from the sale of the option on the convertible notes in the trust.

Broker–Dealer hedges the obligations of the trust under the option contract during the life of the trust.

---

*If the option on the convertible notes is exercised by the option holder during the life of the trust, such notes will be called away from the trust. Under certain provisions specified in the trust documents, upon exercise of the option by the option holder, the trust will be dissolved and trust unit holders receive the net present value (calculated in a specific manner) of any remaining scheduled distributions pertaining to such units. Other events of early dissolution of the trust, such as a change of control of Tomahawk, whereby unit holders can put their units back to the trust, are specified in the trust documents.

coordinated. This is frequently due to internal rivalries between investment banking and capital markets areas and a poor understanding of what new financial products are available and can be created to attain a number of important financial goals of corporations.

An example of how simple some structured financial solutions can be for corporations is described in Chapter 15. Corporations can save a significant amount of money on secondary offerings using a structured shelf and equity distribution program for raising equity capital. This structured program is a simple, low-cost, effective alternative to traditional secondary equity underwritings. Through the use of a little-used SEC shelf registration procedure along with agency sales of equity into the existing secondary order flow, corporations can avail themselves of a program developed by financial engineers that is as effective as a mousetrap for raising equity capital in secondary offerings. The program eliminates expensive banking fees, the costs of preparing offering documents, a great deal of legal work, and "dog and pony" marketing presentations that consume the valuable time of senior corporate executives.

15

STRUCTURED SHELF AND EQUITY DISTRIBUTION PROGRAM FOR CORPORATE ISSUERS, AFFILIATES, AND OTHER SHAREHOLDERS

As an alternative to the expense and time involved with underwritten secondary equity offerings, publicly owned corporations and certain affiliated shareholders may desire a means to access equity funding or monetize concentrated equity positions through the sale of new, registered common stock on an agency basis directly on the floor of a national stock exchange. A structured shelf and equity distribution program allows issuers and related shareholders to sell common stock into the market at such times and prices as desired using a type of shelf registration filed under the SEC's Rule 415.

A structured shelf program provides corporate issuers with a means to raise funds through common stock sales by registering new shares on an equity shelf registration statement filed with the SEC or the common stock portion of a universal shelf. Affiliated individuals or control persons of the corporation and holders of restricted stock positions or stock received pursuant to an acquisition can also sell their holdings through such off-the-shelf structured transactions. The target markets for structured shelf and equity distribution programs includes large, well-known issuers who can raise capital whenever they choose, issuers who have no need to tell their story through highly visible road shows, issuers who wish to access the equity markets during strong market cycles when prices and trading volume are high, issuers who closely manage their capital funding for credit rating purposes, and issuers raising capital for acquisitions or other expenditures. Officers, directors, and affiliated shareholders may avail themselves of the program in seeking a discrete and flexible means to monetize some or all of their holdings at optimal periods of time without depressing the stock price.

Public corporations and shareholders can exploit periodic market opportunities by selling common stock during times of strong stock prices and trading volume. A structured shelf and equity distribution program provides for electronic, unsolicited sales of registered shares into the existing order flow of the primary market where such shares are listed for trading. No active solicitation occurs, and such shares are directed onto the stock exchange trading floor without signaling to the market that additional shares are being sold. On a weekly basis over a period of months, the seller receives sale proceeds equal to the number of shares sold each day times the average of the daily high/low sales prices reported by the primary marketplace. The proceeds from sales of shares at average market prices can also be supplemented through additional agency trades directed to the broker–dealer by issuers and selling shareholders in such amounts and at then current market prices at any time during the life of the program. The structured shelf and equity distribution program provides equity funding and monetization to issuers and shareholders without the possible negative stock price impact often associated with the dilutive effects of publicly announced secondary stock underwritings. Since transaction spreads for such programs are negotiated between the broker–dealer, acting as sales agent, and the issuer and do not involve heavy offering costs and capital commitments (e.g., gross spreads, sales credits, prospectuses, road shows, etc.), equity shelf distribution programs are significantly less expensive than traditional underwritten offerings. The sale of shares is effected through a combination of "best-efforts" underwriting and straight agency trades. Weekly pricing of best efforts shares is based on an independent average market price.

EXAMPLE 1:   The chairman of publicly owned JCB Corporation personally owns 1,000,000 shares of unregistered JCB stock, which currently sells for $40.00 per share. He wishes to sell his JCB stock position but is constrained by the trading and volume limitations of Rule 144. Investment bankers from Broker–Dealer Inc. learn of the CEO's investment goals and recommend the following structured transaction:

They recommend that JCB Corporation file an equity registration and shelf distribution statement for the sale of common stock for the corporation and affiliated shareholders, including the shares held by the chairman.

With Broker–Dealer as advisor to JCB under a sales agency agreement, JCB engages the necessary legal counsel to prepare the registration statement and pays the related SEC filing fees.

Once the shelf is effective at the SEC, Broker–Dealer sells the number of shares designated by JCB, including the CEO's shares, off the shelf directly into the market on an exchange or OTC market.

Broker–Dealer sells a fixed number of JCB shares each week.

Each week Broker–Dealer determines the average weekly share price it received from the sale of JCB shares.

Along with a fixed number of shares, JCB can designate that additional, supplemental shares be sold when its stock is trading at particularly attractive prices.

JCB (through the CEO or CFO) and the designated trader at Broker–Dealer communicate each day or on some other regular basis in order to arrange for the sale of supplemental shares during times of market opportunity.

EXAMPLE 2:   Under the structured shelf and equity distribution program, Broker–Dealer Inc. agrees to make a "best efforts" distribution of up to 50,000,000 common shares of India Corporation through distributions off a shelf registration statement. The sale of shares will be executed by Broker–Dealer's structured product trading desk in coordination with investment banking and operating personnel. The program will be conducted in the following manner:

Prior to commencing the distribution, India Corporation files an S-3 shelf registration statement under Rule 415 with the SEC registering 50,000,000 common shares.

Broker–Dealer is named as the exclusive sales agent in connection with its agreement to distribute India's common stock under the program.

India and Broker–Dealer execute a sales agency agreement setting forth the number of shares to be offered and the method of distribution as follows:

A maximum of 50,000,000 shares will be sold under the program in agreed-upon amounts over a number of pricing periods consisting of five consecutive calendar days each.

Prior to the commencement of a pricing period, Broker–Dealer and India agree upon a number of average market price shares that Broker–Dealer will undertake to sell on a best-efforts basis during each respective pricing period. It is expected that the number of average market price share sold during each pricing period will be approximately 500,000 shares.

During each pricing period, either India or Broker–Dealer can terminate an offering of shares by notifying the other party by telephone, and either party can terminate the program at any time for any reason.

During each pricing period, Broker–Dealer sells the agreed-upon number of average market price shares to the public.

Prior to commencement of trading on any day during a pricing period, India can instruct Broker–Dealer by telephone not to sell any shares during that day unless the sale price meets or exceeds a specified limit order price.

Prior to or on any day during each pricing period in which average market price shares are sold, India and Broker–Dealer can agree to sell additional shares.

At the conclusion of each pricing period, Broker–Dealer will supply India with an end-of-week confirmation including all relevant information concerning the shares sold.

Payment by Broker–Dealer to India of the net proceeds (net of Broker–Dealer's agreed-upon spread) from average market price shares sold will occur on the business day after the end of the pricing period.

Payment for any additional shares sold will occur on a regular way basis.

By the second business day after each pricing period, India will file a one-page prospectus supplement with the SEC indicating the number of shares sold during each pricing period and the net proceeds to India.

INVESTMENT CONSIDERATIONS

Usually the minimum amount of stock offered under a structured shelf and equity distribution program is approximately $10 million in order to produce favorable economics to justify the costs of the transaction. The company engaged in such a program must file a registration statement with SEC and keep it effective until all the stock registered thereunder is sold. The company must be aware that it may be subject to an SEC review in conjunction with the shelf filing.

Affiliated or control stockholders can register and sell shares under the program without violating the restricted stock requirements specified under SEC Rule 144; however, the issuing corporation must provide approval to individual shareholders wishing to dispose of shares through a structured shelf and equity distribution program. As with issuing corporations, selling shareholders participating in a structured shelf program should be aware that they will not receive the proceeds from the sale of stock at one time; payments occur on periodic settlement dates (usually weekly) under the same average pricing mechanism used in determining proceeds to be paid to the issuing corporation (e.g., the weekly average of the average intraday prices obtained by the broker–dealer in selling shares under the shelf).

Structured shelf programs can accommodate unregistered, listed, or OTC-traded common stock of publicly owned companies. A corporation engaging in structured shelf transactions must be qualified as to use the SEC's Form S-3[1] to register common stock. The company should be aware that sales under the shelf registration are made by a specific broker–dealer as the sole manager of an equity offering. The broker–dealer is designated as exclusive sales agent for all capital-raising efforts of the company during the term of the sales agency agreement. The broker–dealer has intraday price risk; if the average price of shares sold is higher than executed prices, the broker–dealer can lose money. (Note: Such risk to the broker–dealer can be avoided or minimized through continuous intraday selling activity.)

The advantages to a company engaged in a structured shelf and equity distribution program include:

Flexibility and Control.   The program can be turned on and off by the company as its equity needs vary and can also instruct the broker–dealer to sell shares via the program, subject to minimum price and volume constraints of its choosing.

Low Cost.   The program's all-in distribution cost to the company is significantly below that of an otherwise comparable underwritten offering.

Reduced Market Impact.   The quiet nature of the shelf filing and the incremental nature of the share selling under the equity shelf and distribution program mitigates potential price pressure on the company's stock and negative market signals associated with overhang of shares is minimized.

Volume Breeds Volume.   The continuous trading activity in the company's stock can generate greater trading volume and interest in the stock, which, in turn, can allow the company to more aggressively sell (when it desires) into volume and stock price strength.

---

[1]Those issuers that have been publicly owned and have been reporting their financial results and business activities to the SEC for at least one year and have a public float (i.e., publicly owned common stock capitalization) of $75 million or more.

No Arbitrage Activity or Postponement of Natural Buying.   Unlike a traditional underwritten offering, in which the announcement of the underwritten transaction causes arbitragers to short the stock and natural buyers to postpone buying, the equity shelf and distribution program minimizes such activity because the public does not know how many shares, at what price and when the company will sell shares.

No Publicity.   Only minimal company disclosure is required for the distribution, apart from the standard public disclosure requirements for registration and sales of shares.

Reduced Time Demands on Management.   Other than the time required for standard due diligence by the broker–dealer, the company's management does not need to devote substantial time and attention on the marketing of its common shares via the program since there are no road shows, analyst presentations, or directed selling efforts.

Potential for Dollar Cost Averaging.   Unlike a traditional underwritten offering, which involves pricing and selling a large block of stock all at one time, the continuous offering of shares via the equity shelf and distribution program allows companies the opportunity to realize higher average net proceeds as stock prices may rise over the term of the program.

Sales Agent Incentive.   The broker–dealer's interests and incentives are aligned with the company's with regard to selling the "best efforts" shares as the broker–dealer earns higher fees both in the form of a discount off of the company's proceeds for the shares sold and to the extent it can sell these shares at prices above the average market price for the stock as reported by the primary marketplace where the shares are listed for trading.

No Interference with Research Coverage.   Unlike a traditional underwritten offering, in which the broker–dealer's research is constrained from publishing during the offering process, a structured shelf and equity distribution program imposes few restrictions, as long as the broker–dealer's research analyst is not brought "over the wall" in terms of being made aware of the program; the analyst can continue publishing research on the company during the distribution process.

The disadvantages to a company engaged in a structured shelf and equity distribution program include the following:

No Bullet Payment.   Company does not get funds all at once as with traditional underwritings.

Low Public Visibility.   Company can not tell its "story" through road shows and other presentations.

Exclusive Relationship.   Company is locked into a relationship with the broker–dealer who directed the establishment of a sale of shares under the program, including all other capital-raising activities during the term of the agency agreement, whether or not there is activity in the equity shelf and distribution program.

CONCLUSION

The description of how corporations can raise equity capital cheaper and more efficiently by using a structure financial solution is emblematic of the types of fresh new ideas and the rethinking of established concepts that is taking place today on Wall Street and in capital markets around the world.

Financial engineering as a profession and as a process is growing rapidly. New concepts tend to be accompanied by an abundance of questions and skepticism. In recent years, structured derivative financial products have been the source of a great deal of controversy among government regulators, politicians, the media, the public, and corporations. The more notorious business misfortunes that have been blamed on derivatives include the collapse of Barings Bank, the bankruptcy of Orange County, California, and the financial misfortunes of a number of blue-chip corporations in the United States, such as Procter & Gamble. It appears that financial problems involving derivatives have resulted from a combination of lax management, lapses in regulatory and compliance oversight, and the tendency of corporate treasury departments to move beyond their risk management capabilities into areas beyond their levels of expertise. Dealers, however, are not without fault. The concerns expressed by regulators and politicians about risk and financial disclosure, customer suitability, and capital adequacy have a great deal of merit. But there is growing evidence that derivative securities and the structured financial products created from them appear to be contributing to a growth in the efficiency of the global financial markets.

The central goal of this book is to advance the development of a favorable consensus of opinion on derivative securities so that needed improvements occur in how they are structured, sold, and regulated, and that their benefits to the world financial markets become more clearly known to broader segments of the national and international investment community and public at large. This book is meant to provide corporate and financial managers, brokers, investors, bankers, traders, lawyers, regulators, government officials, and students with clear explanations, insights, and examples of derivative-based structured financial products.

For more practical information and reference on structured securities, see the Resource Guide that follows. This section provides a great deal of background material supporting the topics covered in the text, including hypothetical structured product presentations to management, information about offering expenses, and activities of structured product working groups, legal, marketing, and pricing information. There are also sample term sheets supporting many of the types of products discussed in this book. A glossary is included as well.

PART FOUR

Resource Guide for Users of Structured Financial Products

This part of the book provides detailed background information supporting discussions throughout the book. It is hoped that readers find the information of interest as it offers distinct insights into many financial engineering, investment banking, legal, trading, risk management, and marketing activities, and various processes involved in originating structured financial products. The documents included take the form of presentations, memorandums, spreadsheets, checklists, letters, schedules, and terms sheets, each of which can be referred to as it is cited in the text. Although the information provided is hypothetical, the general form of the materials is drawn from the experiences of the author. The following information is included:

- Sample Offering Expenses Spreadsheet (p. 173)
- Sample Working Group Checklist (p. 178)
- Sample SEC Rule Filing Comment Letter (p. 184)
- Sample Customer Suitability Memo (p. 188)
- Sample Structured Product Marketing Memos (p. 190)

- Sample Road Show Marketing Schedule (p. 215)
- Sample Syndicate Invitation (p. 218)
- Sample Pricing Spreadsheet (p. 222)
- Sample Questionnaire for Sellers of Restricted Securities (p. 225)
- Sample Structured Product Term Sheets (p. 227)
- Sample Management Presentations (p. 253)
- "Convertibles as Sport" (p. 276)
- "Options as Sport" (p. 279)

SAMPLE OFFERING EXPENSES SPREADSHEET*

Direct Expenses	Aborted DAX Warrants	Actual Bond Yield Warrants	Aborted FX Warrants	Aborted Biotech Notes	Actual Oil Notes	Aborted Yield Curve Warrants	Aborted Health Care Trust	Aborted Japan Index Warrants	Actual FX Index Warrants	Total
Issuers Counsel	($164,945)	($286,715)	($7,340)	($141,654)	($17,440)	($36,750)	($65,000)	($92,826)	($158,541)	($971,211)
Underwriters Counsel/ Blue Sky		(15,953)					(56,152)		(20,000)	(92,105)
Warrant Agent/Trustee		(10,403)		(66,213)					(27,500)	(104,116)
Warrant Agent/ Trustee Counsel		(2,185)		(55,494)			(15,511)	(4,303)	(8,181)	(85,674)
Auditors Opinion		(26,090)						(27,000)	(20,000)	(73,090)
Determination Agent										
Exchange Listing Fee		(22,194)							(20,000)	(42,194)
Agg. Exchange Annual Fees		(3,048)							(21,000)	(24,048)
SEC Registration Fee		(31,250)					(13,875)		(31,250)	(76,375)
NASD Review Fee		(10,500)							(10,500)	(21,000)
Printing Costs Red Herrings		(104,156)		(32,578)			(29,437)	(84,769)	(60,891)	(311,830)
Final Prospectus		(98,196)							(20,297)	(118,493)
Warrant Certificates		(7,813)					(2,040)	(1,550)	(5,000)	(16,403)
CUSIP Nos.		(100)		(168)			(88)	(92)	(100)	(548)
Est. Misc. Fees and Expenses	(4,648)	(18,165)			(17,000)	(5,000)	(20,000)	(5,000)	(20,000)	(89,813)
Total Direct Expenses	($169,593)	($636,768)	($7,340)	($296,107)	($34,440)	($41,750)	($202,103)	($215,540)	($423,260)	($2,026,900)

*See Chapter 3 for a discussion of offering expenses.

173

SAMPLE OFFERING EXPENSES SPREADSHEET

Direct Expenses	Actual Nikkei Warrants	Actual CAC 40 Warrants	Estimated Energy Warrants	Estimated Financial Warrants	Estimated Technology Warrants	Estimated Transport. Warrants	Actual Hang Seng Warrants	Actual Pharm. Warrants	Actual S&P MidCap Notes	Total
Issuers Counsel	($168,500)	($243,340)	($19,427)	($41,082)	($18,652)	($27,471)	($85,000)	($28,773)	($117,160)	($749,405)
Underwriters/ Guarantor's Counsel	(60,300)	(6,977)	(10,000)	(10,000)	(10,000)	(10,000)	(8,175)	(12,000)	(65,000)	(192,452)
Wt. Agent/Registrar/ Trustee		(5,068)	(5,500)	(5,500)	(5,500)	(5,500)	(32,776)	(3,000)	(1,527)	(64,371)
Warrant Agent/ Trustee Counsel			(21,266)	(9,250)			(5,367)		(4,380)	(40,263)
Auditors Opinion	(30,052)	(23,263)					(16,000)		(21,600)	(90,915)
Determination Agent									(5,000)	(5,000)
Exchange Listing Fee	(16,000)	(12,500)	(1,500)	(1,500)	(1,500)	(1,500)	(15,000)	(1,500)	(17,500)	(68,500)
Index License Fee (Lifetime)	(150,000)	(4,327)					(55,000)		(25,000)	(234,327)
Agg. Exchange Annual Fees	(182,968)	(6,500)					(3,913)			(193,381)
SEC Registration Fee		(200,000)								(200,000)
NASD Review Fee	(25,000)	(75,000)								(100,000)
Printing Costs										
Red Herrings	(3,133)	(45,760)					(14,582)		(53,800)	(117,275)
Final Prospectus		(163,472)	(14,745)	(5,000)	(5,000)	(5,000)	(8,633)	(5,614)	(13,449)	(220,913)
Warrant Certificates		(11,116)					(5,000)			(16,116)
CUSIP Nos.									(90)	(90)
Est. Misc. Fees and Expenses	(3,000)	(39,347)	(3,000)	(3,000)	(3,477)	(3,000)	(9,841)	(3,748)	(29,295)	(97,708)
Total Direct Expenses	($638,953)	($836,670)	($75,438)	($75,332)	($44,129)	($52,471)	($259,286)	($54,635)	($353,801)	($2,390,715)

SAMPLE OFFERING EXPENSES SPREADSHEET

Direct Expenses	Aborted US Index Warrants	Aborted Yield Curve Warrants	Actual Amex Hong Kong Wts. Warrants	Aborted DM/$ Warrants	Actual US Yld. Incr. Warrants	Actual Cap Goods Warrants	Actual US Yld. Decr. Warrants	Actual European Warrants Program	Actual "Lookback" Warrants	Total
Issuers Counsel		($30,800)	($67,645)	($13,930)	($5,000)	($16,666)	($16,254)	($42,300)	($6,284)	($198,879)
Underwriters/ Guarantor's Counsel			(155,000)			(2,302)	(2,392)	(10,000)	(5,000)	(174,694)
Warrant Agent/Trustee			(12,379)		(2,027)	(2,027)	(2,500)	(2,027)	(6,331)	(27,292)
Warrant Agent/ Trustee Counsel			(2,806)							(2,806)
Auditors Opinion			(25,750)			(5,500)	(2,800)		(2,800)	(36,850)
Determination Agent										
Exchange Listing Fee			(20,000)		(2,253)	(2,253)	(2,253)	(2,253)	(2,944)	(31,955)
Index License Fee (Lifetime)									(10,000)	(10,000)
Agg. Exchange Annual Fees										
SEC Registration Fee			(250)							(250)
NASD Review Fee										
Printing Costs			(20,000)							
Red Herrings	$55,418									(55,418)
Final Prospectus						(5,646)	(3,743)	(4,999)		(14,388)
Warrant Certificates			(10,761)							(10,761)
CUSIP Nos.			(188)							(188)
Est. Misc. Fees and Expenses		(845)	(13,434)			(4,000)	(4,000)	(4,000)	(3,994)	(30,273)
Total Direct Expenses	($55,418)	($31,645)	($328,213)	($13,930)	($9,280)	($38,394)	($33,942)	($65,579)	($37,354)	($593,754)

SAMPLE OFFERING EXPENSES SPREADSHEET

Direct Expenses	Actual Hong Kong Warrants	Actual Yen/$ Warrants	Aborted Japan Index Warrants	Actual Yen/$ Warrants	Actual OTC Private Placement	Aborted Equity-Linked Notes (ELNs)	Aborted Yield Decrease Warrants	Actual Pharm. Call Warrants	Actual Yen/$ Warrants	Total
Issuers Counsel	($21,605)	($23,161)	($24,103)	($29,838)	($48,061)			($11,997)	($25,755)	($184,519)
Underwriters/ Guarantor's Counsel	(92,686)	(53,732)	(58,859)	(53,480)		($29,716)	($148,007)		(63,662)	(500,143)
QIU										
Warrant Agent/ Trustee	(6,533)	(17,500)		(15,000)					(5,000)	(44,033)
Warrant Agent/ Trustee Counsel	(1,269)	(6,227)		(688)				(2,945)	(1,324)	(12,453)
Auditors Opinion	(27,200)	(19,500)	(2,500)	(30,500)	(7,000)		(25,000)	(8,000)	(29,000)	(148,700)
Determination Agent										
Exchange Listing Fee	(20,000)	(22,500)		(10,000)				(2,500)	(7,744)	(62,744)
Index License Fee (Lifetime)										
Agg. Exchange Annual Fees									(5,523)	(5,523)
SEC Registration Fee	(250)	(250)		(250)						(750)
NASD Review Fee										
Printing Costs										
Red Herrings			(54,441)				(78,118)			(132,559)
Final Prospectus	(87,084)	(56,216)		(63,531)					(55,977)	(262,808)
Warrant Certificates	(16,135)	(6,548)		(4,898)			(1,481)		(6,033)	(35,094)
CUSIP Nos.	(188)	(92)	(188)	(119)			(95)		(123)	(805)
Est. Misc. Fees and Expenses	(9,499)	(9,997)	(2,000)	(9,933)	(500)		(20,000)	(10,000)	(6,385)	(68,315)
Total Direct Expenses	($282,449)	($215,722)	($142,091)	($218,237)	($55,561)	($29,716)	($272,701)	($35,442)	($206,527)	($1,458,446)

SAMPLE OFFERING EXPENSES SPREADSHEET

Direct Expenses	Actual M&A Warrants	Actual FX Warrants	Actual Utility Index Warrants	Aborted Taiwan Export Warrants	Total
Issuers Counsel	($11,741)	($11,741)	($11,570)	($25,000)	($60,052)
Underwriters/ Guarantor's Counsel				(125,000)	(125,000)
QIU					
Warrant Agent/ Trustee	(1,859)	(1,859)	(4,793)	(5,000)	(13,511)
Warrant Agent/ Trustee Counsel				(1,500)	(1,500)
Auditors Opinion	(3,500)	(3,500)		(15,000)	(22,000)
Determination Agent					
Exchange Listing Fee	(5,352)	(5,337)	(2,396)		(23,085)
Index License Fee (Lifetime)					
Agg. Exchange Annual Fees					
SEC Registration Fee					
NASD Review Fee					
Printing Costs					
Red Herrings				(83,000)	(83,000)
Final Prospectus				(20,000)	(20,000)
Warrant Certificates				(5,000)	(5,000)
CUSIP Nos.				(100)	(100)
Est. Misc. Fees and Expenses	(1,129)	(968)	(898)	(10,000)	(12,995)
Total Direct Expenses	($23,581)	($23,405)	($19,657)	($289,600)	($356,244)

Grand Total All Sample Offering Expenses ($6,826,059)

SAMPLE WORKING GROUP CHECKLIST*

ASIAN INDEX PUT & CALL WARRANTS

Proposed U.S. Initial Public Offering

Issuer: U.S. Parent Corporation
Underwriters: U.S. Broker–Dealer, Inc. (Lead Manager and Books),
   Comanager International, Inc. (QIU and Comanager), and
   Comanager Securities, Inc. (Comanager)

Tentative Timetable
(Subject to Revision) [x] = Completed

File Draft Red with Sec: Wed-4-Oct
Sec Sign-Off: Fri-6-Oct±
Print Red Herrings: Fri-6-Oct±
Circulate Red Herrings: Mon-9-Oct±
Commence Marketing: Mon-9-Oct±
Ticketing Deadline: Tue-24-Oct±
Pricing and Trade Date: Wed-25-Oct±

Sample Working Group Checklist
[x] = Assignment Completed

[ ] Meeting Agenda, 9:00 A.M., Friday, September 8th, 39th Floor Deriva-
      tive Conference Room
      [x]   Preliminary pricing discussions
      [x]   Hedging discussions and procedures
      [x]   Underwriting and management fee split
      [x]   Other underwriting members
      [x]   Potential demand
      [x]   Current Nomura research on Japan
      [x]   Index construction
            [x]   Back calculation and start date (10 years)
            [x]   Formal index name
            [x]   Index ownership
            [x]   Copy of exchange rule filing with SEC

---

*See Chapter 3 for a discussion of the working group checklist.

       [x] Index maintenance and dissemination
       [ ] Written index calculation rules
       [x] Update historical index information on computer disk
       [x] Status and timing of exchange rule filing with SEC
       [ ] Comanager International as QIU (NASD Schedule E qualification)
       [x] Miscellaneous business discussions

[x] Latest 10-K, 10-Q, 8-K & proxy from Comanager International

[x] Comanager Options International plc financials to Corp. Credit

[x] *Lead Corp. Banker* obtain mgt., retail, derivative, credit, and risk mgt. green lights (9/26)

[x] *Lead Corp. Banker* retain underwriter's counsel (9/26)

[x] Provide Corp. financials, 10Q & proxy to comanagers

[x] Provide 1994 proxy to underwriter's counsel

[ ] Await 3Q press release

[ ] Sticker press release to red herring? Review with underwriter's counsel

[x] Draft supplement; *Lead Corp. Banker* handling
       [x] Underwriter's counsel providing first draft
       [x] Comments ASAP
       [x] Copies to comanagers
       [x] Table & graph
       [x] Symbols
       [ ] Need Comanager International's approval to start NASD process

[x] Transaction cleared by NASD (compensation & QIU)

[x] Coordination of EDGAR filings; (424 Filing & 8-A) *Issuer's counsel* coordinate

[x] QIU and comanager

[x] Blue Sky work; *Underwriter's counsel* handling

[x] Notify Euroclear/CEDEL

[x] Send Euroclear confirm of terms, closing date, and final prospectus supplement

[ ] Common Code from Euroclear: ____

[ ] ISIN No. from Euroclear: <u>US_____</u>

[ ] CUSIP No.: ____ from S&P

[ ] Provide CUSIP to Euroclear

[ ] Provide term sheet to Euroclear

[x] Comfort letter; notify auditors

[ ] Update financial data in supplement

[x] Determine NASD filing fees (QIU)
[x] Handle $250 SEC 8-A filing fees; RE: EDGAR lockbox
[x] Speak to SEC; RE: timing of filing
[ ] Update table & graph in supplement
[ ] Prepare final chart and table
[x] Notify printer
[x] Notify Banknote Co. RE: warrant certificates
[x] Notify warrant agent
[ ] File 8-A with SEC
[x] *Lead Corp. Banker* obtain red herring count from comanager(s); ____
     providing labels (Corp.: 8,500, Comanager International: _,000, Co-
     manager: _,000 & Extra: 4,500)
[x] Red herring mailing labels
[x] Working group mailing labels
[ ] Final mailing labels
[ ] *Underwriter's Counsel & Lead Corp. Banker* work on listing documents:
     [x] Corp. legal opinion; draft prepared and sent to Exchange
     [x] Corp. legal opinion; execute final
     [x] Draft agreement with warrant agent
     [x] Warrant agreement
     [x] Draft listing application
     [ ] File 8-A with SEC; copy to exchange
     [ ] Final listing application
     [ ] $_0,000 listing fee
     [ ] $_,000 balance of listing fee due
     [x] Listing agreement
     [ ] Exercising holders letter
     [ ] Annual & interim financials; copy to Exchange
     [ ] Listing resolution
     [ ] Underwriter's certification of holders
     [x] Preliminary discussions with SEC market regulation
     [x] Supplement filing with SEC
     [ ] Specimen certificates to exchange
     [x] Warrant agent agreement
     [x] SEC 34-Act approval
     [x] Listing approval
     [x] Select exchange specialist/DPM
[x] Notify DTC of pending offering

[x]   Notify DTC of pricing date
[ ]   Call DTC and confirm initial certification & 45-day conversion
[x]   Underwriting Agreement; *underwriter's counsel* draft (comanagers have previously executed master underwriting agreements with Corp.?)
[ ]   Underwriting Agreement (execute and fax; deliver originals)
[ ]   NASD Rep. letters; file w/NASD by
[x]   Transaction cleared by NASD (compensation & QIU)
[ ]   Final fairness opinion (review draft)
[x]   Fairness opinion from QIU prior to commencement of trading
[ ]   Fax copy of fairness opinion to underwriter's counsel
[ ]   DTC letter of representations
[ ]   Checks for closing
[x]   Due diligence conference call @ 10:30 A.M. EST on _-__-95:
       Derivative banker
       Underwriter's counsel
       Issuer's counsel
       Corp. derivative counsel
       Corp. litigation
       Comanager International derivative banker
       Comanager derivative banker
       Corp. treasurer
       Corp. finance
       Corp. gen. counsel's office
[ ]   Comfort letter from auditor
[ ]   Auditor bring-down/reaffirmation letter
[ ]   Calendar 45-day conversion notice and 10-day advance notice to DTC & Cedel/Euroclear
[ ]   Book-entry conversion; monitor post offering timetable
[x]   Provide deal briefing to management and obtain green light
[x]   Syndicate/selling group list
[x]   Confirm research
[x]   Update management commitment memo
[x]   Reg. Cap; get U.K. model approval
[x]   Confirm Reg. Cap requirements and model approval
[x]   Check vega limit
[x]   Check with credit (provide term sheet)
[ ]   Check final credit sign off; provide copy of written guarantee @ pricing

[x]   Check exchange operational issues

[x]   Institutional price break

[ ]   All retail customers must receive recirculated red herring with Corp. 3Q results stickered on the front

[x]   On new accounts, broker must obtain branch manager approval of option account on *ticketing date,* otherwise, broker loses commission. Option papers must be received by Compliance no more than *15 days* after the ticketing date. [RE: Consent with the SEC according to sales practice examination and review.]

[ ]   Corp. % coverage in secondary market @ $4–6 buy (cumulative) 10% back if down 1/8th, 20% if down 1/4, and 35% if down 1/2

[x]   Preliminary Blue Sky memorandum

[ ]   Final Blue Sky memorandum

[x]   Underwriting expenses

[x]   Underwriting invitations; check with syndicate

[x]   Selling group invitations; coordinate with syndicate

[ ]   Selling group list; set up operations

[ ]   Comanager confirms & international tickets; set up P&S, security code, etc.

[ ]   Draft spreadsheet on pricing data

[ ]   Number of holders

[x]   Syndicate telexes; work with syndicate

[ ]   Review final pricing and terms with syndicate

[x]   Confirm comanager fee split: 1/3rd each; underwriting fee pay underwriting costs and any remainder split 1/3rd each

[x]   Agreement to split offering costs in case of broken deal

[x]   Signed term sheet from comanagers

[ ]   Establish short acct; give to trader

[ ]   Track prices of short covering; coordinate with trader

[ ]   Terminate penalty bid after the close; notify syndicate & retail [Note: Penalty bid is meant to discourage trading during the "stabilization" period immediately after an IPO is launched; lift penalty bid based on trading characteristics: (1) when short position is covered, (2) if security trades down significantly (cover short immediately), or (3) if security trades up significantly (cover short immediately)

[x]   Prepricing discussions

[ ]   Notify wire services of pricing

[ ]   Preclosing

[ ]   Closing memo (closing at underwriter counsel's office)
[ ]   Corp. pricing and takedown approval
[ ]   Size/puts: _,000,000,000 @ $_.__/calls: _,000,000 @ $_.__; broke syndi-
       cate @ _:__ P.M. commence trading @ _:__ on __-__-95.
[ ]   Monitor secondary trading
[x]   Corp. management provide commitment sign-off
[ ]   Obtain final sign-off if deal is upsized
[ ]   Final term sheet for distribution
[x]   Call division sales managers to schedule 9-Oct branch mgr. calls
[x]   Meet with equity syndicate on Thur-5-Oct
[x]   Broker confirm message
[x]   Broker memo to print shop by Thur-4-Oct
[x]   Radio call
[x]   Options page for Broker memo
[x]   FedEx reds to survey brokers
[x]   Fax Broker memo to DSMs
[x]   Internal newspaper article
[x]   Radio spot on Tue-10-Oct
[x]   DSM call Mon-9-Oct:
       - research backdrop
       - terms, timing, request to join in branch calls, conference calls, or
         branch visits
[x]   Follow up with institutional sales personnel
[x]   Follow up with international sales

SAMPLE SEC RULE FILING COMMENT LETTER*

Memorandum to Industry Working Group

SEC Orders Approving Exchange Rule
Changes Relating to the Establishment
of Guidelines for Listing and Trading of
<u>Stock Index, Currency, and Currency-Indexed Warrants</u>

The Securities and Exchange Commission (SEC) published in the Federal Register orders approving rule changes (the Final Rules) to establish listing and trading guidelines for stock index, currency, and currency-indexed warrants (Warrants) on the American Stock Exchange, Inc. (AMEX), the Chicago Board Options Exchange, Inc. (CBOE), the Pacific Stock Exchange, Inc. (PSE), The New York Stock Exchange, Inc. (NYSE), and the Philadelphia Stock Exchange, Inc. (PHLX) (collectively the Exchanges). In addition to filing our comment letter on the proposed rules, we were in regular communication with the Exchanges and the SEC in connection with their discussions concerning the proposed rules.

We are pleased to report that while we were unable to have all of our suggestions incorporated into the Final Rules, we did get a substantial number of our suggestions adopted by the Exchanges and approved by the SEC as outlined below and prevented a number of extremely onerous surveillance requirements from being imposed by the SEC as part of the package authorizing the Final Rules. Preventing the adoption of the surveillance procedures occupied the better part of the past four months and we believe that the procedures that have been adopted are not overly burdensome.

The following outline highlights some of the more important provisions of the Final Rules, the original request by the Exchanges, and the positions that were maintained by the Industry Working Group:

  I. <u>Listing Standards</u>
    A. <u>Summary of Proposal</u>
      Warrant offerings (combined with such offerings by an affiliate) would not be permitted to exceed 25 percent of the issuer's net worth.
    B. <u>Industry Group Recommendations</u>
      (i) Eliminate the 25 percent limit; and/or
      (ii) Adopt hedging and/or netting standards.

---

*See Chapter 3 for a discussion of SEC rule filings.

C. Final Rules

Adoption of alternative standard such that issuer must have either (i) a minimum tangible net worth in excess of $250 million (with no percentage limit on the number of Warrants that can be issued); or (ii) a minimum tangible net worth in excess of $150 million provided that the aggregate original issue price of such Warrant offerings (combined with offerings by its affiliates) do not exceed 25 percent of the warrant issuer's net worth.

II. AM/PM Settlement

A. Summary of Proposal

All equity index Warrants where 25 percent or more of the value of that index is represented by securities whose primary trading market is in the United States shall provide for opening price settlement (A.M. settlement).

B. Industry Group Recommendations

Allow the use of closing settlement prices (P.M. settlement) for all American style Warrants exercised anytime except 48 hours prior to expiration, at which time the A.M. settlement requirement will govern the settlement value.

C. Final Rules

Industry group recommendation was adopted.

III. Option Approval and Customer Protection

A. Summary of Proposal

Warrants may only be purchased or sold for customers who have been preapproved for options trading.

B. Industry Group Recommendations

(i) Create a class of "Warrant Eligible Customers" who are authorized to trade Warrants even if not approved to trade options generally; and

(ii) Allow member firms to accept a representation from a registered investment advisor (IA) that the clients for whom the IA engages in Warrant transactions are either options or "Warrant Eligible" without requiring underlying clients to provide such information to member firms.

C. Final Rules

While refusing to create a special "Warrant Eligible" classification of purchasers and requiring that customers be "option eligible" to purchase Warrants, the SEC expressly left the door open for the creation of a "Warrant Eligible" classification of customers by stating that "as the range of exchange-traded derivative products increases, the SROs might consider in the future as to whether a new derivatives eligibility classification is appropriate."

Provision has now been included in the Final Rules to allow member firms to accept an IA's representation concerning the options eligibility status of its customers.

IV. Position Limits
  A. Summary of Proposal
     The Exchanges have established position limits for stock index Warrants at 75 percent of the level currently in place for index options.
  B. Industry Group Recommendation
     (i)   Position limit levels for Warrants should be at least equivalent to index option position limits;
     (ii) Adopt hedge exemption procedures for Warrants similar to those for listed stock index options; and
     (iii) Provide a mechanism for specific waivers or exemptions for hedgers, market makers, and broker–dealers comparable to the waivers for listed stock options.
  C. Final Rules
     While we were unable to persuade the SEC to modify its position in connection with position limits, the SEC did leave the door open for subsequent modifications to its current stance in a footnote stating that ". . . the hedge exemption for index options was adopted after several years experience with index options trading. Until the SROs gain some experience with domestic index warrant trading, it is difficult to determine the need for a hedge exemption (i.e., that speculative limits are insufficient to meet hedging need)."

V. Surveillance Procedures
  A. Summary of Proposal
     The SEC initially demanded that member firms provide the following data:

(i)   After notice of early exercise has been given but prior to settlement, the nature and size of the hedge unwinds should be reported to the listing exchange; and

(ii)   The number of Warrants exercised to be provided to the exchange where the underlying securities are traded prior to settlement.

B. Industry Group Recommendation

(i)   Eliminate all presettlement notifications and provide for postsettlement notification of hedge unwinds to exchange that lists the Warrants;

(ii)   No new requirements to exchange where underlying securities trade; and

(iii) De minimis exemption for reporting.

C. Final Rules

(i)   The Exchanges will require that all Warrants exercised prior to settlement be reported to the Exchange by 4:30 P.M. on the settlement date for such Warrants and that issuers must report all hedge unwind transactions related to the early settlement of domestic index warrants by the business day following the trade date of such hedge unwind; and

(ii)   Transactions executed in underlying securities as an unwind of a hedge will be subject to reporting on the NYSE's daily program trading report (DPTR) if such activity meets the definition of a "program trade" under NYSE regulation.

As stated in the Federal Register release, many, if not all, of the modifications to the initial proposal were a direct result of an earlier comment letter filed with the SEC as well as subsequent discussions between us, the SEC, and the Exchanges. The entire group effort has, in our view, been extremely successful in delivering an outcome that will hopefully facilitate and encourage the growth of listed Warrants in the United States. We appreciate your help and backing in this project and congratulate the Industry Working Group on its success.

Working Group Legal Counsel

SAMPLE CUSTOMER SUITABILITY MEMO*

Equity New Issue

U.S. Broker–Dealer Incorporated Lead Manager

U.S. Parent Corporation

Taiwan Export Index Put and Call Warrants

U.S. Broker–Dealer Compliance Department and Legal and Advisory Services Division

For Option Accounts Only

Summary of Investor Restrictions

- For primary and secondary trades, customers are required to have option-approved accounts.
- IRA and Custodial Accounts for Minors are prohibited from purchasing the Warrants.
- Branch Manager must approve *new* option account papers on or before the *ticketing* date. Compliance must *receive* signed option papers no later than 15 days from date of Branch Manager *approval* in order for the Investment Executive to retain the sales credit.
- The Warrants are speculative and can expire worthless.

To All Branch Office Managers and Investment Executives

In connection with SEC customer suitability requirements pertaining to Parent Corporation's proposed issuance of *Taiwan Export Index Put and Call Warrants*, please review the suitability of customers wishing to purchase the warrants to confirm their suitability for such purchases. You and the appropriate Investment Executive should review the customer's account information and confirm their suitability prior to the trade date.

---

*See Chapter 3 for a discussion of customer suitability.

Please note that IRA accounts and custodial accounts for minors are prohibited from purchasing the Warrants. Additionally, the appropriate Investment Executive should be reminded to review their institutional investor account files to confirm that the organizational or other relevant documents of such investor permit the purchase of these securities.

Investors in the above-referenced offering are advised to consider carefully the risk factors discussed below prior to investing in the Warrants, as well as the matters discussed under *Risk Factors* and *Certain United States Federal Income Tax Considerations* in the Prospectus.

PROSPECTIVE PURCHASERS OF THE WARRANTS SHOULD RECOGNIZE THAT THEIR WARRANTS MAY EXPIRE WORTHLESS. PURCHASERS SHOULD BE PREPARED TO SUSTAIN A TOTAL LOSS OF THE PURCHASE PRICE OF THEIR WARRANTS. THE WARRANTS ARE APPROPRIATE INVESTMENTS ONLY FOR INVESTORS WITH OPTIONS-APPROVED ACCOUNTS WHO ARE EXPERIENCED WITH RESPECT TO OPTIONS AND OPTION TRANSACTIONS AND WHO ARE ABLE TO UNDERSTAND AND BEAR THE RISK OF A SPECULATIVE INVESTMENT IN THE WARRANTS.

The trading price of a Warrant at any time is expected to be affected by the creditworthiness of U.S. Parent Corporation and a number of interrelated factors including, among others:

- The prevailing level of the stock index
- The volatility of the stock index
- The time remaining to the expiration date of the Warrants
- Dividend rates of stocks in the index
- U.S. and Taiwanese interest rates
- The prevailing currency exchange rate

Equity New Issue

U.S. Broker–Dealer Incorporated Lead Manager

U.S. Parent Corporation

1,000,000 Warrants

U.S. Dollar/Japanese Yen Currency Warrants

> ## Dollar Appears Poised for Rally against the Yen
> ## Warrants Provide Upside Play on Dollar

Major Sales Points

Dollar Appears Oversold—Short-Term Rebound Expected

- Dollar currently trading near record lows of 83.00 yen per dollar.
- Currency forecast projects dollar rebound to 105 yen per dollar (please see the subsequent section on cash settlement and intrinsic value analysis for research discussion).

Financial Leverage of U.S. Dollar Increase Warrants

- Each Warrant controls the cash equivalent of $100 worth of yen.
- Warrant issue price equals 100% time value and 0% cash value.
- Each 1-yen move above the strike adds approximately $1.00 of cash value.

The Warrants are speculative and involve a high degree of risk, including the risk of expiring worthless if the yen/dollar exchange rate does not increase above the strike and due to loss of time value. The Warrants may only be sold by prospectus supplement only to suitable investors with options-approved accounts. This memorandum is for broker use only.

*See Chapter 3 for a discussion of the marketing of structured products.

- Downside risk limited to purchase price of the Warrants; options accounts only.

- Warrants offer currency hedge for existing Japanese investments; pure play on the dollar.

Long-Term Investment Horizon and Liquidity of U.S. Stock Exchange Listing

- One-year term is significantly longer than traditional short-term currency options.

- Exchange traded or exercisable into U.S. dollars on any New York business day.

Offering Summary

Issuer	U.S. Parent Corporation
Issue	IPO of U.S. Dollar/Japanese Yen Currency Warrants
Initial Filing Size	1,000,000 Warrants (can be upsized, based on demand)
Expected Pricing Date	Early April, subject to market conditions
Managers	U.S. Broker–Dealer Incorporated (books) and comanagers
Expiration	1 year from date of issuance
Price Range Per Warrant	$4.75–$5.50, subject to market conditions
Gross Spread	5.00% ($0.25 ± per Warrant)
Selling Concession	3.00% ($0.15 ± per Warrant)
Strike Exchange Rate	At-the-money yen/dollar exchange rate on the pricing date
Spot Yen Quotation Symbol	"JYS.SP" (Quotron - U.S. dollars per yen)
Warrant Listing/Symbol	U.S. Stock Exchange/Symbol: "YEN.WS"
Form and Transfer	Certificates convertible to DTC book entry after 45 days
Exercise and Settlement	"American style" continuous exercise
Cash Settlement Value	If exercised, settlement in U.S. dollars calculated as follows:

The greater of $0 or

$$\$100 - \left[\$100 \times \left(\frac{\text{Strike Yen per \$}}{\text{Spot Yen per \$}} \right) \right]$$

Breakeven Point   88.5 ± yen/dollar, based on an 84 strike
                                  (i.e., the point where the cash intrinsic
                                  value of each Warrant at *expiration* is
                                  equal to the IPO price)

Investor Restrictions   For primary and secondary retail trades,
                                  option-approved accounts required

Product Description

U.S. Parent Corporation (Corp) is offering *U.S. Dollar/Japanese Yen Currency Warrants* expiring one year from the date of issuance (the Warrants). The Warrants are unsecured obligations of Corp and will trade on a U.S. stock exchange. The trading symbol will be "YEN.WS".

The Warrants will have an at-the-money strike price equal to the U.S. dollar/Japanese yen exchange rate at the time of issuance. As puts on the yen, the Warrants are expected to *increase* in value as the number of yen per dollar increases above the strike rate. Alternatively, as the number of yen per U.S. dollar declines below the strike rate, the Warrants are expected to *decrease* in value.

Although the Warrants will be U.S. exchange listed and traded, investors may also elect to exercise them at any time from the date of issuance until expiration. The Warrants will be automatically exercised at expiration and investors will receive a cash settlement value in U.S. dollars based on the cash settlement value formula shown in the preceding *Offering Summary* section.

International Currency Research

- Short-term currency speculation appears to have caused the dollar to be oversold versus the yen.

- U.S. involvement in Mexican crisis, uncertain U.S. trade talks with Japan, and lack of concerted central bank intervention to support the dollar, among other factors, have given the yen a *safe haven* status.

- Political and technical developments often have a short-term influence on currency markets and are reversed as economic fundamentals regain influence.

- Three-month currency forecast is 97 yen per dollar (ranging from 95 to 100).
- Six-month and twelve-month yen/dollar forecasts are 99 and 105 yen per dollar, respectively.
- Caveat: In trying to achieve an economic *soft landing,* the U.S. Federal Reserve may be approaching the top of its tightening cycle while Japan's economy appears to be recovering, the combination of which, among other factors, may produce only a modest dollar recovery, if any.

Cash Settlement/Intrinsic Value Analysis

The following table outlines the cash settlement value of the Warrants (also called "intrinsic value") based on yen/dollar exchange rate increases above a *hypothetical* strike exchange rate of 84.00 yen per U.S. dollar (Note: The actual strike rate will be set on the pricing date.)

Hypothetical Cash Settlement Value of the Warrants

U.S.$ per Yen FX Rate	Yen per U.S.$ FX Rate	U.S.$ Cash Settlement Value of the Warrants
0.009524	105.00	$20.00
0.010000	100.00	16.00
0.010309	97.00	13.40
0.010526	95.00	11.57
0.011111	90.00	6.66
0.011236	89.00	5.61
0.011364	88.00	4.54
0.011494	85.00	1.17
0.011905	**84.00 (Strike)**	**0.00**

Note: The Warrants are puts on the yen. As the yen weakens against the dollar, the Warrants increase in value. Based on a hypothetical strike exchange rate (which could change on the pricing date) of 84.00 yen per U.S. dollar, *exclusive of time value.* The time value of each Warrant will decline as the expiration date approaches, reaching zero on the expiration date. Investors will receive only the cash settlement value (also called intrinsic value) if the Warrants are exercised. When traded on the exchange, investors will receive the *market* value of the Warrants, equal to the cash settlement value plus any remaining time value. Warrants that are in-the-money will be automatically exercised into U.S. dollars at expiration.

Equity New Issue

U.S. Broker–Dealer Incorporated Lead Manager

U.S. Parent Corporation

4,000,000 Hong Kong Index Put Warrants
5,000,000 Hong Kong Index Call Warrants

New Hong Kong Index Warrant Offering

Major Sales Points

- Pure play on Hong Kong; cobeneficiary of growth in China:

  Call Warrants increase as Hong Kong Index *appreciates*. Participate in continued upside growth potential with calls.
  Put Warrants increase in value when Index *declines*. Hedge existing Hong Kong stock or mutual fund profits with Put protection.

- Risk is limited only to the purchase price of the Warrants (100% of invested capital).

- Two-year expiration.

- Fixed exchange rate, denominated and cash settled in U.S. dollars.

- Liquidity:

  U.S. exchange listed and traded.
  Continuous American style exercise any time prior to expiration.

The Warrants are speculative and involve a high degree of risk, including the risk of expiring worthless if the Hong Kong Index does not move from the strike and due to a loss of time value. The Warrants may only be sold by prospectus supplement only to suitable investors with options-approved accounts and by prospectus supplement only. This memorandum is for broker use only.

Offering Summary

Issuer	U.S. Parent Corporation
Issue	IPO of put & call warrants on the Hong Kong Index
Managers	U.S. Broker–Dealer Incorporated (books) and comanagers
Expiration	2 years from issuance

	Put Warrants	Call Warrants
Price Range (assumes index level of <u>600</u> and a 5% gross spread)	$4.75–5.50 per Warrant	$5.50–6.25 per Warrant
Selling Concession (3% net)	$0.14–0.17 per Warrant	$0.17–0.19 per Warrant
US$ Cash Settlement	[(Strike – Spot)/ Divisor]/Fixed FX	[(Spot – Strike)/ Divisor]/Fixed FX
Divisor	3	3
Intrinsic Value Per Index Point	$0.043/Warrant±	$0.043/Warrant±
Filing Size	4,000,000 Warrants	5,000,000 Warrants

Strike Index Level	At-the-money Hong Kong Index at the time of pricing
Spot Index Level	Published globally each day
Currency of Denomination	U.S. dollars
Exercise	American style, continuous exercise into U.S. dollars prior to expiration
Marginability	*Not* marginable, may not be borrowed, may not be sold short
Investor Requirements	For primary and secondary trades, options-approved accounts only
Contacts	Global Derivatives—New York and London, Paris, Hong Kong, Geneva, and Zurich offices

Product Description

IPO of put and call warrants on the *Hong Kong Index* offered by U.S. Parent Corporation (Corp). The U.S. offering provides investors an opportunity to participate in the Hong Kong market. The new warrants will have a cash settlement value for each index point of approximately 4.3 cents. The index is composed of diversified stocks trading on the Hong Kong Stock Exchange and is calculated and disseminated daily.

The put warrants give the holder the right to receive from Corp the cash amount of any *decline* in the Index *below* the specified strike index level. The call warrants give the holder the right to receive the cash amount of any *increase* in the Index *above* the strike index level.

Investors can potentially *profit* from a *decrease* in the Index over two years in the case of the put Warrants or *profit* from an *increase* in the Index over two years in the case of the call warrants by selling the warrants in the open market. The warrants are American style and can also be exercised into U.S. dollars on any New York business day prior to expiration. The Warrants will be priced at-the-money, equal to the starting or strike level of the Index on the new IPO date.

Cash Settlement Value Analysis

The following table outlines the *cash settlement value* (also called the "intrinsic value") of the Warrants based on movements of the Index. The cash settlement value of the new warrant offering will change by approximately $0.043 for every 1-index point move up or down. (Please note that the cash settlement value does not include any remaining time value associated with the warrants.)

Hypothetical Cash Settlement Values of
Hong Kong Index Warrants

Index Level	Proposed Offering (assuming 600 strike) US$ Cash Settlement Value	
	Puts	Calls
850	$0.00	$10.79
800	0.00	8.63
750	0.00	6.47
700	0.00	4.32
650	0.00	2.16
600 (strike)	**0.00**	**0.00**
550	2.16	0.00
500	4.32	0.00
450	6.47	0.00
400	8.63	0.00
350	10.79	0.00

Note: Based on a fixed exchange rate of 7.725 HK$/US$. Please note that all hypothetical cash settlement value figures shown are *exclusive of time value.* The time value of each Warrant will decline as the expiration date approaches, reaching zero on the expiration date. Investors will receive only the cash settlement value if the Warrants are exercised. If traded on the exchange, investors will receive the market value of the Warrants, which includes the cash settlement value plus any remaining time value. At expiration, Warrants that are in-the-money will be automatically exercised.

Research Summary

- The Hong Kong market has tripled in value over the past three years.
- New Hong Kong airport will be the largest infrastructure project in Asia ($15–20 billion).
- Industrial production up 33% in China; Hong Kong companies invest heavily in China.
- China's annual GDP growth has averaged 9% over 10 years.

Hong Kong Reversion to China

When the reversion of Hong Kong to The People's Republic of China occurs, China will be the only emerging country in the world to simultaneously acquire both a world class financial center and the second largest stock market in Asia. Hong Kong is the southern port to China's 1 billion residents. Hong Kong's 5,000,000 residents are 98% Chinese and share a common ancestry and language with The People's Republic of China. There are tremendous potential benefits and risks to political, economic, and social integration.

Political, Economic, and Social Risks in Hong Kong and China

- Death of Deng Xiaoping may cause leadership struggle in China.
- Overheating Chinese economy and inflation threat may cause restraint of credit and growth.
- Failure of democratic reform negotiations between Britain and China; Hong Kong sell-off.
- Under communist rule, Hong Kong market may have fewer investor safeguards.
- Potential civil turmoil in China and human rights violations; negative world reaction.
- Loss of Most Favored Nations status with U.S.; cut Hong Kong growth rate in half.
- Elimination of fixed HK$/US$ exchange rates; possible currency devaluation.

Equity New Issue

U.S. Broker–Dealer Incorporated Sole Manager

U.S. Parent Corporation

3,000,000 Units
Index-Linked Notes on the S&P MidCap 400 Index

**A Unique Investment Opportunity Providing
Above-Market Equity Returns, Principal
Preservation, and Liquidity**

Major Sales Points

- **Above-market equity returns**

  At maturity, 120% of the appreciation of the S&P MidCap 400 Index.

- **Downside protection: no risk to principal**

  Return of $10 per unit initial investment at maturity.

- **Liquidity**

  The securities will be U.S. exchange listed for trading.

Index-Linked Notes are most appropriate for retirement and tax deferred accounts. Investors should be aware that if the Final Value of the S&P MidCap 400 Index is not in excess of the Initial Value, Unitholders will be entitled to receive repayment of initial investment but no Supplemental Redemption Amount. Payment at maturity will be made by Parent Corporation ("Corp"); the Securities are subordinated obligations of Corp. This memorandum is for broker use only.

Offering Summary

Issuer	U.S. Parent Corporation (Corp)
Sole Manager	U.S. Broker–Dealer Incorporated (Inc)
Offering	Units of Index-Linked Notes on the S&P MidCap 400 Index (the Securities)
Initial Filing Size	3,000,000 units
Offering Price	$10.00 per unit
Minimum Purchase	100 units
Selling Concession	$0.20 per unit (2.0%)
Listing	U.S. stock exchange listed
Term	The Securities will mature 7 years from the date of issue and are noncallable prior to maturity
Obligation	The Securities are subordinated obligations of Corp, rated ____ by Moody's and ____ by Standard & Poor's
Use of Proceeds	Corp use proceeds for general funding purposes and to purchase financial assets to hedge its obligations with respect to the Securities
Initial Value of the Index	The S&P MidCap 400 Index value will be set at the level of the Index on the issue date of the Securities
Payment at Maturity	At maturity, a unit holder will be entitled to receive the $10 initial investment per unit plus a supplemental redemption amount, if any, based on 120% of the final value of the S&P MidCap 400 Index, calculated as follows:

$$\$10 \text{ Initial Investment } + \$10 \times \frac{\text{Final Value} - \text{Initial Value}}{\text{Initial Value}} \times 120\%$$

Calculation Agent	Bank of New York
Investor Restrictions	The Securities are most appropriate for retirement and tax-deferred accounts; however, certain restrictions apply (see Note at end of memo)
Delivery	Book entry
Contacts	Structured products, retail equity, prospectus department, retail equity new issues desk, and ERISA desk

Product Description

Corp is offering 3,000,000 units of index-linked notes on the S&P MidCap 400 Index (the Securities). The Securities are subordinated obligations of Corp and will be exchange listed for trading.

At maturity, a unit holder will receive the $10 per unit initial investment plus a supplemental redemption amount, if any, based on 120% of the appreciation of the S&P MidCap 400 Index from the issue date to the maturity date of the Securities. In no event will the supplemental redemption amount be less than zero. Payment per unit at maturity will be calculated as follows:

$$\$10 \text{ Initial Investment} + $$
$$\$10 \times \frac{\text{Final Value} - \text{Initial Value}}{\text{Initial Value}} \times 120\%$$

The initial value of the S&P MidCap 400 Index will be set at the level of the Index on the issue date of the Securities. The final value of the S&P MidCap 400 Index will be determined by the Bank of New York and will equal the average of the closing values of the Index on five business days prior to maturity, beginning on the tenth business day prior to maturity.

S&P MidCap 400 Index

The S&P MidCap 400 Index, published by Standard & Poor's Corporation, measures the stock price performance of the middle "growth" sector of the U.S. equities market. The Index includes 400 companies, of which 265 are listed on the New York Stock Exchange, 12 on the American Stock Exchange, and 123 on the NASDAQ National Market System. The market capitalizations of the companies included in the S&P MidCap 400 Index range from $200 million to $5.2 billion. The S&P MidCap 400 Index is quoted under the symbol MID.

Major Sales Points

• **Above-Market Equity Returns**

The Securities are designed to return 120% of the appreciation of the S&P MidCap 400 Index at maturity. The following table shows hypothetical returns of the Stock Index Return Securities based on historical movements of the S&P MidCap 400 Index in each seven-year period since 1981:

Period	S&P MidCap 400 Index		Index-Linked Notes	
	Annualized Return	Percent Change in Index Value	Annualized Return	Per Unit Value at Maturity[a]
1981–1987	9.75%	91.82%	10.85%	$20.56
1982–1988	11.90	119.77	13.17	23.77
1983–1989	13.97	149.74	15.38	27.22
1984–1990	9.64	90.49	10.72	20.40
1985–1991	16.40	189.55	17.97	31.80
1986–1992	13.55	143.34	14.93	26.48

[a]Assumes return of $10 per unit initial investment plus 115% of the appreciation on the S&P MidCap 400 Index.

The following chart displays potential investor returns per $10 unit based on hypothetical values of the S&P MidCap 400 Index at maturity. The starting Index level is assumed to be 160.

Hypothetical Index Value	Percent Change in Index Value	Per Unit Value at Maturity	Annualized Rate of Return[a]
80	–50%	$10.00	0.00%
120	–25	10.00	0.00
160[b]	0	10.00	0.00
240	50	15.75	6.60
280	75	18.63	9.08
320	100	21.50	11.24
360	125	24.38	13.14
400	150	27.25	14.85
440	175	30.13	16.39
480	200	33.00	17.80

[a]Calculated on a semiannual bond equivalent basis.
[b]Assumes an Initial Value of the S&P MidCap 400 Index of 160.

- **Downside Protection to Principal**

The Securities provide downside protection to principal even in the event of a decline in the S&P MidCap 400 Index. At maturity, investors receive their $10 initial investment. The Securities are subordinated obligations of Corp.

- **Liquidity**

The Securities will be exchange listed. Liquidity is an important feature for investors wishing to sell the Securities prior to maturity. The value of the Securities will fluctuate with changes in the value of the S&P MidCap 400 Index and interest rates, among other factors.*

Questions and Answers

What are the prospects for the S&P MidCap 400 Index?

In the slow-growth, low-inflation, and low-interest-rate environment of the 1990s, growth stocks are expected to be the best performers. Midcap stocks are medium-size companies that can offer greater growth potential than the larger blue-chip stocks with more stability than small-cap stocks. Some of the advantages enjoyed by midcap companies include the opportunity for market share growth, impact of new products, participation in faster-growing market sectors, and entrepreneurial management.

What factors may affect the trading value of the Securities in the secondary market?

The value of the Securities is expected to fluctuate with changes in certain key variables, primarily the level of the S&P MidCap 400 Index and current interest rates. Other interrelated factors such as volatility of the S&P MidCap 400 Index, time to maturity, and dividend rates on the stocks comprising the S&P MidCap 400 Index will also affect the trading value of the Securities in the secondary market.

What is the credit underlying the Securities?

The Securities are unrated; however, they are subordinated debt securities of Corp, rated ____ by Moody's and ____ by Standard & Poor's.

---

*The price at which Units may be sold prior to maturity may be at a discount from the $10 initial price if, among other things, the S&P MidCap 400 Index is below, equal to, or not significantly above the level of such Index at issuance.

Why can't I create this security by purchasing a combination of bonds and options?

A combination of a zero-coupon bond and a seven-year call option is currently unavailable in the market. Seven-year options are not available to most investors and utilization of a rollover strategy to create such an option would result in market risk and extremely high transaction costs.

Are there any similar products trading in the market currently?

There are no other products that offer investors the opportunity to outperform the growth of the S&P MidCap 400 Index over a seven-year period while providing principal protection and liquidity. There are other listed index-linked notes available to investors, however, for shorter durations and on different indexes

What is the opportunity cost of purchasing the Securities?

By purchasing the Securities instead of "buying" the S&P MidCap 400 Index, an investor is forgoing the dividends on the S&P 400 stocks. The current dividend rate on the S&P MidCap 400 Index is approximately 1.9%. This can be viewed as the cost to investors of ensuring a return of their initial investment at maturity.

What are the tax considerations of purchasing the Securities?

There is no current tax liability associated with the Securities while held in a *tax-advantaged retirement account.* Any tax consequences are deferred until the proceeds are withdrawn from the tax-advantaged account.

In a *non-tax-advantaged account,* the tax treatment is complex and investors are encouraged to read the offering materials and to consult their tax advisor regarding their particular situation.

Sample Investor Profiles

Clients interested in participating in potential long-term equity appreciation who do not want any risk to principal, especially new and existing retirement and tax-advantaged account investors (IRAs and IRA rollovers). The Securities should not be marked as a trading vehicle because there can be no assurance that appreciation in the S&P MidCap 400 Index will be fully reflected, if at all, in the market value of the Securities prior to maturity.

- Conservative investors who do not typically invest in the equity markets because of risk to principal. The Securities provide the potential for above-market equity returns with guaranteed return of initial investment.
- Investors seeking diversification of their retirement and education savings who are traditionally fixed income investors but desire a level of controlled exposure to the equity markets without risking principal.
- Investors holding zero-coupon bonds who have reaped the benefits of a declining interest rate environment and would like to reinvest capital gains while protecting principal.
- Retirement and education account investors for whom a seven-year maturity is appropriate. The Securities provide such investors with a unique opportunity to invest for equity-linked returns in a finite-life vehicle without risk of principal.

Because the tax implications of investing in the Securities are complex, the Securities are strongly recommended for retirement and other tax-advantaged accounts. There are proposed tax regulations that render current tax treatment of the Securities unclear, including tax regulations that treat the Security as consisting of a zero-coupon portion and an option portion, each having separate and distinct tax implications.

Note

The purchase of these securities by employee benefit plans that are subject to ERISA and for which Inc or its affiliates is a service provider may constitute a prohibited transaction under ERISA. Before any pension or employee benefit plan can purchase these securities, it must be confirmed that these ERISA provisions do not apply or that an exemption is available for the purchase. Potential investors should consult with their counsel on this matter.

Equity New Issue

U.S. Broker–Dealer Incorporated Lead Manager

U.S. Parent Corporation

1,000,000 IBM
Equity-Linked Notes (ELNs)

A Unique Investment Opportunity on IBM Stock Providing Enhanced Yield and Equity Appreciation Potential

Major Sales Points

- **Enhanced yield**

  ELNs have a much higher yield than IBM common stock.

- **Appreciation potential**

  ELNs provide principal payout at maturity up to a cap of 25% to 30% *above* the current price of IBM common stock.

- **Trading liquidity**

  The ELNs will be U.S. exchange listed and traded.

  The sale of IBM stock and purchase of ELNs will not be treated as a wash sale; investors realize any tax loss on sale of IBM.

Investors should be aware that they can lose their entire principal investment based on, among other things, (i) the performance of the common stock of IBM and (ii) the creditworthiness of U.S. Parent Corporation. Even though ELNs are debt securities, investors have price risk similar to common stock investments. If the price of IBM is more than 25 to 30 percent above the issue price at maturity, investors would not participate in price appreciation above the cap level. Investors should review the prospectus for the tax treatment of the ELNs. ELNs are direct, unsecured, and subordinated obligations of U.S. Parent Corporation. This memorandum is for broker use only.

Offering Summary

Issue and Maturity	IBM Equity-Linked Notes (ELNs)
Obligation & Issuer	Direct, unsecured, and subordinated debt of U.S. Parent Corporation
Issuer's Debt Rating	Subordinated Debt, S&P: ____, Moody's: ____
Redemption	Noncallable
Managers	U.S. Broker–Dealer Incorporated (books) and comanagers
Underlying Equity	International Business Machines common stock/ NYSE Symbol: IBM
Initial Filing Size	1,000,000 ELNs
Issue Price	The NYSE closing price of IBM on the pricing date
Gross Spread	1.85% of the offering price
Selling Concession	1.00% of the offering price
Minimum Purchase	100 ELNs
Use of Offering Proceeds	Parent Corporation will use the funds from the offering for hedging its ELN obligations and general funding purposes
ELN Interest Payments	4.75% to 5.25% per annum payable quarterly in arrears
ELN Payment at Maturity	

> The *lesser* of:
>
> (A) 125–130% of the ELNs issue price or
>
> (B) The average closing price of IBM for the
>   10 trading days prior to maturity

Trustee	Citibank, N.A. (registration, transfers, and payments)
Investor Suitability	ELNs may only be sold to investors for whom an investment in IBM common stock would be suitable and who have sufficient knowledge and investment experience to understand the risk characteristics of ELNs
Delivery	Fully registered certificates
Contacts	Structured products (New York), retail equity new issues (New York), institutional sales and prospectus dept.

Product Description

U.S. Parent Corporation (Corp) is offering IBM equity-linked notes (ELNs); direct, unsecured, and subordinated debt obligations of Corp.

ELNs are a new type of hybrid debt obligation that combines elements of both debt and equity providing investors with an enhanced yield relative to an underlying common stock in exchange for a limit or cap on the upside appreciation of the common stock. They are similar to buy/write or covered call-writing investment strategies. ELNs convert a portion of the appreciation potential of common stock into significantly higher dividend payments. Investors benefit from increased current income while continuing to participate in possible stock price increases. Throughout the life of the ELNs, holders receive a 4.75% to 5.25% annual yield* (payable quarterly) and at maturity, the lesser of:

(A) 125% to 130% of the ELNs issue price, or
(B) the average closing price of IBM for the 10 trading days prior to maturity.

Investors benefit from increased current income while continuing to participate in possible stock price increases. Investors should be aware that they can lose their entire principal investment in the ELNs based on, among other things, the performance of IBM's common stock and the creditworthiness of Corp. ELNs pay a stated yield until maturity, but the invested principal is exposed to the same risk of price declines as if the investor were holding IBM common stock. Investors should be made aware that they will not participate in any appreciation of IBM's common stock above a 25% to 30% cap over the ELNs issue price.

The issue price of the ELNs will be set on the pricing date of the offering and will equal the closing price of IBM common stock as reported by the New York Stock Exchange. Interest on each ELN will be paid quarterly in arrears over a two-year period commencing on June 15 and each June 15, September 15, December 15, and March 15 thereafter, until maturity.

---

*The exact yield, issue price, and appreciation limit will be set on the pricing date.

International Business Machines

IBM develops, manufactures, and sells advanced information processing products, including computers and microelectronic technology, software, networking systems, and information technology–related services through its worldwide business units. Its common stock trades on the NYSE under the symbol IBM.

Sample Sales Points and Investment Risks

- **Enhanced Yield Backed by Parent Corporation**

ELNs on IBM will have a constant yield of 4.75% to 5.25% versus the current yield on IBM common stock of 1.88%.

Interest and final cash payout backed by Corp (subject to its ongoing creditworthiness).

- **Upside Appreciation and Downside Risk**

ELNs provide principal payout at maturity up to a maximum of 25% to 30% above the price of IBM common stock of the pricing date of the ELNs.

Investors will not participate in gains of more than 25% to 30% above the market price for IBM common stock on the pricing date of the ELNs.

ELNs allow investors to convert a portion of the upside growth potential of IBM into a higher current yield while maintaining IBM in their portfolios.

Investors should be aware that when the ELNs mature, if IBM common stock is lower than when the ELNs were issued, they will receive the cash value of such lower amount from Corp.

- **Liquidity**

The ELNs will be U.S. exchange listed for secondary trading. Liquidity is an important feature for those investors wishing to sell the ELNs prior to maturity. The value of the ELNs will fluctuate with changes in the value of IBM common stock, interest rates, and interest payment dates, among other factors.*

ELNs may not be called prior to maturity.

---

*The price at which ELNs may be sold prior to maturity may be at a discount from the initial price if, among other things, the price of IBM common stock is lower than when the ELNs were issued.

The sale of IBM stock and simultaneous purchase of IBM ELNs is not a wash sale for tax purposes. Investors may realize any tax loss on their sale of IBM and buy IBM ELNs.

Questions and Answers

Why buy IBM ELNs if IBM is rated "unattractive"?

Although IBM investment opinions vary on Wall Street, Corp's technology analyst rates IBM as "unattractive." IBM's mainframe sales were down 50% this year and similar declines are expected next year. IBM's software and maintenance businesses are beginning a slow secular decline (see published research reports).

For investors who wish to hold IBM as a long-term investment, ELNs allow them to:

Sell IBM and realize any existing tax losses.
Simultaneously buy IBM ELNs issued by Corp at the current market price of IBM.
Avoid wash sale tax treatment on the sale of IBM stock and immediate purchase of IBM ELNs.
More than double the current yield they are receiving from IBM stock
Retain significant upside potential if IBM appreciates over the next three years.

Are ELNs debt or equity securities?

ELNs are hybrid securities, containing elements of both debt (coupon payments) and equity (appreciation potential). They are direct, unsecured, and subordinated debt obligations of Corp that are currently rated by S&P and by Moody's.*

---

*Corp's *senior* debt is rated BBB+ by S&P and A3 by Moody's.

What is the investor's maximum downside exposure?

Investors can potentially lose their entire principal investment in the ELNs if IBM stock falls to zero. Quarterly interest payments will continue being made by Corp (subject to its ongoing creditworthiness) based on the yield set on the pricing date.

Will I receive IBM common stock from Corp upon maturity of the ELNs?

No. The value of the ELNs at their maturity (up to the 25% to 30% cap) will be paid to investors in cash by Corp.

Are there any voting rights attached to the ELNs?

No.

Are investors locked into this investment for three years?

No. The ELNs will be U.S. exchange listed for secondary trading. Investors can sell them prior to maturity.

How do ELNs differ from PERCS?

With ELNs, the investor will receive a cash payout at maturity. With PERCS, common stock is delivered.
ELNs are debt securities. PERCS are a form of preferred stock.
Corp is the issuer of the ELNs. IBM is the issuer of both IBM common stock and PERCS on IBM.

What factors may affect the trading value of the ELNs in the secondary market?

Although it is not possible to predict how the ELNs will trade in the secondary market, it is expected that they will be affected by IBM stock price fluctuations, the value of quarterly ELN interest payments, and the value of the imbedded cap option or 25% to 30% appreciation limit in the ELNs. In order to get an enhanced yield, ELN holders have, in effect, sold off possible price appreciation above the cap. As IBM common stock rises, ELNs are not expected to rise as quickly because the cap becomes less valuable as IBM trades up to the cap limit. If IBM trades above the cap, the ELNs are expected to trade around the cap level. Conversely, if IBM stock falls in price, ELNs should decline more slowly because of the increased value of the imbedded cap and the higher current income of ELNs versus IBM. Also, ELNs may decline in value on quarterly interest payment ex dates. At maturity, holders will receive the final ELN interest payment plus 125% to 130% of the issue price or the average closing price for the last 10 trading days prior to maturity, whichever is *less*.

Are there any similar products trading in the market currently?

Yes. For example, other ELNs (also known as ELKs, YEELDs, and CHIPS) trade on the following stocks:

Stock/Symbol	ELN Symbol
Merck/MRK	MCP
Amgen/AMGN	AYN
Amgen/AMGN	AEK
Digital/DEC	DLK
Hewlett/HWP	HLK
Microsoft/MSFT	MEK
Oracle/ORCL	LYN
Oracle/ORCL	OLK

Can investors create this security by holding or purchasing IBM and selling covered call options?

Yes, however, the IBM option position would have to be reestablished whenever the underlying option contract expires, creating roll risk or the possibility that the sale of future option positions will not produce the premium income needed to maintain the same mix of income and appreciation potential of ELNs. Transaction costs must also be taken into account when establishing an ELN-like position.

What is the credit underlying the ELNs?

ELNs are unrated. However, the ELN performance obligation is the direct, unsecured, and subordinated debt of Corp. Corp's subordinated debt is rated by Moody's and by Standard & Poor's.*

---

*Corp's *senior* debt is rated BBB+ by S&P and A3 by Moody's.

What is the opportunity cost of purchasing ELNs?

Although investors will receive higher current income and participate in some upside growth, those who purchase ELNs instead of holding or buying IBM common stock run the risk of forgoing potential appreciation above the 25% to 30% appreciation cap set on the pricing date.

What are the tax considerations of purchasing the ELNs?

(Investors should refer to the prospectus supplement for a full discussion of ELNs tax treatment.)

There is no current tax liability associated with the ELNs while held in a *tax-advantaged retirement account*. Any tax consequences are deferred until the proceeds are withdrawn from the tax-advantaged account.

In a *non-tax-advantaged account*, interest payments are expected to be treated as ordinary income and sales as a capital gain or loss, subject to IRS rulings to the contrary. Investors are strongly encouraged to consult their tax advisors regarding their particular tax circumstances.

The sale of IBM common stock and the purchase of ELNs will *not* be considered a wash sale for tax purposes.

Non-U.S. investors avoid dividend withholding tax on ELNs because the income is treated as interest and not subject to the withholding tax.

Sample Investor Profiles

- Investors seeking higher current income than typical equity securities.

- Current holders of IBM common stock who want to remain invested but believe growth prospects are limited during the term of the ELNs.

- Retired investors seeking current income.

- IRA investors that want to build savings through income generation and appreciation potential.

- Institutions that need fixed income investments but seek to retain equity exposure.

- Income-oriented institutional investors seeking equity exposure but requiring yields of 5% or more.

- Money managers seeking to enhance yield of IBM common stock required to be held in portfolio.

- Insurance companies, pension fund and mutual fund managers, and convertible bond portfolio managers seeking current income but required to hold dividend-paying stocks.

Important Note on ERISA Rules

The purchase of ELNs issued by Parent Corporation by employee benefit plans that are subject to ERISA and for which Broker–Dealer Incorporated or its affiliates is a "service provider," may constitute a prohibited transaction under ERISA rules. Before any pension or employee benefit plan can purchase these securities, it must be confirmed that these ERISA provisions do not apply or that an exemption is available for the purchase. Potential investors should consult with their counsel on this matter.

SAMPLE ROAD SHOW MARKETING SCHEDULE*

Long Bond Yield Warrants Sample Road Show Marketing Schedule

Key: B1 = Banker 1, B2 = Banker 2, B3 = Banker 3

Midwest Offices

B3	Minneapolis, MN
B3	Wayzata, MN
B3	St. Paul, MN
B3	Chicago, IL
B3	Northbrook, IL
B3	Pittsburgh, PA
B1	Denver, CO

Northeast Offices

B3	Boston, MA
B3	Wellesley, MA
B3	Darien, CT
B3	New Haven, CT
B3	Stamford, CT
B3	White Plains, NY
B3	Pearl River, NY
B3	Hackensack, NJ
B3	Princeton, NJ
B1/B3	NYC

West Coast Offices

B1	Los Angeles, CA
B1	Pasedena, CA
B1	Beverly Hills, CA
B1	Century City, CA
B1	Mission Viejo, CA
B1	Palos Verdes, CA
B1	San Francisco, CA
B1	Oakland, CA
B1	Seattle, WA

Southern Office

B2	Richmond, VA
B2	Atlanta, CA
B2	Memphis, TN
B1	Ft. Worth, TX
B1	Houston, TX
B1	Miami, FL
B1	Boca Raton, FL

THUR-12-JAN
Seattle, WA, 120 Third Ave, Suite 400, Zip 98101   25 Brokers
1:00 P.M. Lunch
Tom Jasper, (206) 556-4001

Hotel: Four Seasons, Tel: (206) 621-1700

FRI-13-JAN
San Francisco, CA, 2100 California St., 9th Floor, Zip 94111   25 Brokers
7:30 A.M. Breakfast
Bill Hutton, (415) 454-7000

---

*See Chapter 3 for a discussion of marketing structured products.

Oakland, CA, 9900 Harrison St., Suite 700, Zip 94612   10 Brokers
10:30 A.M.
Jack Thompson, (510) 522-4110

Hotel: Stanford Court, Tel: (415) 989-3500

MON-16-JAN
Los Angeles, 2333 Grand Ave, Zip 90071   50 Brokers
7:30 A.M.
Scott Gallagher, (213) 254-3385

Pasadena, CA, 300 Los Robles, Zip 91101   20 Brokers
10:30 A.M.
Johnathan Valle, (213) 680-0102

MON-16-JAN
Newport Beach, CA, 755 MacArthur Ct, Zip 92660   22 Brokers
1:00 P.M.
Jerry Hinson, (800) 548-2221

TUE-17-JAN
Los Angeles, CA, 257 Figueroa St., Zip 90017   50 Brokers
1:00 P.M. Lunch
Steve Curry, (213) 729-5111

Hotel: (Jan 14 & 15) Shutters, Santa Monica, Tel: (310) 458-0030
Hotel: (Jan 16) Beverly Wilshire, Tel: (310) 275-5200

WED-18-JAN
Denver, CO, 703 15th St., Zip 80202-9807   25 Brokers
11:30 A.M. Lunch
Frank Rich, (303) 208-0905

Hotel: (Jan 17 & 18) Brown Palace, Tel: (303) 297-3111

THUR-19-JAN
Houston, TX, 1112 Oiler St., Suite 5100, Zip 77002   30 Brokers
Noon Lunch
Bill Parker, (713) 546-2550

Houston, TX, 544 Post Oak Road, Zip 77027   20 Brokers
<u>3:15 P.M.</u>
Ann Berry, (713) 409-8002

Hotel: The Warwick, Tel: (713) 526-1991

FRI-20-JAN
Dallas, TX, 601 Elm St., Zip 75201   15 Brokers
<u>10:00 A.M.</u>
Steve Barrow, (214) 987-0596

Fort Worth, TX, 4301 Commerce St., Zip 76102   25 Brokers
<u>Noon Lunch</u>
Larry Page, (817) 353-7314

SAMPLE SYNDICATE INVITATION*

Re: 1,000,000 Puts   [Date]
       1,000,000 Calls

U.S. Parent Corporation
Taiwan Export Index Put and Call Warrants

We are pleased to invite you to participate in these captioned offerings. Please call the Equity Syndicate Department at U.S. Broker–Dealer as soon as possible to indicate your interest in participating in either or both of these offerings. Questions or comments may also be directed to the Structured Products Group. Preliminary prospectuses are available upon request. The pricing date for the offerings is expected to be two weeks from the date hereof.

Terms

Issuer	U.S. Parent Corporation (Corp)
Managers	U.S. Broker–Dealer and comanagers
Shelf Registration	Effective
Expiration	2 years from date of issuance
Settlement upon Exercise	Cash payment in U.S. dollars
Call Features	Noncallable
Strike Index Level	Strike will equal the at-the-money index level on pricing date
Warrant Strike Level	100% (at-the-money)
Exercise Features	American style (continuously exercisable)
Cash Settlement Value/Puts	$\dfrac{[\text{TBD}] \times (\text{Strike Index Level} - \text{Spot Index Level})}{\text{Fixed Yen/Dollar Exchange Rate}}$
Cash Settlement Value/Calls	$\dfrac{[\text{TBD}] \times (\text{Spot Index Level} - \text{Strike Index Level})}{\text{Fixed Yen/Dollar Exchange Rate}}$

Note: [TBD] = to be determined.

*See Chapter 3 for a discussion of syndicating structured products.

Terms (cont.)

Initial Foreign Exchange Rate	Fixed at-the-money on pricing date
Currency Protection Features	Currency exposure is fully hedged; investor receives U.S. dollar payment based on index fluctuations
Issue Premium/Puts	14.25%–15.1% of underlying value; $4.50–$5.50 per Warrant
Issue Premium/Calls	15.25%–16.1% of underlying value; $5.00–$6.00 per Warrant
Issue Price	$$\frac{\text{Issue Premium} \times [\text{TBD}] \times \text{Spot Index Level}}{\text{Initial FX Rate}}$$
Listing	U.S. Stock Exchange
Symbol	ABC.WS–Puts
	XYZ.WS–Calls
Offering Date	Late October
Underwriting Spread	5% gross spread subject to breakpoint pricing set forth below with 66.6% for selling concession

Hypothetical Warrant Cash Settlement Value Assumptions

- Strike Index Level   200
- Issue Premium–Puts   15.1%
- Issue Price–Puts $5.134
- Issue Premium–Calls   16.1%
- Issue Price-Calls $5.474
- Issue Multiplier   17
- Yen/Dollar FX Rate   100

Hypothetical Warrant Cash Settlement Values

Index Level at Exercise	Put Cash Settlement Value	Call Cash Settlement Value
100	$17.00	$0.00
120	13.60	0.00
140	10.20	0.00
160	6.80	0.00
180	3.40	0.00
200 (Strike)	**0.00**	**0.00**
220	0.00	3.40
240	0.00	6.80
260	0.00	10.20
280	0.00	13.60
300	0.00	17.00

Offering Highlights

- Taiwanese exports may rebound—after a 60% decline since 1990, the Taiwanese equity market is rebounding and a weakening Yen may fuel a rise in export stocks.

- Brand names and high tech—The *Taiwan Export Index* has outperformed the *Taiwan Stock Average* over the past 10 years. It includes 40 top Taiwanese export companies representing some of the world's most popular brand names.

- A play on Asia and world trade—Taiwanese export companies are well positioned to benefit from rapidly expanding Pacific economies and growth in world trade.

- Weaker currency—Reversal in currency exchange rate stands to benefit Taiwanese exporters.

- The Warrants will be U.S. exchange listed. The *Taiwan Export Index* is calculated and disseminated daily under the symbol TEX.

- The breakeven TEX annualized growth rate for an investor holding the Call Warrants until maturity is 7.75% (assuming the assumptions shown above).

- If the TEX rises 25% in the next six months, Call Warrant investors should enjoy a return on the warrants of about 79%.

- If the TEX declines by 25% in the next six months, Put Warrant investors should enjoy a return on the warrants of approximately 72% (based on the assumptions mentioned above).

Price Break

For orders of 100,000 Warrants or more, investors will receive a 2.5% discount on the purchase price of the Warrants. Investment executives should note that in such breakpoint sales, the sales credit will be reduced from 3% to 1.5%. Warrants subject to breakpoint pricing will be delivered to investors at the closing of the offering less 2.5% of the Warrants, which will be held by Corp for 45 days. If an investor that receives such breakpoint pricing sells any Warrants held during the 45-day holding period, the 2.5% of the Warrants held by Corp will be forfeited by the investor. If the investor holds the Warrants past the 45-day holding period, the 2.5% of the Warrants held by Corp will be released to the investor (see the *Underwriting* section of the Prospectus Supplement for further details).

Please advise of your interest in this offering.

Structured Products Groups
Equity Syndicate
U.S. Broker–Dealer Incorporated

SAMPLE PRICING SPREADSHEET*

	Final Pricing Nikkei Warrants	Final Pricing CAC 40 Warrants	Final Pricing US Long Bond Yld. Decr. Wts.	Final Pricing Hang Seng Warrants	Final Pricing HK Index Warrants	Final Pricing HK Index Warrants	Final Pricing Dollar FX Wts. on Yen	Final Pricing Dollar FX Wts. on Yen	Final Pricing Dollar FX Wts. on Yen
Puts									
Strike Level	29,249.06	1,633.15	8.35%	5,897.90	440.09	541.73	105.40	99.90	83.25
Forex Rate Per US Dollar	159.8000	4.9795	N/A	7.8000	7.7290	7.7260	105.40	99.90	83.25
Term of Warrant (Years)	3.00	3.00	2.00	2.00	2.00	2.00	2.00	2.00	1.00
Number of Warrants	12,000,000	6,400,000	3,500,000	56,000,000	5,000,000	6,300,000	5,000,000	1,300,000	1,050,000
Total $ Premium	$46,171,839	$7,609,013	$10,200,000	$0	$23,567,506	$33,935,512	$16,250,000	$8,554,000	$5,722,500
$ Notional Amount	$439,285,006	$139,935,870	—	$42,343,897	$142,350,239	$147,247,347	$250,000,000	$130,000,000	$105,000,000
$ Straddle	$7.95	N/A	N/A	N/A	$9.42	$11.00	N/A	N/A	N/A
Term	3 Years	3 Years	2 Years	2 Years	2 Years	2 Years	2 Years	2 Years	1 Year
$ Institutional Put Price/Warrant	$3.20	—	—	—	$4.67	—	—	—	$4.17
$ Retail Put Price/Warrant	—	$3.17	$4.25	—	—	$5.125	$3.25	$6.58	$5.45
% Premium–Institutional	8.75%	14.50%	—	—	13.80%	15.75%	5.30%	4.69%	4.17%
% Premium–Retail	—	—	—	—	16.40%	21.93%	6.50%	6.58%	5.45%
Divisor/Multiplier Puts	5	15	$0.10	—	2	3	$50.00	$100.00	$100.00
Expected GrossVolatility Sold	—	—	—	—	—	—	20.00%	16.40%	18.40%
Expected Net Volatility Sold	24.00%	25.00%	—	—	33.00%	41.00%	14.50%	15.58%	17.48%
Expected Realized Volatility	22.00%	22.00%	—	—	23.00%	28.00%	12.50%	12.60%	14.82%
Expected Net Less Assumed Vol.	2.00%	3.00%	—	—	10.00%	13.00%	2.00%	2.98%	2.66%
Historical Vol. Range (Term of Wt)	15%–50%	—	—	—	21.00%	24.00%	9.53%	9.90%	11.40%

*See Chapter 4 for a discussion of pricing structured products.

Implied Vol. @IPO (Term of Wt)	41.00%	—	—	26.00%	34.00%	12.50%	12.60%	14.82%
Intrinsic Value/1-Index Point Puts	$0.0013	$0.0134	—	$0.0647	$0.0431	$0.4700	$0.9911	$11.1869
Index Points Move = BE Puts	2,559	237	—	72	119	7	7	4.59
Index % Move = Breakeven Puts	9%	14%	—	16.40%	21.93%	6.56%	6.65%	5.52%
Number of Puts	7,000,000	2,400,000	—	2,400,000	4,100,000	5,000,000	1,300,000	1,050,000
$ Gross Spread per Warrant	$0.23	$0.22	—	$0.23	$0.25	$0.16	$0.33	$0.27
$ Gross Spread Aggregate	$1,610,000	$528,000	$0	$552,000	$1,025,000	$812,500	$427,700	$286,125
Gross Spread %	7.18%	5.18%	—	4.93%	5.00%	5.00%	5.00%	5.00%
$ Sales Credit per Warrant	$0.14	$0.14	—	$0.14	$0.15	$0.10	$0.20	$0.16
$ Sales Credit Aggregate	$980,000	$336,000	$0	$336,000	$630,335	$487,500	$256,620	$171,675
Sales Credit %	4.37%	3.29%	—	3.00%	3.00%	3.00%	3.00%	3.00%
Calls								
Strike Level	29,249.06	1,633.15	5,897.90	440.09	541.73	105.40	99.90	83.25
Forex Rate Per US Dollar	159.8000	4.9795	7.8000	7.7290	7.7260	105.40	99.90	83.25
Term of Warrant (Years)	3.00	3.00	2.00	2.00	2.00	2.00	2.00	1.00
Number of Warrants	12,000,000	6,400,000	56,000,000	5,000,000	6,300,000	5,000,000	1,300,000	1,050,000
Total $ Premium	$46,171,839	$7,609,013	$0	$23,567,506	$33,935,512	$16,250,000	$8,554,000	$5,722,500
$ Notional Amount	$439,285,006	$139,935,870	$42,343,897	$142,350,239	$147,247,347	$250,000,000	$130,000,000	$105,000,000
$ Straddle	$7.95	N/A	N/A	$9.42	$11.00	N/A	N/A	N/A
Term	3 Years	3 Years	2 Years	2 Years	2 Years	2 Years	2 Years	1 Year
$ Institutional Call Price/Warrant	—	—	$0.14	$4.75	$5,875	—	—	—
$ Retail Call Price Warrant	$4.75	—	—	—	—	—	—	—
% Premium–Institutional	—	—	—	14.00%	17.60%	—	—	—
% Premium–Retail	25.95%	—	17.90%	16.70%	25.14%	—	—	—

SAMPLE PRICING SPREADSHEET (*continued*)

	Final Pricing Nikkei Warrants	Final Pricing CAC 40 Warrants	Final Pricing US Long Bond Yld. Decr. Wts.	Final Pricing Hang Seng Warrants	Final Pricing HK Index Warrants	Final Pricing HK Index Warrants	Final Pricing Dollar FX Wts. on Yen	Final Pricing Dollar FX Wts. on Yen	Final Pricing Dollar FX Wts. on Yen
Divisor/Multiplier Calls	10	—	—	1,000	2	3	—	—	—
Expected Gross Volatility Sold	—	—	—	—	—	—	—	—	—
Expected Net Volatility Sold	24.00%	—	—	36.00%	29.50%	43.00%	—	—	—
Expected Realized Volatility	22.00%	—	—	26.00%	23.00%	28.00%	—	—	—
Expected Net Less Assumed Vol.	2.00%	—	—	10.00%	6.50%	15.00%	—	—	—
Historical Vol. Range (Term of Wt)	15%–50%	—	—	22.00%	21.00%	24.00%	—	—	—
Implied Vol. @IPO (Term of Wt)	22.00%	—	—	26.00%	26.00%	34.00%	—	—	—
Intrinsic Value/1-Index Point Calls	$0.0006	—	—	$0.0001	$0.0647	$0.0431	—	—	—
Index Points Move = BE Calls	7,591	—	—	—	73	136	—	—	—
Index % Move = Breakeven Calls	26.00%	—	—	0.00%	16.70%	25.14%	—	—	—
Number of Calls	5,000,000	—	—	—	2,600,000	2,200,000	—	—	—
$ Gross Spread per Warrant	$0.34	—	—	—	$0.24	$0.29	—	—	—
$ Gross Spread Aggregate	$1,700,000	—	—	—	$624,000	$646,217	—	—	—
Gross Spread %	7.16%	—	—	—	5.05%	5.00%	—	—	—
$ Sales Credit per Warrant	$0.21	—	—	—	$0.21	$0.18	—	—	—
$ Sales Credit Aggregate	$1,050,000	—	—	—	$546,000	$387,730	—	—	—
Sales Credit %	4.42%	—	—	—	4.42%	3.00%	—	—	—

SAMPLE QUESTIONNAIRE FOR
SELLERS OF RESTRICTED SECURITIES*

(To be completed and signed by the proposed seller of restricted securities.)

1. What is the full name of the person or entity selling the securities (the Seller)?

2. What is the address of the Seller?

3. Who is the issuer of the securities being sold?

4. What is the class of the securities being sold?

5. What is the par value of the securities being sold?

6. What quantity of the security is being sold?

7. Who is the person to contact if questions should arise concerning this transaction, and what is the person's telephone number and address?

8. Was the transaction in which the Seller acquired the securities a transaction exempt from registration under the Securities Act of 1933, as amended?

9. What is the basis for exemption from registration?

10. From whom did the Seller purchase these securities?

11. Did the Seller acquire the securities for its own account?

12. Did the Seller purchase the securities for the purpose of investment?

13. Since the Seller acquired the securities, have such securities been fully paid and not pledged to secure any obligation?

14. Has the Seller been the sole beneficial owner of the securities since first acquiring them?

15. Did the Seller pay the full purchase price of the securities when the securities were acquired?

16. On what date did the Seller acquire the securities?

17. On what date did the Seller pay the full purchase price of the securities?

---

*See Chapter 13 for a discussion of customer due diligence relating to structured product monetization and hedging strategies.

18. Has the Seller engaged in a general advertising of solicitation of persons to purchase the securities?

19. In what activities has the Seller engaged in selling the securities?

20. Is the Seller or any of its affiliates, officers, directors, or partners, as applicable, a director or officer of the issuer?

21. Is the Seller controlled by, controlling, or under common control with the issuer (i.e., an affiliate of the issuer)?

22. Is the Seller in a position to influence or control the management of the issuer?

23. Is the Seller acting with any other holder of similar securities in selling these securities?

24. Were the securities ever converted or exchanged? If no, stop here and turn to the last page for your signature. If yes, please respond to the remaining questions.

25. On what date did the conversion or exchange occur?

26. What were the securities converted into or exchanged for? Explain fully.

27. Was any consideration paid by the Seller in connection with this conversion or exchange?

28. Prior to the conversion or exchange, on what date did the Seller purchase the original securities?

I certify that, to the best of my knowledge and belief after due investigation, the foregoing information is true and complete this _____ day of _____.

Seller's Signature: _____

Print Name: _____

Co. Name of Restricted Stock: _____

SAMPLE STRUCTURED PRODUCT TERM SHEETS*

Oil Price Inflation Notes
S&P 500 Index "Bull" Market Notes
S&P 500 Index "Bull" Market Notes with Interest Payments
Call Warrants on a Basket of Pharmaceutical Stocks
EuroTop 100 Index Call Warrants
Hang Seng Index Put and Call Warrants
Nikkei 225 Index Put and Call Warrants
U.S. Dollar Increase Warrants on the German Deutsche Mark
U.S. Long Bond Yield Decrease Warrants
German Bund Yield Decrease Warrants
Yield Curve Spread-Tightening Warrants
Synthetic PERCS Trust
Stock Income Participation Trust

Oil Price Inflation Notes

Issue	U.S. IPO of *Oil Price Inflation Notes*
Issuer	U.S. Parent Corporation (takedown off SEC shelf; Subordinated Debt, S&P: AA–)
Underwriter(s)	U.S. Broker–Dealer (books) and [TBD]
Offering Price	$1,000 per Note
Maturity Date	2 years from date of issuance
Spot/Strike Oil Level	West Texas Intermediate (WTI)/at-the-money spot WTI per barrel at the time of pricing
Annual Coupon	3.00% (semiannual payments)
Principal Protection	100% return of principal at maturity by Parent Corporation
Oil Price Participation	50% of any WTI price appreciation from the Strike Oil Level to the Determination Date
Determination Date	10 New York banking days before maturity

Note: [TBD] = to be determined; [ ] = preliminary terms/subject to change.

*See Chapter 3 for a discussion of the structured product creation, development, and offering process and the use of term sheets.

Minimum Return	Annual Coupon plus 100% return of principal
Maximum Return	Annual Coupon plus 100% return of principal plus 50% times any appreciation of WTI from the Strike Oil Level
Gross Spread	1.66%
Sales Credit	1.00%
Secondary Market	U.S. stock exchange or upstairs market-making by U.S. Broker–Dealer Equity Derivative Desk

Hypothetical Example: Investor buys $10,000 of the *Notes.* During the term of the *Notes,* Investor collects $300 annual coupon payments (3% per year paid semiannually). On the Determination Date, WTI Spot Oil is 25% higher than the Strike Oil Level. At maturity, Investor receives

> + $10,000 return of principal
> + $1,250 ($10,000 × 12.5% = $1,250) (12.5% = 50% participation × 25% WTI appreciation)
> + $150 final coupon payment
> = $11,400 at maturity
> = Total Return of $11,850, or 8.00% IRR (principal + 4 coupon payments + WTI appreciation)

S&P 500 Index "Bull" Market Notes

Issue	U.S. IPO of *S&P 500 Index "Bull" Market Notes*
Issuer	International Corporation (IC) (S&P: AAA), exempt transaction
Principal Amount	$100 to $200 million aggregate
Underwriter	Broker–Dealer
Offering Price/ Maturity	$1,000 per Note/6 years
Annual Coupon	1.25% (paid annually)
Funding Cost to IC	LIBOR less 10 basis points

Note: [TBD] = to be determined; [ ] = preliminary terms/subject to change.

Strike Index Level	At-the-money S&P 500 Index level at the time of pricing
Option Proceeds to IC	14% Volatility (22.5646% premium) paid to IC out of the offering proceeds
Principal Protection	100% return of principal to investors by IC at maturity
Index Participation	100% of any increase in the S&P 500 Index from the Strike Index Level on the IPO date to the Determination Date
Determination Date	10 New York banking days before maturity
Minimum Return	100% return of principal
Maximum Return	100% return of principal plus 100% times any percentage increase of the S&P 500 Index from the Strike Index Level
Gross Spread	Paid by Broker–Dealer
Offering Expenses	Paid by Broker–Dealer
Secondary Market	U.S. Stock Exchange

Transaction Overview: IC to issue the 1.25%, 6-year notes at sub-LIBOR cost of funding and receive out of the offering proceeds the midmarket volatility (e.g., 14%) to hedge its risks associated with the imbedded S&P 500 call option. IC will negotiate and obtain a back-to-back hedge from a counterparty acceptable to IC. As consideration for issuing the notes, and in addition to sub-LIBOR funding, IC will retain the spread between midmarket and bid volatility quotations at the time of pricing.

Tax Considerations: It is expected that any gain or loss on the Notes will be treated under long-term capital gains/loss tax rules or short-term gain/loss if held less than one year.

Hypothetical Example: Investor buys $10,000 of the *"Bull" Market Notes.* On the Determination Date of the *Notes,* the S&P 500 Index is 10% **higher** than the Strike Index Level. At maturity, Investor receives $11,000 as follows:

Note: [TBD] = to be determined; [ ] = preliminary terms/subject to change.

+ $10,000 return of principal
+ $1,000 ($10,000 × 10% = $1,000) (Note: 10% = 100% index
  participation × 10% S&P 500 index increase)
= $11,000 Total Return at maturity (30–33 months); 10% ROI
  and principal protection

S&P 500 Index "Bull" Market Notes with Interest Payments

Issue	U.S. IPO of *S&P 500 Index "Bull" Market Notes*
Issuer	International Corporation (IC) (S&P: AAA)
Estimated Pricing Date	Mid-July, subject to investor demand and market conditions as mutually agreed upon by Broker–Dealer and PaineWebber and IC
Estimated Closing Date	30 days after the pricing date
Principal Amount	$100 to $200 million aggregate
Underwriter	Broker–Dealer
Offering Price/ Maturity	$1,000 per Note/6 years from issuance
Annual Coupon	1.25% (paid annually by IC)
Note Funding Cost to IC	LIBOR less 25 basis points (e.g., 1 yr: 5.41%, 2 yr: 5.48%, 3 yr: 5.59%, 4 yr: 5.71%, 5 yr: 5.78%, and 6 yr: 5.865%, quoted on a bond equivalent yield basis)
Option Proceeds to IC	Offered-side volatility at time of pricing (e.g., 22.20% to 22.40% Premium)
All-In Funding Cost to IC	LIBOR/Par Swap Rates less 36 to 42 basis points, subject to market conditions as mutually agreed upon by Broker–Dealer and IC; paid to IC on the closing date
Strike Index Level	At-the-money S&P 500 Index level at the time of pricing
Principal Protection	100% return of principal to investors by IC at at maturity

---

Note: [TBD] = to be determined; [ ] = preliminary terms/subject to change.

Index Participation	100% of any **increase** in the S&P 500 Index from the Strike Index Level on the IPO date to the Determination Date
Determination Date	10 New York banking days before maturity
Minimum Return	100% return of principal
Maximum Return	100% return of principal plus 100% of any increase of the S&P 500 from the Strike Index Level
Offering Expenses	Paid by Broker–Dealer
Secondary Market	U.S. Stock Exchange (Bond Desk)

Transaction Overview: IC is proposed to be the issuer of 1.25%, 6-year *S&P 500 "Bull" Market Notes.* IC will receive sub-LIBOR funding. Broker–Dealer will underwrite the note offering. It is proposed that IC will receive the following out of the offering proceeds:

- The net present value of the notes based on the coupon, term, and sub-LIBOR funding rate agreed upon.

- The dollar value of the imbedded 6-year S&P 500 call option will be available to IC to hedge its risks (i.e., the "offered" institutional volatility, presently indicated at approximately 14%), such amount as determined by Broker–Dealer and agreed to by IC. IC will then negotiate and obtain a hedge with terms identical to the notes from a counterparty acceptable to IC. In addition to sub-LIBOR funding, IC will retain the dollar amount of the institutional bid/offered volatility spread quoted at the time of pricing.

Tax Considerations: It is expected that any gain or loss on the Notes will be treated under long-term capital gains/loss tax rules or short-term gain/loss if held less than one year.

Hypothetical Example: Investor buys $10,000 of the *"Bull" Market Notes.* Investor receives $625 of coupon payments over 5 years ($125 per annum). On the Determination Date in year 6 of the *Notes,* the S&P 500 Index is 90% **higher** than the Strike Index Level. At maturity, investor receives $19,125 as follows:

Note: [TBD] = to be determined; [ ] = preliminary terms/subject to change.

+ $10,000 return of principal
+ $9,000 ($10,000 × 90% = $1,000) (Note: 90% = 100% index participation × 90% S&P 500 index increase over 6 years)
+ $125 final coupon payment
= $19,125 at maturity
= Total Return of $19,750, or 97.50% ROI over 6 years plus principal protection

---

Call Warrants on a Basket of Pharmaceutical Stocks

Issue	*Call Warrants on a Basket of Pharmaceutical Stocks*
Issuer	International Corporation
Manager	International Broker–Dealer
Index	Price-weighted index; calculated as the sum of the closing prices of 12 pharmaceutical industry common stock prices as traded on the New York Stock Exchange
Warrant Style	American style call warrants (continuous exercise)
Term/Expiration	2 years from date of issuance
Premium	14.70%
Gearing	6.80×
Price	[US$7.26] (based on a premium level of 14.70% at a strike level of the basket of 493.625 and a divisor of 10 [(493.625 × .1470)/10] = $7.26)
Strike Price	At-the-money, set at the time of pricing; the index level will equal the price of the basket on the night before pricing
Index Units/ Warrant	10 Warrants control 1 Basket Unit (i.e., a divisor of 10, or each warrant gives the holder the ability to call the basket at 493.625/10 = 49.3625)
Selling Concession	3.00% (US$0.22 per warrant)
Settlement Date	[TBD]
Listing	European Stock Exchange

Note: [TBD] = to be determined; [ ] = preliminary terms/subject to change.

Basket Stocks (listed in order of decreasing volatility)

Company Name	Ticker	% Div. Yield	$Price
Glaxo	PLCGLX	2.67	18.625
Marion Merrell	MKC	3.84	24.375
Upjohn Co.	UPJ	4.50	29.250
Pfizer Inc.	PFE	1.97	63.125
Abbott Labs	ABT	2.12	26.125
Baxter Int'l	BAX	2.62	30.125
J & J	JNJ	1.95	43.500
Merck	MRK	2.24	37.625
Warner Lambert	WLA	3.21	64.000
Bristol Myers	BMY	4.32	58.125
Eli Lilly & Co.	LLY	3.51	55.250
Rhone Poulenc	RPR	2.02	43.500
Total:		2.90	493.625

Exercise Notice	Notice of exercise shall be given to the Warrant Agent not later than 10:00 A.M. Brussels time for Valuation as of the close of the Exercise Day (the "Valuation Date"); the proceeds shall be determined using the closing level of the Pharmaceutical Basket on the Valuation Date
Exercise Settlement	Cash settled in U.S. dollars on the fifth New York banking business day following the Valuation Date
Minimum Trade Size	100 Warrants
Minimum Exercise	1,000 Warrants
Maximum Exercise	250,000 Warrants
Euroclear #	[TBD]
ISIN #	[TBD]

Note: [TBD] = to be determined; [ ] = preliminary terms/subject to change.

EuroTop 100 Index (E-100) Call Warrants

Issue
EuroTop 100 Index (E-100) Call Warrants, a capitalization/GNP-weighted, European Currency Unit (ECU)-denominated stock index published since mid-1990 by the European Options Exchange in Amsterdam. The *E-100* includes 100 primary U.K. and continental European companies and represents trends on nine major European stock exchanges. The *E-100* index level is calculated and published continuously and is available live in the U.S. until 11:30 A.M. New York time each business day.

Issuer/Underwriter/
QIU
Parent Corporation/U.S. Broker–Dealer/[TBD]

Term
3 Years

Gross Spread/
Sales Credit
5.00% / 3.00%

Index Strike
At-the-money

Estimated Price
per Warrant
[TBD]

Exercise
American Style/Continuously exercisable, automatically exercised at expiration into U.S. dollars

Customer
Suitability
Option papers required

Listing
U.S. stock exchange

Index Symbol
"TOP"/"EOE Index"/".EUR"

Note: [TBD] = to be determined; [ ] = preliminary terms/subject to change.

Constituent Countries

Country	% Weighting	No. of Stocks
Britain	22	22
Germany	15	15
France	15	15
Netherlands	8	8
Switzerland	10	10
Italy	10	10
Spain	8	8
Belgium	4	4
Sweden	8	8

Exercise	American Style/Continuously exercisable, automatically exercised at expiration into U.S. dollars
Cash Settlement Value Formula	Puts: {[(Strike Index Level – Spot Index Level) / Divisor] / Fixed HK$ per 1 US$ Exchange Rate} Calls: {[(Spot Index Level – Strike Index Level) / Divisor] / Fixed HK$ per 1 US$ Exchange Rate}
Customer Suitability	Option suitability required

Hang Seng Index Put and Call Warrants

Issue	*Hang Seng Index Put and Call Warrants,* a price-weighted, continuously calculated, Hong Kong dollar-denominated equity index based on [33]-stocks traded on The Stock Exchange of Hong Kong Ltd. and published since 1969 by HSI Services Limited, a wholly owned subsidiary of Hang Seng Bank Limited, Hong Kong. Constituent

Note: [TBD] = to be determined; [ ] = preliminary terms/subject to change.

	stocks in the Index represent four Hong Kong industry sectors: Commerce and Industry, Finance, Properties, and Utilities. Issue and underwriting to occur offshore. Payment through PW-HK.
Issuer	International Corporation
Underwriter	Cayman Islands Broker–Dealer
Senior Debt Rating	Investment Grade: "A" (Moody's) "A+" (S&P)
Investors	Hong Kong retail and Asian "professional persons"
Term	2 years from date of issuance
Total Warrants	[75,000,000+]
Total Premium	[HK$74,000,000+ / US$10,000,000+]
Strike Level	At-the-money, to be set at the time of pricing
$ Price/Warrant	Puts: [HK$0.99]
	Calls: [HK$1.03] (Net of Gross Spread and based on a 4,978 Index level)
Gross Spread	5.00%
Selling Concession	3.00%
Multiplier	[HK$0.001 per Index point]
Exercise Formula	Puts: [(Strike Index Level – Closing Index Level) × Multiplier]
	Calls: [(Closing Index Level – Strike Index Level) × Multiplier]
Exercise	European Style/Automatically exercised at expiration into Hong Kong dollars
Form	Registered Certificates
Index Valuation	Continuous calculation, 15-minute updates, daily rebalancing for corporate events (capital changes, dividends, stock splits, etc.)

Note: [TBD] = to be determined; [ ] = preliminary terms/subject to change.

Index Dissemination	International print and electronic media
License/ Management	HSI Services Ltd./Advisory Committee provides quarterly review of the Index constituents
Listing Date/ Market	[February 9, 1993]/The Stock Exchange of Hong Kong Ltd. ("HKSE")
Registrar	[Citibank-HK]
Warrant Agent	[Citibank-HK]
Clearance/ Settlement	[IPO Booking: PW-UK; Secondary Trades: HKSE and Warrant Agent]
Hong Kong Agent	PW-HK/IPO Placement order commitments and ticketing

Comments: Initial demand for the *Hang Seng Index Warrants* indicates a predominant preference for calls over puts. The primary hedge for these securities upon issuance would be created initially by buying a proportion of correctly weighted stocks representing the Hang Seng Index. The proportion is determined by the delta of the warrants themselves, which is simply the changes in price of the Warrants due to changes in the underlying index. This delta will change over time as a function of price, time to expiration of the Warrants, and interest rates. Changes in the delta over time will signal to us, on a periodic basis, to both buy and sell the constituent Index stocks or Index futures, whichever is more efficient to execute at the time. Based on initial estimates of demand and pricing of the Warrants, approximately US$25 million of stocks in the Hang Seng Index will be bought as the initial hedge, upon issuance of the Warrants. It is important to note that the subsequent adjustment of the hedge will create incremental liquidity on the Stock Exchange of Hong Kong as both stock and Index futures purchases will be executed. At no point during the life of the Warrants will any selling of the underlying securities occur in a greater notional amount than the original demand.

Note: [TBD] = to be determined; [ ] = preliminary terms/subject to change.

Nikkei 225 Index Put and Call Warrants

Issue	*Nikkei 225 Index Put and Call Warrants*
Issuer	Parent Corporation
Managers	U.S. Broker–Dealer and Comanagers TBD
Warrant Style	American (continuous exercise)
Gross Spread	7.00%
Selling Concession	4.20%
Strike Price	At-the-money, to be set at the time of pricing; the level will be equal to the spot price of the Nikkei on the night before pricing
Divisor/Warrant	5 for the put warrants and 10 for the call warrants (the old Nikkei warrants had a 5 divisor on the Puts and a 10 on the Calls)
Currency	Currency hedged (i.e., fixed exchange rate; the first Nikkei Warrants had a fixed rate on the Puts and Floating on the Calls—i.e., "quanto")
Investor Restrictions	Option-qualified accounts only

Pricing Matrix

	Put (3 Year)	Call (3 Year)
Premium	14.9%	26.9%
Dollar Price	$5.20	$4.70
Nikkei Spot	21,581	21,581
Yen/Dollar Spot	123.50	123.50
Breakeven Point	18,365	27,386
100% Return Point	15,150	33,191

Old Warrant Pricing

	Put (3 Year)	Call (3 Year)
Premium	8.75%	25.95%
Dollar Price	$3.20	$4.75
Currency Hedged	Yes (at 158.9)	No
Nikkei Spot	29,249	29,249
Yen/Dollar Spot	158.90 158.90	

Note: [TBD] = to be determined; [ ] = preliminary terms/subject to change.

U.S. Dollar Increase Warrants on the German Deutsche Mark

Issue	*U.S. Dollar Increase Warrants on the German Deutsche Mark* (calls on the dollar, puts on the D-mark)
Warrant Style	American (continuous exercise)
Warrants Issued	3,000,000
Gross Spread	7.00%
Selling Concession	4.20%
Strike Price	At-the-money, to be set at the time of pricing; the level will be equal to the spot price of the currency on the night before pricing
Index Units/ Warrant	Based on $50 investment
Intrinsic Value	50 × (1-Spot/Strike) or the greater of $50 × the appreciation in the spot from the strike, or zero
Listing	U.S. stock exchange
Investor Restrictions	Option-qualified accounts only

Pricing Matrix

	1 Year	*2 Year*	*3 Year*
Premium	8.50%	11.50%	12.90%
Dollar Price	$4.25	$5.75	$6.45
Spot	1.57	1.57	1.57
Breakeven Point	1.70	1.75	1.77
100% Return Point	1.84	1.93	1.98

Exercise Notice	Notice of exercise shall be given to the Warrant Agent not later than 3:00 P.M. New York time for Valuation as of the close of the Exercise day (the "Valuation Date"). The Valuation Date shall be the next New York Business day after the

Note: [TBD] = to be determined; [ ] = preliminary terms/subject to change.

Exercise Date. The proceeds shall be determined using the New York Federal Reserve noon buying rate for dollar/D-mark on the Valuation Date.

Exercise Settlement	Cash settled on the fifth banking business day following the Valuation Date
Minimum Exercise	1,000 Warrants
Maximum Exercise	250,000 Warrants

U.S. Long Bond Yield Decrease Warrants

Issue	*U.S. Long Bond Yield Decrease Warrants*
Long Bond Yield	The value of the Warrants throughout their lives will be determined by reference to the yield to maturity of a *specific* 30-year U.S. Treasury "Long" Bond issued and sold by the U.S. government, which, at the time of pricing the Warrant offering, will be the **highest yielding** Long Bond with the **longest** remaining period of time to maturity
Issuer	Parent Corporation
Underwriters	U.S. Broker–Dealer (books)/[TBD]
Exercise	American Style (continuous exercise)
Term/Expiration	3 or 4 years/October 1997 or 1998
Number of Warrants	2,000,000 Warrants (filing size)
Registration	Takedown off existing SEC shelf registration
Indicative Issue Price	[3 year: $6.75] (Range: $6.50–$7.00 based on an 8.14% yield on the 8.75% May '20 Long Bond)
	[4 year: $7.25] (Range: $7.00–$7.50 based on an 8.14% yield on the 8.75% May '20 Long Bond)
Total Filing Size	[$13 to 15 million ±]

Note: [TBD] = to be determined; [ ] = preliminary terms/subject to change.

Total Notional	[$175 to 200 million ±]
Strike Yield	At-the-money; determined by reference to the yield to maturity of a specific 30-year U.S. Treasury "Long" Bond issued and sold by the U.S. government, which, at the time of pricing the Warrant offering, will be the **highest yielding** Long Bond with the **longest** remaining period of time to maturity
Premium (3-Yr. Wt.)	8.29% {[$6.75 / (814 basis points × $0.10 per basis point)] = 8.29%}
Premium (4-Yr. Wt.)	8.91% {[$7.25 / (814 basis points × $0.10 per basis point)] = 8.91%}
Gearing (3-Yr. Wt.)	12.05 × {[(814 basis points × $0.10 per basis point) / $6.75] = 12.05 ×}
Gearing (4-Yr. Wt.)	11.22 × {[(814 basis points × $0.10 per basis point) / $7.25] = 11.22 ×}
Cash Settlement	Cash settled in U.S. dollars; each Warrant, upon exercise or at expiration, will have a cash settlement value of U.S.$0.10 per basis point yield below the Strike Yield [$0.10 × (8.14% – Spot Yield)]; automatically exercised at expiration
Breakeven Yield (3-Yr. Wt.)	7.46% (68 basis point yield decrease from 8.14% hypothetical strike yield)
Breakeven Yield (4-Yr. Wt.)	7.41% (73 basis point yield decrease from 8.14% hypothetical strike yield)
Gross Spread	5.00% [$0.34–$0.36 per Warrant]
Selling Concession	3.00% [$0.20–$0.22 per Warrant]
Listing	U.S. stock exchange
Suitability	Sales only to customers with options-approved accounts

---

Note: [TBD] = to be determined; [ ] = preliminary terms/subject to change.

German Bund Yield Decrease Warrants

Issue	*German Bund Yield Decrease Warrants* based on the most recently offered 10-year German Federal Government bond (the "Bund") having the longest remaining time to maturity
Issuer	International Corporation (AA for senior debt)
Issue Date	October 1992
Underwriters	U.S. Broker–Dealer and Comanager [TBD]
Pricing Agent	[TBD]
Number of Warrants	[3–5] million (plus 15% over allotment option)
Issue Size	[$23–38 million]
Notional Value	$[TBD] million
Price Sensitivity	1-Basis point in yield equals US$0.10
Strike Yield	[7.42%] ATM, to be set at the time of pricing
Spot Yield	The official 12:00 Noon Frankfurt Stock Exchange "Kassa" price of the most recently issued 10-year Bund, as provided by [Reuters/Telerate/Knight Ridder/Quotron/Telekurs et al.]
Exchange Rate	Fixed deutsche mark/U.S. dollar
Term/Expiration	2 years from date of issuance
$ Price Per Warrant	[$6.10–$6.35] (including gross spread)
Gross Spread	5.00% ([$.31–$.32] per warrant)
Selling Concession	3.00% ([$.18–$.19] per warrant)
Breakeven Point	[6.80%] Bund Yield at Expiration (Bund yields were last at 6.80% in July 1989)
100% Return Point	[6.20%] Bund Yield at Expiration (Bund yields were last at 6.20% in November 1988)

Note: [TBD] = to be determined; [ ] = preliminary terms/subject to change.

Listing	U.S. stock exchange
Investor Restrictions	Option Level "A" approval required
Bund Quote/ US Dissemination	Daily Frankfurt Stock Exchange "Kassa" price/ disseminated once per day in the U.S.
Exercise/Settlement	American Style/continuous exercise into U.S. dollars
Business Day	A Business Day is any day other than a Saturday or Sunday or other day on which the Amex, NYSE, or banks in New York City or Frankfurt, Germany, are authorized or required under applicable law or order to remain closed, or a day on which the LIFFE or DTB is closed
Exercise & Valuation	Notice for exercise of the Warrants shall be given to the Warrant Agent not later than 3:00 P.M. on any New York Business Day, the Exercise Date; the next Business Day after the Exercise Date shall be the Valuation Date, at the close of business on the Frankfurt Stock Exchange
Cash Settlement Value	The Cash Settlement Value shall equal the product of (A) $.10 *times* (B) the Spot Yield *minus* the Strike Yield on the Valuation Date
Minimum Exercise	1,000 Warrants
Maximum Daily Exercise	1,000,000 Warrants total; 250,000 Warrants per person
CUSIP Number	[TBD]
Warrant Agent	Citibank, N.A.

Overview of the German Federal Government Bond Market: Since the lifting in 1985 of the remaining controls and restrictive practices affecting it, the German federal government bond market has become more accessible to international investors, growing to become the third largest

---

Note: [TBD] = to be determined; [ ] = preliminary terms/subject to change.

government securities market, behind the U.S. and Japan. German agency debt is issued with the full faith and credit of the federal government ("Bunds"), the Federal Railway ("Bahns") and Post Office ("Posts"), and, more recently, German Unity Fund Bunds. Other issues include limited-guarantee European Reconstruction Program bonds (ERPs) and federally guaranteed "Treuhand" financing obligations for the purchase of East German industrial companies. Although federally guaranteed, the ERPs and Treuhands are not considered to be "Bunds." Bund maturities range from 6 to 12 years (there have been a limited number of 30-year maturities offered) but the 8.5-year to 10-year Bund (collectively referred to as the "10-year Bund") is the benchmark German government issue. Offering schedules are not predetermined but occur almost every month (8 to 10 times per year). The 10-year Bund represents the largest sector of the German government debt market in terms of amount of deutsche marks outstanding and secondary market turnover. In 1991, the Bundesbank introduced an open auction process (participants must have bank status) for the sale of government debt. The Bundesbank intervenes regularly to support or regulate bond prices. Bunds are noncertificated loan stock rights that are entered in the Federal Debt Register. They trade on the Frankfurt Stock Exchange, where official closing price fixings are published, as well as over-the-counter. Bund futures are most actively traded in London on the LIFFE and also trade in Frankfurt on the DTB. LIFFE and DTB Bund contracts are not fungible; they each have different legal definitions of what a "Bund" is.

Yield Curve Spread-Tightening Warrants

Issue
: *Yield Curve Spread-Tightening Warrants* based on the spread between the U.S. government 30-year bond and the 2-year Note

Issuer
: Parent Corporation (BBB+ senior rating)

Manager
: U.S. Broker–Dealer

Note: [TBD] = to be determined; [ ] = preliminary terms/subject to change.

Warrant Style	American (continuous exercise)
Expiration	[TBD]
Warrants Issued	3,000,000
Gross Spread	7.00%
Selling Concession	4.20%
Issue Size	[TBD]
Premium	[TBD]
Price	[TBD]
Strike Price	At-the-money, to be set at the time of pricing; the level will be equal to the difference in the 30-year bond and the 2-year Note on the night before pricing
Listing	U.S. stock exchange
Investor Restrictions	Option-qualified accounts only
Exercise Notice	Notice of exercise shall be given to the Warrant Agent not later than 3:00 P.M. New York time for Valuation as of the close of the Exercise Day (the "Valuation Date"). The Valuation Date shall be the next New York Business day after the Exercise Date. The proceeds shall be determined using the closing level of the USDX Index on the Valuation Date.
Exercise Settlement	Cash settled on the fifth banking business day following the Valuation Date
Minimum Exercise	1,000 Warrants
Maximum Exercise	250,000 Warrants
CUSIP Number	To be obtained
Warrant Agent	Citibank

Note: [TBD] = to be determined; [ ] = preliminary terms/subject to change.

Synthetic PERCS Trust

Issue	*Synthetic PERCS Trust,* which consists of common stocks of the individual companies listed as follows, and a swap agreement with International Investment Bank that requires a fixed dividend payment to the Trust in exchange for the right to call the individual common stocks in the Trust at the specified call prices
Underwriter	U.S. Broker–Dealer
Expiration	3 years from date of issuance
Yield	7.50%, or a quarterly dividend of $0.35 per Trust share, less any administrative expenses
Call Premium	30% for each individual stock
Shares Issued	3,000,000 (3,450,000 if the over-allotment option is exercised)
Price	$18.74, equal to the price of the common stock, divided by the divisor (187.38/10 = 18.74)
Divisor	10
Selling Concession	2.00%, or $0.37 per share based on an assumed basket level of 187.38
Listing	U.S. stock exchange
Stocks in Trust	One Share of the following stocks, except as noted:

Share Name	Price ($)	Dividend Yield (%)
Compaq Computer	35.00	0.00
Microsoft (½ Share)	61.38	0.00
Sun Microsystems	33.50	0.00
Novell	57.50	0.00
Total	187.38	0.00

Note: [TBD] = to be determined; [ ] = preliminary terms/subject to change.

Swap Counterparty   International Investment Bank

Counterparty Credit   A+

Dividend Distributions: The dividends from the underlying common stocks will be distributed to the holders of the Trust as the Trust receives the dividends. Simultaneously, the swap payment will be distributed to the holders of the Trust for a single quarterly payment. The dividend pass-through payments will be characterized as dividend income, although the 70% dividend exclusion might not hold. The swap payments will be characterized as **tax free** payments until exercise or maturity, at which point the payment would be characterized as capital gain. The tax impact is preliminary and will need further refinement from U.S. tax counsel.

Trust Activity: The Trust, managed by International Investment Bank of potentially a third party general partner, will enter into a swap agreement with International Investment Bank, which will make quarterly payments specified fixed payments to the Trust for the right to call the underlying common stocks in the Trust. The swap payments will end when and if all the common stocks in the Trust are called away. The Trust will be entitled to the dividends from the underlying common stocks until the stocks are called away or the Trust is terminated.

Management Fee: The only fees will be for administrative services; no management fees will be charged as the Trust will not be actively managed.

Administrative Fee: Expected to be ___ (will contact Trustee to determine appropriate amount).

Trust Termination: The Trust will terminate at the end of the 3 years or upon the exercise of each of the swap agreements on the individual common stocks, whichever comes first. Upon termination, all the holders of Trust units will receive pro rate cash distributions from the liquidation of the common stocks up to the level of each call price. The Trust unit holders are not guaranteed to receive their principal investments at maturity. No securities will be distributed upon termination.

Note: [TBD] = to be determined; [ ] = preliminary terms/subject to change.

Return Analysis: Maximum Return (assumes all stocks hit the Trust call price and the Trust is terminated at the end of each year)

	Year 1	Year 2	Year 3
Total Return	37.50%	37.50%	37.50%
Annualized	37.50%	21.07%	16.05%

Standstill Return: Assuming the stocks do not change in price, the return will be equal to the yield on the Trust of 7.50% versus 0% return from the underlying stock.

Expected Trading Levels: Because the Trust will have limited appreciation, due to the call price, the Trust should trade at a discount to the common stock if the common stock appreciates more than roughly 10% a year. If the common stock appreciates above the call price, the Trust should trade close to the level of the call price, giving the holder a "secure" 7.50% return, except for the risk of being called. If the stocks in the Trust remain flat or decline, the Trust should trade at a premium to the underlying common stocks. If the common stocks decline significantly, the Trust will trade at a "present value of the dividends" amount higher than the common stock, slowly declining to the level of the common stock at maturity.

Other Issues

- Tax aspects have been reviewed by underwriter's counsel.
- Corporate relationships could be adversely affected by issuing synthetic PERCS and having the underlying company complain about negatively impacting their ability to issue a PERCS.
- Could be done for any relatively large cap stocks or for select foreign stocks (with opportunity to hedge the currency exposure). Foreign stocks might reduce corporate relationships problems and create a truly unique security for investors, if they have enough information about the underlying company.
- Could be expanded to baskets of companies.

Note: [TBD] = to be determined; [ ] = preliminary terms/subject to change.

- Purchasing the call from the Trust should be free of credit concerns because the Trust will hold the common stocks.

- Transactions would require coordination with Block Trading Desk to facilitate purchases for the Trust, possibly adding to our block trading capabilities.

Target List of Stocks

Company Name	Common Ticker	Common Yield (%)	Trust Yield (%)	Cap (%)	Ranking
American Express	AXP	5.25	8.42	35	NR
Hanson PLC	HAN	7.33	8.35	30	NR
Sears Roebuck	S	5.65	7.50	30	3
British Gas PLC	BRG	5.95	7.10	30	NR
Dow Chemical	DOW	5.27	6.90	35	3
BAT Ind. PLC	BTI	5.51	6.90	30	NR
IBM	IBM	5.23	5.90	30	2

Note: The above pricing assumes a 2.25% gross spread and 0.75% in fees for 3 years. Additionally, the call option is sold at the 2-year historic volatility level; no market quotes were obtained.

General PERCS Terms

Company Name	Common Yield (%)	Trust Yield (%)	Cap (%)
General Motors	3.86	8.00	30
K-Mart	4.00	7.75	30
Texas Instr.	2.47	7.75	33
Broad	1.53	8.53	35
RJR	0.00	8.25	35

Note: [TBD] = to be determined; [ ] = preliminary terms/subject to change.

Stock Income Participation Trust

Issue	*Stock Income Participation Trust* consists of common stock of the individual companies listed in the following, and treasury strips that pay a quarterly payment. The Trust also enters into a contract that limits the capital appreciation of stocks to 30%.
Underwriters	U.S. Broker–Dealer and comanagers [TBD]
Expiration	3 years from date of issuance of Trust units
Yield	See following table
Call Premium	See following table
Shares Issued	2,000,000
Price	$15.00 per Unit
Divisor	Adjusted to give $15.00 price
Gross Spread	3.00%
Selling Concession	1.80%, or $0.27 per Unit
Listing	U.S. stock exchange
Pricing Table	

Yield to Investor (%)	Cap on Appreciation (%)
6.00	42
6.25	40
6.50	37
6.75	35
7.00	32
7.25	30

Stocks in Trust: One Share of the following stocks, except as noted:

Note: [TBD] = to be determined; [ ] = preliminary terms/subject to change.

Share Name	Price ($)	Dividend Yield (%)
Baxter Intl.	37.00	1.85
U.S. Surgical	119.50	0.27
Medtronic	87.63	0.54
Medco Contain.	33.25	0.05
Humana	28.00	3.34
Biomet	25.00	0.00
Bausch & Lomb	54.00	1.24
National Med Ent.	16.75	2.72
Nat Health Labs	25.75	0.92
St. Jude Medical	47.75	0.00
Becton Dickinson	69.63	1.75
Stryker	44.00	0.10
T2 Med	60.00	0.00
Bard C R	33.25	1.56
Sci Med Life	80.00	0.00
	Average	0.75

Dividend Distributions: The dividends from the underlying common stocks will be distributed to the holders of Trust units on a pro rata basis as the Trust receives the dividends. Simultaneously the treasury strip payments will be distributed to the holders of Trust units for a single quarterly payment. The dividend pass-through payments will be characterized as dividend income, although the 70% dividend exclusion might not hold. The treasury strip payments will be characterized as **tax free** payments until exercise or maturity, at which point the payment would be characterized as capital gain. Additionally, the holders will be taxed on OID from the strip.

Trust Manager   Three independent Trustees will be appointed.

Management Fee: No management fee.

Administrative Fee: Expected to be approximately 10 basis points per year.

Note: [TBD] = to be determined; [ ] = preliminary terms/subject to change.

Trust Termination: The Trust will terminate at the end of the 3 years. The Trust holder is not guaranteed to receive the principal at maturity. Holders will have the right to receive the securities upon distribution.

Return Analysis   Maximum Return (assumes all stocks hit the Trust call price)

	Year 3
Total Return	51.75%
Annualized	16.00%

Standstill Return: Assuming the stocks do not change in price, the return will be equal to the yield on the Trust of 7.30% versus 1.09% return from the underlying stocks.

Expected Trading Levels: Because the Trust will have limited appreciation, due to the call price, Trust units should trade at a discount to the common stock if the common stock appreciates more than roughly 10% a year. If the common stock appreciates above the call price, the Trust units should trade close to the level of the call price, giving the holder a "secure" 7.30% return, except for the risk of being called. If the stocks in the Trust remain flat or decline, the Trust units should trade at a premium to the underlying common stocks. If the common stocks decline significantly, the Trust will trade at a "present value of the dividends" amount higher than the common stock, slowly declining to the level of the common stock at maturity.

Advantages of Trust Units over PERCS

- Potential for higher dividend yield with increases in the underlying stock dividends.
- Diversified portfolio in single transaction.
- Nondilutive to Issuer, should result in superior relative performance to stock prices.
- Tax free nature of distributions until maturity.

Note: [TBD] = to be determined; [ ] = preliminary terms/subject to change.

SAMPLE STRUCTURED PRODUCT
MANAGEMENT PRESENTATIONS*

Proposal to Issue and Sell Currency Warrants
Proposal to Issue and Sell Hong Kong Index Put and Call Warrants
Proposal to Issue and Sell Index-Linked Notes on the S&P MidCap 400 Index
Proposal to Issue and Sell IBM Equity-Linked Notes (ELNs)

Proposal to Issue and Sell
Currency Warrants

Summary

U.S. Parent Corporation (Corp) will issue *Currency Warrants* (the Warrants) from its *Currency Exchange Rate Warrants* shelf registration with the SEC. U.S. Broker–Dealer Inc. (Inc) will act as lead underwriter of the offering and distribute the Warrants through its U.S. retail and worldwide institutional distribution networks. Comanager, Inc. will comanage the deal and act as qualified independent underwriter.

General Issue Structure

Corp issues the Warrants while simultaneously purchasing an identical option from its U.K. subsidiary, Financial Products Inc. (Financial).

Inc, as underwriter, purchases the Warrants from Corp and will then resell the Warrants to its retail network as a takedown under a prospectus supplement to Corp's *Currency Exchange Rate Warrants* shelf registration.

The Warrants will be U.S. exchange listed for secondary trading.

Financial will then hedge its long position in the Warrants with an equal and offsetting position using OTC currency options, listed currency futures and options on futures, and the underlying currency.

---

*See Chapter 2 for a discussion of management responsibilities associated with structured derivative product transactions.

Capital

Corp will sell the products and, as a holding company, will not have any capital requirements.

Corp will purchase an identical and offsetting security from Financial to avoid becoming a U.S. broker–dealer.

Subject to market conditions, Financial will then hedge the risks associated with the Warrants using listed currency futures, options on futures, cash, and the currency underlying the Warrants. The hedge will consist of OTC currency options purchased from counterparties whose creditworthiness will be reviewed by and found acceptable by Corp's credit department.

Financial has no additional regulatory capital requirement associated with the issuance of the Warrants.

Term Sheet

Issue	*Currency Warrants*
Issuer Rating	U.S. Parent Corporation (Corp) / Moody's A2 and S&P A1
Registration	Takedown off Corp's *Currency Exchange Rate Warrants* shelf
Term	1 year from date of issuance
Underwriters	Inc and Comanager
Filing Size	1,000,000+ Warrants (can be upsized to match demand)
Issue Price	$4.75–$5.50 per Warrant
$ Premium	$5,250,000+ (aggregate)
% Premium	4.75% to 5.50%
1-Year Historical Volatility	11.1%
1-Year Implied Volatility	13.5%
Strike FX	At-the-money
Gross Spread	5.00% ($0.24–$0.28 per Warrant)
Selling Concession	3.00% ($0.14–$0.17 per Warrant)
Warrant Symbol/Listing	"XYZ.WS"/U.S. Stock Exchange

Exercise/Settlement	American style/continuous exercise into U.S. dollars
Cash Settlement Value	The greater of (i) 0 and (ii) [$100–{$100 × (Strike per/Spot per $)}]
Investor Restrictions	Option-approved accounts only; no IRAs or UGMAs

Marketing Plan

Investor profile: U.S. retail and institutional accounts.

Major sales points:

- Leveraged ability to hedge debt or equity currency rate exposure in Japanese yen
- Ability to speculate on currency rate movements without the capital levels required for foreign currency trading
- Liquidity of exchange listing (the Warrants will trade as *equity* warrants not as currency options)
- One-year maturity allows greater time frame for currency rate movements than traditional foreign currency option products

Options suitability is required for all customers.

Sales will be integrated among U.S. retail equity, institutional, and international customers.

Currency Research*

Short-term currency speculation appears to have caused the dollar to be oversold versus the yen; currently trading at 79 yen per dollar.

Political and technical developments often have a short-term influence on currency markets and are expected to be reversed as economic fundamentals regain influence.

Corp's 3-month currency forecast is 97 yen per dollar (ranging from 95-100).

Corp's 6-month and 12-month yen/dollar forecasts are 99 and 105 yen per dollar, respectively.

---

*Based on yen/dollar currency forecasts by Corp's International Economics Group, *Global Currency and Interest Rate Strategy* report.

Caveat: U.S. involvement in Mexican crisis, uncertain U.S. trade talks with Japan, and lack of concerted central bank intervention to support the dollar, among other factors, have given the yen a *safe haven* status.

Caveat: In trying to achieve an economic *soft landing*, the U.S. Federal Reserve may be approaching the top of its tightening cycle while Japan's economy appears to be recovering, the combination of which, among other factors, may produce only a modest dollar recovery, if any.

Contribution to Corp

Assumes $5,250,000 minimum issue size (1,000,000 Warrants @ $5.25 per Warrant) sold 25% by Inc and 75% by Comanager (lifetime estimates).

	Structuring and Trading	Retail	Total Corp
Revenues			
Gross Spread Breakdown (5%)			
Management fee (1%)	$ 2		$ 2
Underwriting (1%)	53		53
Sales credit (3%)		$39	39
Estimated Trading Revenue	2,000		2,000
Total Revenue	$2,055	$39	$2,094
Direct Expenses			
Legal (issuer/underwriter/ wt. agent/Blue Sky)	(100)		(100)
Printing (preliminary and final)	(50)		(50)
Warrant agent	(5)		(5)
Stock exchange (initial listing)	(15)		(15)
Auditor (comfort letter)	(30)		(30)
Miscellaneous expenses	(5)		(5)
Direct retail payout	—	(18)	(18)
Total Direct Expenses	(205)	(18)	(223)
Gross Contribution to Corp	1,850	21	1,871
Discretionary Compensation	(648)	(3)	(651)
Assumed Profit to Corp	$1,202	$18	$1,220

Note: In U.S. $ (thousands).

Corp Profit/Loss Assuming Different Realized Volatilities (Lifetime Estimates)

Realized Volatility (%)	Estimated Profit (Loss) on Hedge (U.S. $, thousands)
11.5	2,530
12.5	2,205
13.5[a]	2,000
14.5	1,835
15.5	970
16.5	605
17.5[b]	0
18.5	(365)
19.5	(730)
20.5	(1,095)

[a]Assumed realized volatility.
[b]Expected volatility sold.

Risks

Credit. To the extent Corp uses OTC options, credit risk is a factor.

Volatility. If the volatility realized at each roll point over the term of the Warrants is greater than the volatility sold, Corp could lose money. Volatility assumptions are as follows:

Expected Volatility Sold	17.5%
Expected Volatility Sold (net of gross spread and direct expenses)	16.0%
Assumed Realized Volatility	13.5%
1-Year Historical Volatility	10.1%
1-Year Implied Volatility (future estimate)	13.5%

Required Management Approval

Approve shelf takedown and issuance of *Currency Warrants*.

Proposal to Issue and Sell
Hong Kong Index
Put and Call Warrants

Summary

U.S. Parent Corporation (Corp) proposes to issue *Hong Kong Index Put and Call Warrants* (the Warrants).

Expected Product

Corp proposes to issue put and call warrants on the Hong Kong Index and distribute them through U.S. Broker–Dealer Incorporated (Inc) and co-managers to U.S. retail investors and to institutional investors in the United States and Europe. The Warrants will have an at-the-money strike and will expire 2 years from issuance. The reversion of Hong Kong to The People's Republic of China is expected to occur on June 30, 1997.

The Hong Kong Index was created in June 1993. Presently, there are four put and two Hong Kong Index call warrant issues trading (including Corp's first offering of puts and calls). Constituent stocks in the Index represent the following Hong Kong industry sectors: commerce, industry, transportation, finance, property development, and utilities. The Index is a market-weighted, Hong Kong dollar-denominated equity index calculated once per U.S. business day, based on the closing prices of stocks traded on the Hong Kong Stock Exchange. The index value is disseminated worldwide.

Corp issued 2-year put and call warrants on the Hong Kong Index at $4.50 and $4.75 per warrant, respectively. The strike index level was 450. Sixty days after the offering, the warrants were trading at $4.75 and $11.00, respectively, and the index was at 626, up more than 40% from the strike.

General Issue Structure

The Warrants are similar in structure to other index, yield, and currency warrant offerings.

Corp issues the Warrants while simultaneously purchasing an identical off-setting position from Corp's U.K. subsidiary (International).

Inc, as the U.S. underwriter, purchases the Warrants from Corp and will then resell the Warrants to its retail network as a takedown under a prospectus supplement to Corp's *Stock Index Warrants* shelf registration.

The Warrants will be listed in the United States for secondary trading. The Index value will be updated once each day in New York and continuously disseminated worldwide.

International will then hedge its long Warrant position with an equal and offsetting position in Hong Kong cash, futures, listed options, or OTC positions.

Capital

Corp will issue the Warrants and, as a U.S. holding company, will not have any capital requirements.

Corp will purchase an identical and offsetting security from International to avoid being deemed a U.S. broker–dealer.

Subject to market conditions, International will then hedge the risks associated with the Warrants with a combination of offsetting Hong Kong cash, futures, listed options, or OTC positions purchased from counterparties whose creditworthiness will be reviewed by and found acceptable by Corp's credit department.

International has determined that its capital surplus will be subject to a capital charge of approximately $3,500,000 under regulatory requirements outside the United States.

Term Sheet

Issue   *Hong Kong Index Put and Call Warrants* are based on stocks traded on the Hong Kong Stock Exchange. The Index represents the following Hong Kong industry sectors: commerce, industry, transportation, finance, property development, and utilities. The Index is market-weighted, denominated in Hong Kong dollars, and calculated once per U.S. business day, based on closing Hong Kong Stock Exchange stock prices.

Issuer	U.S. Parent Corporation
Pricing	Mid-January
Term	2 years from date of issuance
Underwriters	U.S. Broker–Dealer Incorporated (books) and two other comanagers
Size	Puts: 4,000,000±; Calls: 5,000,000±
$ Premium	$51,120,000± (aggregate)
Estimated Price/ Warrant	Puts: U.S.$5.13± (based on a 626 Index level and an HK$7.725/US$ FX rate) Calls: U.S.$6.12± (based on a 626 Index level and an HK$7.725/US$ FX rate)
Listing/Index License	U.S. Stock Exchange
Warrant Agent	Citibank, N.A.
Exercise	American style, continuously exercisable, automatically exercised at expiration; the Warrants will be cash-settled in U.S. dollars based on a Hong Kong dollar/U.S. dollar exchange rate fixed at the time of the IPO
Customer Suitability	Option-approved accounts only; no IRAs or UGMAs

Marketing Plan and Research

Investor profile: U.S. retail and institutional investors in the United States and Europe.

Major sales points:

- Reset strike with new warrant offering after 40% run-up in the Hong Kong market
- Leveraged ability to speculate on the Hong Kong equity market
- Convenient U.S. time zone/U.S. traded instruments for hedging existing stock positions in the Hong Kong equity market
- Liquidity of exchange listing (will trade under *equity* rules as a warrant not as an option or future)
- Two-year maturity allows greater time frame for equity index movements than existing futures contracts in Hong Kong
- Exchange-traded or exercisable any time prior to expiration

Issued by Corp and underwritten by Inc and comanagers to U.S. retail investors and to institutional investors in the United States and Europe.

There are a significant number of research reports published by Inc on Hong Kong and China, as follows:

"Oriental Sun Rising" (10/22/93)   "Fortune Cookies" (3/23/93)
"Country Outlook" (1/92–12/93)   "Tigers Lillies" (12/19/92)
"Chinese Cooking" (4/9/92)   "Hot Chopsticks" (4/12/92)
"Pacific Pickup" (7/28/91)

In Corp's December 1993 *Investment Report*, Hong Kong was said to be experiencing "just the start of a historical economic event." China's GNP growth has averaged 9% per year over the past 10 years; it was over 12% last year and 14% this year, and is officially forecast to grow 10% next year, despite government efforts to control inflation.

Customer suitability: The Warrants will only be sold in primary and secondary transactions to investors whose accounts are option approved.

Contribution to Corp

Assumes $51.120 million total issue size sold and hedged 100% by U.S. Broker–Dealer Incorporated (lifetime estimates). Note: Although comanaged, the following economics assume a sole-managed deal.

	Inc Structuring and Trading	Retail	Total Corp
Revenues			
Gross Spread Breakdown (5%)			
Management fee (20%)	$ 511		$ 511
Underwriting (20%)	511		511
Sales credit (60%)		$1,534	1,534
Estimated Trading Revenue	11,000		11,000
Total Revenue	$12,022	$1,534	$13,556
Direct Issuer Expenses of Corp			
Legal (issuer, Blue Sky, warrant agent)	(70)		(70)
Printing	(60)		(60)
Warrant agent	(5)		(5)
Stock exchange listing	(20)		(20)
Auditor (comfort letter)	(25)		(25)
Warrant certificates	(9)		(9)
Miscellaneous expenses	(20)		(20)
Direct retail payout	—	(690)	(690)
Total Direct Expenses	(209)	(690)	(899)
Gross Contribution to Corp	11,813	844	12,657
Discretionary Compensation	(4,135)	(127)	(4,262)
Assumed Profit to Corp	$ 7,678	$ 717	$ 8,395

Note: In U.S. $ (thousands).

Corp Profit/Loss Assuming Different Realized Volatilities (Lifetime Estimates)

Realized Volatility (%)	Estimated Profit (Loss) on Hedge (U.S. $, thousands)
27	12,828
29[a]	11,000
31	8,428
33	6,268
35	3,708
37	1,548
38[b]	0
39	(612)
41	(2,770)

[a]Assumed realized volatility.
[b]Expected volatility sold.

Risks

Credit. To the extent we use OTC options, credit risk is a factor.

Volatility. If the volatility realized is greater than the volatility sold, Corp could lose money. Volatility assumptions are as follows:

Expected Volatility Sold (net of gross spread and expenses)	38%
Assumed Realized Volatility	29%
2-Year Historical Volatility	23%
Current Implied Volatility	31%

Required Management Approval

Approve shelf takedown, underwriting, and issuance by Corp of *Hong Kong Index Put and Call Warrants*. Final terms and pricing will be submitted for approval on the pricing date.

Proposal to Issue and Sell
Index-Linked Notes on the
S&P MidCap 400 Index

Summary

U.S. Parent Corporation (Corp) will issue *Index-Linked Notes on the S&P MidCap 400 Index* as a takedown off its existing *Medium-Term Note* shelf registration with the SEC. U.S. Broker–Dealer Incorporated (Inc) will act as underwriter of the offering and distribute the Notes through its U.S. retail network.

Expected Product

Corp proposes to issue *Index-Linked Notes on the S&P Midcap 400 Index* (the Notes). Inc will act as the Underwriter of the offering and distribute the Notes through its U.S. retail network.

The S&P MidCap 400 Index is a capitalization-weighted index designed and published since 1991 by Standard & Poor's Corporation. The MidCap measures the performance of the middle growth sector of the U.S. equities market (400 companies with market capitalizations from approximately $200 million to $5 billion).

Investors will "beat" the price return of the S&P Midcap Index over the term of the Notes. At maturity, each investor's principal investment will be returned along with an interest payment equal to 120% of the appreciation of the MidCap Index over 7 years.

The S&P MidCap Index has appreciated an average of 14.7% per year over the past 10 years. Corp Research calls for potential P/E growth and earnings expansion in the U.S. growth stock sector. Growth stocks, such as those comprising the S&P MidCap 400 Index, are expected to outperform the overall market over the term of the Notes.

General Issue Structure

Imbedded in each Note is the equivalent of a zero-coupon bond and a 7-year call option on the S&P MidCap 400 Index. Corp issues the Notes. A portion of the offering proceeds will be used to purchase an option from

Corp's International subsidiary (International) identical to the MidCap Index option imbedded in the Notes. The zero-coupon bond portion of the offering proceeds (discounted Corp's cost of capital as subordinated debt) will be used by Corp for general corporate funding purposes. Corp will repay investors $10.00 per Note face value at maturity.

Inc, as the underwriter, purchases the Notes from Corp and will then resell them into its U.S. retail network under a registration statement filed with the SEC.

The Notes will be U.S. exchange listed for secondary trading.

International will then hedge its long MidCap option position by purchasing equal and offsetting OTC index options, listed index options, index futures and options, and common stocks in the MidCap Index.

Capital

Corp will issue the Notes and, as a holding company, will not have any regulatory capital reserve requirements.

Corp will purchase an identical and offsetting security from its U.K. subsidiary (International) to avoid being deemed a U.S. broker–dealer.

Subject to market conditions, International will then hedge the risks associated with the Notes using OTC and listed S&P MidCap Index options and index futures and options, as well as certain common stocks that comprise the index. All OTC index options will be purchased from counterparties whose creditworthiness will have been reviewed and found acceptable by Corp's credit department.

International will have approximately a $6,000,000 additional offshore regulatory capital requirement that will be charged against International's capital surplus.

Term Sheet

Issue	*Index-Linked Notes on the S&P MidCap 400 Index*
Ranking	Subordinated Debt
Issuer	U.S. Parent Corporation
Issuer's Senior Rating	Moody's __ / S&P ____

Underwriter	U.S. Broker–Dealer Incorporated
Term	7 years
Issue Price	$10 per certificate
Interest Cost to Corp	145 basis points over the 7-year U.S. Treasury Bond rate (7.20%±)
Issue Size	$25–35 million
Call Provision	Noncallable for the life of the certificates
Principal Return	Return of principal at maturity
Interest at Maturity	Interest will be paid in the form of a single payment at maturity equal to approximately 120% (set on the pricing date) of the appreciation of the S&P MidCap 400 Index from the date of offering to the date of maturity; investors are guaranteed to get their principal back and "beat" the return of the MidCap after 7 years
Gross Spread	3.00% ($0.30 per Unit)
Selling Concession	3.00% ($0.30 per Unit)
Listing/Symbol	U.S. Stock Exchange/"ABC"
Calculation Agent	The Bank of New York

Annualized 7-Year Price Returns on the S&P MidCap 400 Index and Notes

Rolling 7-Year Periods[a]	Annualized 7-Year Returns (%)	Note Dollar Value After 7 Years	
		@110%	@120%[b]
1981–1987	9.75	20.10	21.02
1982–1988	11.90	23.17	24.37
1983–1989	13.97	26.47	27.97
1984–1990	9.64	19.95	20.86
1985–1991	16.40	30.85	32.74
1986–1992	13.55	25.77	27.20

[a]S&P does not provide historical MidCap 400 Index levels prior to 1981.
[b]Return of principal plus 110% and 120% of the appreciation of the MidCap over 7 years.

Marketing Plan

Retail investor profile:

- New and existing IRA investors
- Investors pursuing yield enhancement by extending maturities through medium-term instruments
- Middle-aged customers investing for retirement
- Young families seeking to finance future college expenses
- Parents shifting assets to children (Uniform Gifts to Minors)

Liquidity of exchange listing.

Extended 7-year maturity allows investors to "climb" the yield curve while pursuing a 1990's growth stock investment strategy through a well-known and diversified U.S. growth stock index. Corp research calls for potential P/E growth and earnings expansion in the U.S. growth stock sector. Growth stocks, such as those comprising the S&P MidCap 400 Index, are expected to outperform the overall market throughout most of the 1990s.

Sales will be integrated between U.S. retail equity and institutional customers.

Contribution to Corp

Assumes $30 million total issue size, sold 100% by Inc, U.S. retail (lifetime estimates). Note: As a sole-managed deal, the management fee and underwriting fee are not shown as they are incorporated in the estimated trading revenue.

	Structuring and Trading	Retail	Total Corp
Revenues			
Gross Spread Breakdown (3.00%)			
Management fee (0%)			
Underwriting (0%)			
Sales credit (100%)		$900	$ 900
Estimated Trading Revenue	$1,000		1,000
Total Revenue	$1,000	$900	$1,900

(continued)

	Structuring and Trading	Retail	Total Corp
Direct Expenses			
Legal (issuer, underwriter, Blue Sky)	(150)		(150)
Printing	(70)		(70)
Stock exchange listing fee	(18)		(18)
Auditor's financial review	(12)		(12)
Calculation agent	(5)		(5)
S&P MidCap 400 Index license	(25)		(25)
Miscellaneous expenses	(20)		(20)
Direct retail payout	—	(405)	(405)
Total Direct Expenses	(300)	(405)	(705)
Gross Contribution to Corp	700	495	1,195
Discretionary Compensation	(105)	(74)	(179)
Assumed Profit to Corp	$ 595	$421	$1,016

Note: In U.S. $ (thousands).

Corp Profit/Loss Assuming Different Realized Volatilities (Lifetime Estimates)

Realized Volatility (%)	Estimated Profit (Loss) on Hedge (U.S. $, thousands)
14	1,884
16	1,428
18[a]	1,000
20	477
22[b]	0
24	(483)

[a]Assumed realized volatility.
[b]Expected volatility sold.

Risks

Credit. To the extent Corp uses OTC options, credit risk is a factor.

Volatility. If the volatility realized at each MidCap Index option and future roll point over the term of the Notes is greater than the volatility sold, Corp could lose money. MidCap volatility assumptions are:

Expected Volatility Sold (net of gross spread and expenses)	22%
Assumed Realized Volatility	18%
7-Year Historical Volatility	14%
Current Implied Volatility	18%

Required Management Approval

Approve debt shelf takedown, issuance, and underwriting of *Index-Linked Notes on the S&P MidCap 400 Index*. Final terms and pricing will be provided for approval on the pricing date.

Proposal to Issue and Sell
IBM Equity-Linked Notes
(ELNs)

Summary

U.S. Parent Corporation (Corp) proposes to issue *IBM Equity-Linked Notes* (the ELNs) as a takedown off its existing *Medium Term Note* shelf registration with the SEC.

The offering proceeds will be used for risk management and quarterly coupon commitments, and as a below-market funding source for Corp.

U.S. Broker–Dealer Incorporated (Inc) will act as lead underwriter of the offering and distribute the ELNs through its U.S. retail and institutional network. An underwriting syndicate is expected to include comanagers.

General Issue Structure

Corp proposes to issue the ELNs, and Inc will act as the underwriter of the offering and distribute the ELNs through its U.S. retail and institutional network.

ELNs are hybrid instruments (debt/equity) based on common stocks that have little or no dividend yields. They are similar to buy/write transactions where the investor holds the equivalent of:

- A common stock on a low dividend paying company
- An out-of-the-money covered call written against the stock position
- An enhanced coupon/dividend yield

The proceeds from the sale of the call are used to provide investors with an enhanced coupon/dividend yield (i.e., 4.75–5.25%) and also allow for limited participation in any appreciation of the underlying stock 25% to 30% above the strike IBM price level over the 3-year term of the ELNs.

ELNs will be treated as medium-term debt of Corp (approximately 3-year term), the net proceeds of which will be available to Corp for general funding purposes. Redemption of the ELNs at maturity will be a taxable event for Corp. If the underlying common stock appreciates, the redemption of the ELNs will create a capital loss to Corp (redemption value is greater than issue price), reducing Corp's tax liability in the year of redemption. If the underlying stock depreciates in value (redemption value is less than the issue price), the amount of the redemption is treated as a capital gain, generating a tax liability to Corp. A taxable gain or loss at redemption could be partially offset by a gain or loss on the hedge.

Inc, as the underwriter, purchases the ELNs from Corp and resells them into its U.S. retail and institutional network as a shelf takedown from its existing medium-term note registration statement filed with the SEC.

The ELNs will be listed on a U.S. stock exchange.

Capital

Corp will sell the ELNs and, as a holding company, will not have any capital requirements.

Corp will enter into an identical and offsetting swap transaction with Corp's U.K. subsidiary (International) to avoid being deemed a U.S. broker–dealer.

International will then hedge the risks associated with the ELNs using the underlying common stock.

Based on the parameters set forth in the following Term Sheet, International will have approximately a $2,160,000 additional regulatory capital requirement charged against its capital surplus. Based on the assumed profit to Corp of approximately $1.681 million (see the following Contribution to Corp spreadsheet), return on regulatory capital over the 3-year term of the ELNs is expected to be approximately 26%.

Term Sheet

Issue and Maturity	*IBM Equity-Linked Notes (ELNs)*
Obligation and Issuer	Direct, unsecured, and subordinated debt of Corp
Issuer's Debt Rating	Subordinated: Moody's _____ / S&P ____
Underwriters	Inc and comanagers
Redemption	Noncallable
Underlying Stock	IBM
Initial Filing Size	1,000,000 ELNs or $53,375,000 notional value
Indicative Issue Price	The NYSE closing price of IBM on the pricing date (currently $53.375)
Gross Spread	1.85% of the offering price
Selling Concession	1.00% of the offering price (approximately $0.52 per ELN)
Listing/Symbol	U.S. stock exchange/ELN
ELN Interest Payments	4.75% to 5.25% per annum payable quarterly in arrears
Payment at Maturity	The *lesser* of (A) 125% to 130% of the ELNs issue price, or (B) the average closing price of IBM for the 10 trading days prior to maturity
Trustee	Citibank, N.A. (registration, transfers, and payments)
Investor Suitability:	ELNs may only be sold to investors for whom an investment in IBM common stock would be suitable and who have sufficient knowledge and investment experience to understand

the risk characteristics of ELNs. Branch Managers and Investment Executives must certify as to each investor's suitability for ELNs purchases and that such investor understands and can bear the risk of investing in ELNs.

Delivery: Fully registered certificates

Marketing Plan

IBM is covered by Corp research (currently rated Unattractive). Corp investors still hold IBM. Investors that continue to hold IBM despite research sell recommendations can buy IBM ELNs to receive higher yield and still participate in potential appreciation up to the 25% to 30% cap.

Retail investor profile:

- Investors seeking higher current income than typical equity securities
- Retired investors seeking current income
- IRA investors that want to build savings through income generation and appreciation potential

For investors who wish to hold IBM as a long-term investment, ELNs allow them to:

- Sell IBM and realize any existing tax losses
- Simultaneously buy IBM ELNs issued by Corp at the current market price of IBM
- Avoid "wash sale" tax treatment on the sale of IBM stock and immediate purchase of IBM ELNs
- More than double the current yield they are receiving from IBM stock
- Retain significant upside potential if IBM appreciates over the next three years

Institutional investor profile:

- Institutions that need fixed income investments but seek to retain equity exposure
- Insurance companies, pension fund and mutual fund managers, and convertible bond portfolio managers seeking current income but required to hold dividend-paying stocks

- Money managers seeking to enhance yield of IBM common stock required to be held in portfolio

- Income-oriented institutional investors seeking equity exposure but requiring yields of 5% or more

Liquidity of exchange listing.

Sales will be integrated between U.S. retail equity and institutional customers.

Contribution to Corp

Assumes $54 million total issue size sold 100% to U.S. retail and institutional investors (lifetime estimates).

	Structuring and Trading	Inc Retail	Total Corp
Revenues			
Gross Spread Breakdown (1.85%)			
Management fee (.42%)	$ 227		$ 227
Underwriting (.43%)	232		232
Sales credit (1.00%)		$540	540
Estimated Trading Revenue	2,110		2,110
Total Revenue	$2,569	$540	$3,109
Direct Expenses			
Legal (issuer, underwriter, Blue Sky)	(175)		(175)
Printing	(50)		(50)
Stock exchange listing	(15)		(15)
Auditor's financial review	(20)		(20)
Miscellaneous expenses	(20)		(20)
Direct retail payout	—	(243)	(243)
Total Direct Expenses	(280)	(243)	(523)
Gross Contribution to Corp	$2,289	$297	$2,586
Discretionary Compensation	(801)	(104)	(905)
Assumed Profit to Corp	$1,488	$193	$1,681

Note: In U.S. $ (thousands).

Corp Profit/Loss Assuming Different Realized Volatilities (Lifetime Estimates)

Realized Volatility (%)	Estimated Profit (Loss) on Hedge (U.S. $, thousands)
20	(1,380)
24[a]	0
25	350
30[b]	2,110
35	3,870
40	5,640

[a]Expected volatility sold.
[b]Assumed realized volatility.

Balance Sheet Impact of Issuing ELNs (Assumes $54 Million Offering)

Entity	Assets	Liabilities
U.S. Parent Corporation	Cash: $27 million Intercompany receivable from International: $27 million Total: $54 million	3-Year debt: $54 million Equity-Linked Notes Total: $54 million
U.K. International (parent subsidiary)	Net inventory: $27 million Total: $27 million	Intercompany payable from PWG: $27 million Total: $27 million
U.S. Broker–Dealer Incorporated	No impact	No impact

Risks

Volatility. Profitability flows from Corp's purchase of a relatively inexpensive out-of-the-money call option on the IBM common stock underlying the ELNs. If the volatility realized is lower than the implied volatility paid, Corp could lose money. Volatility assumptions are as follows:

Expected Volatility Paid (net of gross spread and expenses)	24%
Assumed Realized Volatility	30%
3-Year Historical Volatility	28%
Current Implied Volatility	32%

Required Management Approval

Approve terms, underwriting, and issuance of *IBM Equity-Linked Notes* (ELNs) from Corp's *Medium-Term Note* shelf registration with the SEC. Final terms and pricing will be submitted for approval on the pricing date.

"CONVERTIBLES AS SPORT"*

Option prices can be understood by comparing various stages in an option's life to periods of a basketball game (see *Options as Sport*). The basketball analogy is easily applied because options are relatively simple creatures whose life spans are known with certainty. The only thing missing from the option-basketball paradigm is the possibility that the game might go into overtime (i.e., that the option's life might be extended past its stated expiration). This cannot happen with traditional options, but the concept of overtime gives us an interesting framework to compare convertible bonds with the sport of *baseball*.

Convertible bonds typically have two key reference dates. One is the first call date, at which point the issuer of the bonds may redeem them, generally by forcing bondholders to convert the bond into the underlying stock when the market value of the stock is significantly higher than the bond's redemption price. The other is the bond's stated maturity, a date more useful for theoretical valuations than for understanding how convertible securities behave, since most issuers call in their convertibles before they mature; those that do not usually go bankrupt. We will focus here on the motivations of an issuer as we look at a callable convertible bond using the analogy of a baseball game.

Consider a hypothetical World Series (best of seven games). Team A has won three of the first five games, but Team B is leading late in the sixth game, which it must win to keep the series alive. Team B's ace pitcher has pitched the eighth inning. As Team A comes to bat in the ninth inning, Team B's manager faces this dilemma:

- If he leaves his ace pitcher in for the ninth inning, the pitcher's arm will wear out and he will not be nearly as effective for tomorrow's seventh game (assuming they win the game tonight and there is another game tomorrow).

- If he takes his ace pitcher out early, the manager runs a much bigger risk of blowing the game and losing the series.

Excerpted from a paper by and published with the permission of Bill Feingold, First Vice President, PaineWebber Incorporated, 1996.
*See Chapter 7 for a discussion of convertible securities.

Team B's manager will base his decision on two factors: the size of his team's lead in this game and the difference in capabilities between his ace pitcher and his less capable relief pitcher. The bigger the lead, the more likely the manager will bring in his less capable relief pitcher. The more the two pitchers differ in ability, the more the manager will be inclined to leave his ace pitcher in the game.

Now, consider for a moment a corporation that has issued a convertible bond. The issuer could call the bond at 103 when its value is currently 125. The company needs to raise substantial new capital for expansion in the next year and wants to turn the debt into equity by forcing conversion. If the issuer calls the bond now, arbitrage-related selling of the stock may trigger a panic, which could push the bond's conversion value below 103. The company would then have to raise new capital just to refinance the existing bond it has just called, since holders will prefer the cash call price of the bond to its conversion value and will therefore decide not to convert. In order to raise funds to pay off its existing bond obligation plus the new capital it needs to raise for its expansion plans, the issuer will probably have to price its new debt on terms more favorable to investors than to itself.

On the other hand, if the company does not attempt to force conversion by calling the bonds, and the stock market falls apart several months later, taking the company's stock down, for example, 25 percent, the company will have missed a tremendous opportunity to use a strong stock market to strengthen its balance sheet. Its chief financial officer may also have to seek new employment.

The company's decision to attempt a forced conversion will depend on two main factors. One is the difference between the bond's conversion value and its call price (i.e., the size of the team's lead). The other is the stock's volatility (i.e., the difference in the quality of the pitchers). A company with low stock volatility might safely call a bond with conversion value of 120; one with rollercoaster stock prices and high volatility might not be able to call the bond even with a conversion value above 140, for fear of having to raise cash during a period when the stock price is low.

Calling the bond and attempting to force conversion is similar to Team B bringing in its less capable relief pitcher, attempting to capitalize on its current lead in the game in the hope that it will continue to play well (i.e., the conversion value stays well above the call price). If the strategy works, the company will need to raise less cash on better terms and Team

B's ace pitcher will be available for the seventh game. If the strategy back-fires, the company will be at the mercy of the capital markets. Team B loses tonight's game and the series is over.

To attempt to synthesize the investor's view of convertible securities into our baseball format, consider a hot dog vendor selling his dogs at the ball game. While an issuer of a convertible bond wants to end the bond's life as soon as possible (i.e., by ending the game after nine innings), the hot dog vendor (i.e., the investor) wants as much money to flow in as possible from his sale of all the hot dogs he has brought to the game (i.e., the bond investor wants to receive as many coupon payments from his convertible as possible). The hot-dog-vendor-cum-investor hopes for extra innings, so as to sell more of his product at a profit to hungry fans. If the game goes into extra innings, the vendor makes more money. The hot dog vendor, ex-pecting a long game, has invested in as many hot dogs as possible. If the game goes a mere nine innings and the innings are quick, many of the ven-dor's hot dogs will go unsold. Think of the unsold hot dogs as the premium an investor pays for a convertible bond over and above the cash flows it promises to the investor up to the bond's first call date. The premium paid by an investor is money well spent if the convertible remains outstanding beyond its call date. It is money wasted if the stock price goes straight up and the bond is called by the issuer at the first possible call date.

It is important to recognize the limitations in the hot dog vendor/in-vestor analogy. A "natural" owner of convertibles (i.e., one who buys a convert to gain exposure to the underlying stock while collecting coupon payments) will prefer that the underlying stock price go up as far as possi-ble (i.e., that the baseball game is a blowout). The bond will certainly be called: its premium will disappear, but its absolute dollar value will be very high. The hot dog vendor is like an arbitrageur* (i.e., an arbitrageur who has hedged a convertible bond by taking an offsetting short position in the stock) who hopes to recoup income far in excess of the premium paid for the convert with the bond remaining outstanding far beyond its call date (i.e., that the baseball game is played late into the night).

---

*An arbitrageur is one who takes advantage of price disparities in the market, such as buying something cheap one place and selling it somewhere else at a profit.

"OPTIONS AS SPORT"*

Understanding how option prices change in response to change in other variables can be tricky. The Greek (delta, gamma, and theta) and pseudo-Greek (vega) names used to measure option sensitivities do not necessarily make things clearer. Options do, however, make intuitive sense if they can be viewed in an easily understood framework. With this in mind, basketball is a sport that lends itself to understanding options. Please note that the following examples involve references to hypothetical bets on the performance of imaginary teams. The examples are used strictly to help explain option pricing concepts, not as an endorsement of pure speculation or betting. Rather, options are instruments that investors can use to tailor their portfolios to their own expectations and to reduce or increase risk.

Delta (Probability of an Option Expiring In-the-Money)

An option's delta is its most frequently observed characteristic. *Delta* is most commonly thought of as a hedge ratio, but it also generally approximates the likelihood that an option will finish its life in-the-money (e.g., that a call option will expire with the underlying asset at a higher price than the call's strike). A nearly exact analogy in a basketball game is the probability that one of the teams will win.

Suppose Teams A and B are about to play and the game is considered a toss-up. Before the game starts, each team has an equal chance of winning. With options, 50 percent is a typical *delta* for an at-the-money option with a relatively short term to expiration, say three months. The fact that the option is "at" the money (i.e. the underlying asset's price is equal to the option's strike price) is important for preserving the basketball analogy because each team is neither ahead nor behind, just as the option is neither in- nor out-of-the-money.

In a hypothetical basketball game, Team A is a heavy favorite. It has a delta of 80 percent. Since the game has not yet begun, we must still say that the option is at-the-money. How can an at-the-money option have such a high delta? It can if there is strong reason to believe the underlying asset

---

Excerpted with permission from "Options as Sport," by Bill Feingold, in *Handbook of Equity Derivatives* (Irwin, Illinois, 1994).

*See Chapter 4 for a discussion of option pricing and valuation.

will exceed the strike price at expiration (we will continue to use calls in our example, although the logic can also be used for puts). What might be the rationale for such a belief?

Consider a 10-year at-the-money call option on an index of non-dividend-paying stocks. Because the opportunity cost of keeping money in stocks for this long a period is quite high (money invested in risk-free securities could easily double in value because of compounding interest over a 10-year period), it seems highly unlikely to expect the stock index to have a lower nominal value at the end of the period than at the beginning. Just as Team A is heavily favored to beat Team B, a 10-year at-the-money call option is heavily favored to finish in-the-money. Consequently, the delta, or probability of the option being in-the-money in 10 years, will be much greater than neutral (50 percent is neutral). Note that this logic clearly does not apply to short-term options, since their value is dictated by price moves over a handful of days and the randomness of these moves will dominate the relatively minor amount of forgone interest income over such a short period of time.

Gamma (Rate of Increase of the Probability of an Option Expiring In-the-Money)

Suppose now that the basketball game is underway and one of the teams has taken the lead. It makes sense that the team in front now has a higher probability of winning than it did at the beginning of the game, and that the greater the team's lead, the more the odds have swung in its favor. Moving back to options, this is equivalent to a stock going up and raising the delta of what was originally an at-the-money call. But how much should the delta go up? In option language, this is measured by *gamma*, which is much higher as the option nears expiration than at the beginning of its life. But if this is Greek to you, go back to basketball!

Let's look again at a basketball game where the teams are considered to have even odds. The game starts and Team A wins the jump ball and scores on a quick layup. It leads 2 to 0. Realistically, Team A has only a marginally higher change of winning than it did before the game started; perhaps now its delta is 51 percent instead of 50 percent. In other words, its *gamma* is 1 percent. Nothing significant has happened. But skip ahead to the last minute of the game. The score is tied 76–76 with just seconds to play. Each team's delta should be around 50 percent. When Team A scores right before the end of the game, its delta goes up from 50 percent to 98 percent, a much higher rate of increase, or gamma, than when it scored the first basket of the game. Of course, if the game had been one-sided throughout, with Team A dominating the game, the last basket before the buzzer would not affect the delta at all.

This example shows how gamma is at its highest for near-the-money options approaching expiration. A single favorable move in the underlying stock makes it almost certain to finish in-the-money, while an unfavorable move makes it virtually certain to expire worthless. On the other hand, using the basketball game example, buying a long-dated option gives you the luxury of scoring your way out of a bad start. You still have plenty of time to catch up.

Theta (Time Decay of an Option)

Consider two 5-minute stretches in an imaginary basketball game between Teams A and B. In each case, Team A begins the first 5-minute stretch leading by 8 points, and the margin is unchanged at the end of the stretch. Let's say the first stretch was early in the game, beginning with 17 minutes left in the first half and ending with 12 minutes to go in the half. The second 5-minute stretch, on the other hand, begins with 6 minutes left in the game and ends with only 1 minute left.

In each case, Team B fails to score and reduce its point deficit as time passes. How much should the value of a bet on Team B fall? Let's imagine an initial pregame bet of $1.00 that Team B will win. In the first case, after Team B has quickly fallen behind by 8 points early in the game, that bet loses some of its value, but is probably still worth around $0.85. Almost the whole game is left and perhaps Team A just happened to be the first team to have a hot streak (equivalent to a noticeable move in the underlying asset very early in the life of an option). After more time has passed and Team B's point deficit remains at 8 points, the value of the bet on Team B will have fallen more, from say $0.85 to $0.80. The 5-cent drop in the value of the bet on Team B over a 5-minute stretch early in the game (or 1 cent per minute) is the *theta,* or loss of value per unit of time passage, of a bet on the losing team.

Now let's look at the second example, where Team B trails by 8 points late in the game. Clearly, time is a huge factor now; Team B's failure to gain any ground should cause a big drop in the value of a bet on it, say from $0.20 to $0.01. In this case the theta would be $0.19 over 5 minutes, or almost $0.04 per minute, a much higher theta, more than earlier in the game when theta was only $0.01 per minute.

In other words, when a given amount of time passes with nothing happening to the value of the underlying security, the amount by which an option's value decays depends primarily on how far the option is from expiration. When expiration is still relatively far off, the passage of some time will have a modest negative effect on the option. But as expiration approaches, the passage of that same absolute amount of time will cause a much larger drop in the options' value, both in absolute and percentage terms.

Notice that the example uses the losing team. This was not arbitrary. The winning team wants time to pass without the score changing, assuming it is only concerned with winning and not with the margin of victory. If a bet on the losing team has properties similar to those of an option, a bet on the winning team must be similar to the position of someone who has written (sold) an option. Such a person is said to have "sold volatility" and wants the score of the basketball game or, in the case of options, the underlying asset to remain as they are.

Vega (Amount of Option Price Change for Each Percent Change in Volatility)

Vega is not only *not* a real Greek letter, but it is also in some sense an artificial measure of how option values change. This is because vega is defined as the amount an option's value changes if its *implied* volatility changes by one percentage point. However, the only way to find implied volatility is to look at the market price of the option and determine the volatility based on the price. In other words, there is a bit of a chicken-and-egg problem: Is the option expensive because volatility is high, or is implied volatility high because the option is expensive?

On the other hand, this description is a bit unfair to vega. Volatility, as represented in numerical terms, is usually defined as the annual standard deviation of price changes in the underlying security. To simplify, this means that a $100 stock with a volatility of 30 percent can be expected to have a price between $70 and $130 at the end of a year.* The key is that a given level of volatility has different implications for likely absolute price changes for different periods of time. The longer the time, the more a stock can be expected to move up or down.

Now let's get back to basketball. First, imagine Team A whose best player always scores 20 points per game. He almost never does better or worse. He has very low volatility and so does his team when he is playing. Let's say the team's volatility with "Steady Eddie" is 10 percent. It scores on average 60 points per game, with a range of 54 to 66 points. But the team also has a talented freshman named "Wild Thing," who can score 40 points when he is hot, but might not score any points on a bad night.

With Wild Thing replacing Steady Eddie, the team still scores an average of 60 points, but now the team's volatility is, say, 30 percent instead of 10 percent. The team might score between 42 and 78 points. If the team expects to be able to hold its opponent's score under 50 points, it should go with Steady Eddie, but against a high-scoring opponent expected to score 75 points or more, the team has to take its chances with Wild Thing. Before the start of the game, Team A's coach has to assess the possible scoring potential of Wild Thing and Steady Eddie. But what if the team makes a mistake in scouting Team B? Let's say Team A goes with Steady Eddie and finds itself unexpectedly far behind at halftime, say by 45 to 30. Team A now expects Team B to score 30 points in the second half, so they know they (Team A) will need more than a total of 75 points (more than 45 points in the second half) to win. With Steady Eddie, the best the team can reasonably hope to score is 34 points in the second half, which is unlikely to be enough to win.

At halftime the coach turns to Wild Thing. But before the coach can speak, the freshman, who knows option theory, says, "It's too late, coach. You only get a half game of my volatility now, and the best we can score in

---

*A bit of pure math is necessary here. Time does not influence option prices linearly but as a square-root function. Consider two options, identical in all respects except that one has twice as much time to expiration as the other. The longer-duration option will not be worth twice as much as the shorter one. The factor is, instead, the square root of 2, or about 1.4. This may make intuitive sense to you when you think about the economic principle of diminishing marginal returns. If not, don't worry about it. Getting back to our stock, after six months the stock can be expected to have a price range centering roughly around 100, with the lower end around 15/1.4 or 11 points below the center and the upper end a similar amount higher (i.e., a six-month range of $89 to $111).

the second half with me playing is probably 43 points, which won't quite do it. Increasing our volatility from 10 to 30 percent for half a game only increases our upside potential from 10 to 30 percent for a half-game only. That only increases our upside potential by 9 points (i.e., $[(18 - 6)/1.4] = 9$). If you had put me in when the game started, then you could have increased our upside potential by 12 points. Volatility is like fine wine, coach. You've gotta give it time."

GLOSSARY

affiliates: Holders of greater than 5 percent of the common stock of a company (i.e., either individuals or corporations).

agency trades: Securities transactions by and between broker–dealers as opposed to stock exchanges or other markets or investors.

at-the-money: When puts or calls trade at the strike they are said to be trading at-the-money and have no cash intrinsic value.

barrier options: Options that are triggered when an underlying asset price moves to a given price level. Knock-in barrier options are activated when a specified price level is reached, and knock-out options are canceled when a specified price level is reached. Barrier options are path dependent and can be canceled or "brought back to life" when the underlying asset or index crosses a specified level before the option expires.

basis risk: Cash market or other position risk exposure versus futures or other derivative markets.

basis swaps: Contracts to exchange interest payments based on different interest rates, such as the exchange of LIBOR-based (i.e., London Inter Bank Offer Rate) cash flows for U.S. Treasury rates.

basket options, sector options, and sector warrants: Securities based on specific custom-made portfolios of equities, currencies, commodities, and bonds that are bundled, usually in order to take advantage of fast-moving market events.

best efforts: The basis under which underwriting and selling-group members work in a syndicated offering in selling securities; an agreement to make a good faith attempt at selling as many securities as possible in an initial public offering as opposed to a firm commitment to sell a specified number of securities.

breakeven: Used to describe the time it would take a convertible to recoup the premium paid over common through its yield pickup. The premium paid over common refers to the convertible's conversion premium. Yield pickup refers to the amount by which a convertible's current yield exceeds the common stock's dividend yield. An easy formula to compute breakeven time is:

$$\text{Breakeven time (in years)} = \frac{\text{Conversion premium}/(1 + \text{Conversion premium})}{\text{Convertible current yield} - \text{Common dividend yield}}$$

For example, if a convertible trades with a 20 percent conversion premium, a 6 percent current yield, and the common pays a 2 percent dividend yield, the convertible's breakeven is 4.17 years [(0.2/1.2)/(0.06 − 0.02)].

break syndicate: All orders that have been placed by syndicate and selling group members are considered final.

broad-based index: A large group of stocks (e.g., from 15 to 5,000 or more stocks) whose values are calculated together to produce a single value that is viewed as representative of entire markets as a whole.

call date: Certain DECS can be called prior to maturity with the initial call price set at a small premium to the issue price. Typically, the call price declines to the issue price at maturity. The higher the common's trading level above the call price, the greater the probability that it will be called for redemption prior to maturity.

calls: The right but not the obligation to buy the underlying asset from the option writer.

comanager: An investment bank that joins the lead investment banking manager and takes a major role in distributing securities in an underwritten offering; usually earns a portion of the underwriting fee.

Commodity Future Trading Commission (CFTC) and the Commodities Exchange Act (CEA): The CFTC has regulatory jurisdiction over all futures and commodity option transactions. In 1982, Congress amended the CEA and the federal securities laws dividing jurisdiction over options and futures contracts on financial instruments between the CFTC and the SEC. Pursuant to these amendments, the CFTC was granted exclusive jurisdiction over all futures on stock indexes, and options on futures contracts, leaving jurisdiction over stock options, certificates of deposit, and stock indexes to the SEC. Adding to the convolution of U.S. securities regulatory regimes, both the CFTC and SEC retain regulatory authority over currency options.

commodity swaps: The exchange of cash flows linked to a commodity price index (e.g., U.S. Dollar Index, Natural Gas Index, etc.).

concentrated equity positions: Large stock positions that are difficult to liquidate by traditional means and often represent a significant portion of an individual's net worth.

conversion premium: The premium over conversion value at which a convertible trades. For example, a $100 convertible with a $50 conversion value has a 100 percent conversion premium. Conversion premium is one measure of a convertible's equity sensitivity. The lower the conversion premium, the greater the equity sensitivity. Conversely, the higher the conversion premium, the lower the convertible's sensitivity to common stock movements.

conversion price: The price of common above which, at maturity, a holder should convert into common stock rather than accept the redemption value. At maturity if the common trades below the conversion price, accept the redemption value. If the common stock trades above the conversion price, the convertible is in-the-money. If a convertible is in-the-money at maturity, an investor should convert into common stock rather than accept par value. The conversion price is computed by dividing the convertible's par value by its conversion ratio. Therefore, a $1000 face value convertible bond that converts into 50 shares has a $20 conversion price (i.e., par value of $1000/conversion ratio of 50 = $20 conversion price). Remember, corporate bond prices are quoted as a percentage of par. Therefore, price quotes appear in 100 bond point and not in 1000 dollar terms.

conversion ratio: The number of shares of common stock received upon conversion. A convertible can be converted at any time, in most cases, into the number of shares of common stock equal to the conversion ratio.

conversion value: The value of common stock represented by each convertible. Conversion value is computed by multiplying the price of the underlying common stock by the conversion ratio. With regard to convertible bonds, divide the conversion value by 10 as bond prices as quoted in 100's and not in 1000's.

counterparties: Participants in a swap or other transaction.

coupon/dividend: Convertible bonds pay a fixed annual coupon, typically paid semiannually. Coupons are normally expressed as a percent of par. Convertible preferred stocks pay a fixed dollar dividend, typically paid quarterly.

credit quality: A measure of default risk by an issuer of an obligation or investment contract. Credit ratings assigned by Moody's and Standard and Poor's (S&P) are widely used measures of an issue's credit quality. Companies with the highest credit quality receive AAA ratings from both agencies. Companies in default, on the other hand, are rated D.

credit risk: The possibility of default by a counterparty to a transaction.

currency exchange rate risk: Risk to foreign currency fluctuations that arises through long or short positions held.

currency swaps: The counterparties to the swap contract agree to swap principal and interest payments denominated in different currencies based on an agreed-upon currency exchange rate with specified interest at fixed or floating rates.

current yield: A convertible's coupon or dividend payment divided by its current price. Current yield is a measure of a convertible's current income.

deconstructing, stripping, or bifurcating a security: The process segregating the components of a financial instrument into discrete economic categories (e.g., a convertible security comprises debt and an equity option, a Treasury security has principal and income components; common stock can have appreciation and dividend components).

delta (index or stock risk): The percentage amount an option's price changes in response to a change in the price of the underlying asset.

delta hedging: Refers to a risk management strategy whereby an offsetting option position is established in an underlying security equal to the option position multiplied by the value of its delta.

derivatives: A generic term to describe a wide variety of financial instruments ranging from standardized, exchange-listed products to custom-made, over-the-counter instruments whose values are linked to, depend on, and are derived from the price or value of one or more underlying assets, including indexes, exchange rates, interest rates, or commodity prices. Derivative securities and contracts are the elemental building blocks of structured products. Elemental derivative instruments fall into two categories: *forward-based,* such as forward contracts, futures, and swaps; and *option-based,* including put and call equity options, caps, floors, interest rate, currency, and exotic options.

digital options: Pay a predetermined amount at such time as a certain specified trigger point is reach relating to the underlying asset.

discontinuance of index calculation: Contract document provision that provides for an alternative method of index calculation if the primary calculator fails to update the index values or the cash securities underlying the index cease to trade.

dividend yield risk: Risk of changes in stock dividend rates; difficult to hedge but usually a marginal risk that is smaller than interest rate risk.

dropping tickets: Customer orders placed by brokers that are received electronically by the syndicate desk.

due diligence: Meetings held among co-underwriting managers to review and confirm the acceptability of all material legal and financial matters relating to the issuer of a security.

dynamic hedging: A risk management strategy that includes changing the structure of a risk management strategy employed in response to or in anticipation of market events; for example, selling stock index futures in order to protect stock portfolios from adverse price movements, thus eliminating market risk without incurring stock transaction fees, which are higher than for futures instruments, and without losing dividend cash flows from the stocks themselves.

exotic options: Financial instruments that often have unique, custom-made terms as opposed to standardized options.

expiration date: The end of an option or warrant's term; if not exercised by the end of its term, both put and call options expire worthless.

fairness opinion: A written document provided by a qualified independent underwriter attesting to the equitable pricing of the instrument to investors; provided to the lead underwriter.

fair value: The value of the security based upon our pricing model. Fair value = common + present value of income pickup – short option value. A trading level below fair value improves the risk/reward of a PERCS or ELKS relative to common.

financial engineers: Those who engage in structured product origination activities.

forward start swaps: Swaps whose start date and subsequent exchange of interest payments are deferred to some time in the future.

gamma (actual volatility): The percentage amount by which an option's delta will change in price in relation to the price of the underlying security.

grantor trust: A contractual arrangement that provides a legal "container" into which a variety of assets can be deposited and resold in smaller economic units to investors that might otherwise be unable to participate in certain type of markets (e.g., oil or other commodities or currencies); publicly offered trusts are regulated under the Securities Exchange Act of 1940 (the Investment Company Act), but private trust transactions are generally unregulated.

gross spread: The gross spread is the amount added to the price of an offering and can range from 1 percent to 7 or 8 percent, depending on the type of security being offered. The 5 percent gross spread is usually divided into a 40 percent management fee (1 percentage point), 40 percent underwriting fee (1 percentage point), and 60 percent as a sales credit (3 percentage points).

hard call protection: A convertible cannot be called for redemption prior to its hard call date. The time remaining to the call date is known as call protection. Since a convertible typically pays a higher yield than common, the greater the length of call protection, the greater the income pickup over common.

hedging: Protecting investments from market risk; requires the ability to quantify and manage risk over time; firms may hedge a portion of the risk associated with a market position by using listed options, futures, options on futures, as well as replicating the index with securities in the underlying cash market. On occasion, a portion of the hedge may consist entirely of OTC currency options purchased from creditworthy counterparties.

holder: The buyer of an option contract.

implied or future volatility: Unknowable and must be estimated from calculations using the option model pricing parameters (i.e., strike, price, term, interest rates, and dividend rates). Implied volatility can be solved for when all the other option pricing variables are given.

index amortizing swaps: The economic equivalent of a swap with an embedded option.

index- and asset-linked notes: Debt securities that offer investors principal preservation (i.e., return of the principal investment at maturity) and potential capital appreciation (called a kicker) linked to the movement of an index or other asset (equity, debt, commodity, or exchange rate).

in-the-money: When the underlying asset price moves below the strike, the puts are said to be trading in-the-money. Calls increase in value as the underlying asset price moves above the strike and are then said to be trading in-the-money.

intrinsic value: An amount by which an option is in-the-money (above the strike if it's a call and below the strike if it's a put).

investment premium: The premium over investment value at which a convertible trades. The lower a convertible's investment premium, the better its price support. Busted convertibles typically trade at low investment premiums and possess little equity sensitivity. At the other extreme, equity sensitive convertibles trade at high investment premiums and possess little price support.

investment value: The value of a convertible below which it should not fall regardless of common declines. Investment value is based upon a convertible's credit quality, term to maturity, yield, and the spread to Treasuries on similar risk nonconvertible fixed-income securities. Computing investment value is a two-step process. First, determine the discount rate on a comparable-risk non-convertible bond of the same maturity. Computing the discount rate involves determining the spread to Treasuries that a comparable-risk corporate bond trades at. The value of the convertible based on the computed discount rate is known as its bond value or its investment value.

legal risks: Risks associated with customer suitability for certain types of investments, compliance with securities regulations, disclosure materials, copyrights, etc.

leveraged swaps: A type of investment contract generally involving a series of variable-rate interest payments that adjust at some specified multiple of actual interest rate movements.

liquidity risk: A type of market risk arising from a low level of trading volume and float (i.e., the number of shares or contracts of a security that is outstanding) that may make it difficult to set a hedge and manage position risk.

lookback options: Provide investors with the ability to "reset" the strike price to a more favorable level if one occurs during a specified period of time after the option is sold; if a position moves against an investor, a lookback feature protects his position by resetting the strike to an at-the-money level (i.e., so that it is no longer out-of-the-money).

lowest call price: The call price at maturity or the cap price. If the PERCS trades above the call price at maturity, the PERCS will be called for redemption and the PERCS holder will receive the call price in cash or common. With respect to an ELKS, holders receive in cash the lesser of the call price or the value of one share of common stock.

management fee: Part of the gross spread; the management fee is split among the comanagers on a negotiated basis, often equally; but in some cases with a higher portion of the split going to one firm or another, depending on placement capability or as a sweetener to join the underwriting.

market disruption events: Usually covered in contract documentation that provides certain limits or cancellation of exercise rights if liquidity in certain cash and futures markets fails to exist.

market value of an option: The market value of an option consists of two main parts: intrinsic value and time value.

maximum annualized yield to maturity: The annualized rate of return earned on a PERCS or ELKS if the common stock trades above the call price at maturity. The rate of return includes the income earned on the security as well as any capital gain or loss.

monetizing collar: A zero-cost collar transaction combined with a margin loan; proceeds to investor are typically greater than a conventional margin loan.

monetizing equity swap: Investor exchanges cash flow obligations with a counterparty relating to investor's restricted stock or concentrated equity position in exchange for the returns of another asset or diversified index; transaction generates temporary cash proceeds to the investor who retains stock ownership and voting rights but is still exposed to market price risk.

naked: When a financial position is unhedged or at risk for some portion or possibly all of its notional market exposure.

new product risks: Risks arising from incorrect assumptions or errors made in structuring a new product or about the underlying asset or market.

notional: The aggregate dollar amount of underlying assets that are controlled by a derivative instrument; the amount that serves as the basis for calculating the potential payoff to investors, and the amount that is at risk and must be hedged by the issuing party. In the case where a derivative instrument controls a multiple of the underlying asset, the issue price of each unit times the number of units sold times the multiplier equals the notional amount. For example, if a derivative is priced at $50 but it sells better if priced to investors in $5 units, the multiplier is $10 ($50/$5 = $10). If 5,000,000 units are sold, the notional amount of the offering is $250,000,000 ($5 × 5,000,000 × $10 = $250,000,000).

options: Financial instruments used alone for speculation on asset price movements and also used for risk management purposes, mitigating risk as they preserve investors' opportunities to benefit from favorable price movements in the underlying asset; options are valued using the strike of the underlying asset, the underlying stock, bond or other asset price(s), the time until expiration of the option, dividend rate (stocks) or yield (bonds), interest rate assumptions, and the volatility of the underlying asset.

options on futures: OTC and exchange-listed options that give the holder the right to acquire or sell a specified futures contract at a predetermined price.

option writer: The originator or seller of an option contract.

out-of-the-money: When puts decrease in value, the asset price on which they are based moves above the strike, whereupon the puts are said to be trading out-of-the-money. As the asset price decreases below the strike, calls are said to be trading out-of-the-money.

over-the-counter (OTC) markets: Nonpublic transactions where privately negotiated contractual arrangements among institutions and sophisticated individual investors are largely unregulated; the various counterparties can consummate transactions in days or hours; the OTC structuring process has fewer steps than a publicly traded transaction offered to retail investors.

par or redemption value: Convertibles are typically issued with a $1000 face value and are redeemed for that amount at maturity. Preferred stocks, on the other hand, are issued with face values of either $25 or $50 and do not carry a mandatory redemption date.

position risk: The market, credit, or other exposure to a specific securities holding or book of holdings by a firm through its trading desk.

premium: The dollar amount paid for or received for an option or warrant.

present value of income pickup: The present value of the amount by which the yield on a PERCS and ELKS exceeds the yield on common.

private equity sales: Discounted private sale by investor or restricted stock to counterparty who holds stock until it is freely tradable or otherwise further monetizes it or sells it pursuant to an exemption from registration; investor loses all control and equity ownership in the stock and receives less than 100 percent of the current market value of the stock, but has no economic risk in the position going forward.

private placements: Custom-made, OTC transactions for institutional clients and individual or groups of accredited investors; Section 4(2) or Regulation D transactions are exempt from registration under the Securities Act of 1933, as amended; private placement exemptions eliminate registration delays associated with exchange-traded products; products can include equity and debt and structured products such as warrants, equity-linked notes, and other securities.

provisional call protection: Aside from hard call protection, some convertibles also possess provisional call protection. That is, they cannot be called prior to the provisional call date unless the common trades above a certain price, typically 40–50 percent above the conversion price, for a specified period of time.

purchase of put options: Investor obtains downside price protection on equity position by purchasing a put option; investor retains control over stock and all appreciation potential.

puts: The right but not the obligation to sell the underlying asset to the option holder.

qualified independent underwriter (QIU): A written fairness opinion from a QIU is required under NASD (National Association of Securities Dealers) Schedule E requirements relating to the fairness to the investor of the pricing of the structured product to be issued. This requirement relates to situations in which potential conflicts of interest could arise where the issuer and the lead underwriter are affiliated entities. A QIU provides comfort to investors in that the pricing of the instrument being offered is fair relative to other publicly traded instruments and market conditions affecting the asset upon which the structured product is based; the fairness opinion is provided to the lead underwriter and cited in the prospectus supplement.

relative performance options: Financial instruments that give investors the right to receive the price return of one asset or index of assets over and above the return of another index (also called "better of" or "outperformance" options).

reset options, warrants, and notes: A provision in an option, warrant, or index-linked note that allows for the strike price to be moved or reset to the then-current asset or index level to which the instrument is linked.

rho (interest rate risk): The dollar amount of change in an option price due to changes in interest rates.

road shows: Organized marketing presentations of pending securities offerings to brokers in branch offices.

roll point and roll risk: A period in time that occurs when some or all of a hedge position is reestablished because of the expiration of one of its component securities (i.e., a listed option or future). The chance that money is lost while trying to reestablish such a hedge is called roll risk.

Rule 144: Two-year holding period and the trading volume requirements pursuant to SEC Rule 144. Rule 144 is part of the Securities Act of 1933, the main purpose of which is to require SEC registration of securities sold to the public. However, registering stock is time consuming and expensive. For this reason, issuing companies often sell unregistered stock privately and often choose not to register control and restricted stock for resale to the public. In the absence of registration, the only practical way for holders to sell restricted or control stock is in accordance with the requirements of Rule 144 or in a private transaction. Two categories are subject to selling restrictions:

control stock: Any stock of an issuer (including registered and unregistered shares) owned by an affiliate or the issuer (i.e., an officer, director, or other person who, through stock ownership or otherwise, controls the management policies of the issuer). Requirements: (1) Current public information must be available regarding the issuer; (2) no minimum holding period; (3) number of shares that may be sold by a holder within a three-month period is subject to volume limitations equal to the greater of 1 percent of the shares of the same class outstanding or the average weekly trading volume (averaged over the prior four calendar weeks); all Rule 144 sales of securities of the same class (restricted or nonrestricted) by or on behalf of the owner and certain persons related to the owner must be aggregated; (4) sales must be made by the owner to a market maker in the stock or by a broker on behalf of the owner to purchase in unsolicited agency transactions; and (5) Form 144 Notice of Sale must be filed with the SEC and the principal exchange (if any) for the stock no later than the day on which the sell order is entered.

restricted stock: Unregistered stock owned by an affiliate or nonaffiliate that was sold by the issuer or an affiliate in a private transaction. Requirements: (1) current public information must be available regarding the issuer; (2) two-year holding period commencing upon the acquisition of the securities from the issuer or an affiliate of the issuer in a private transaction (and fully paid for); one who acquired restricted stock in a private transaction from a nonaffiliate can tack to the holding period of the nonaffiliate; one who acquired any stock (restricted or nonrestricted) from an affiliate in a private transaction takes on a new two-year holding period; (3) number of shares that may be sold by a holder within a three-month period is subject to volume limitations equal to the greater of 1 percent of the shares of the same class outstanding or the average weekly trading volume (averaged over the prior four calendar weeks); all Rule 144 sales of securities of the same class by or on behalf of a *nonaffiliate* owner and certain persons related to the owner must be aggregated and all Rule 144 sales of securities of the same class by or on behalf of an *affiliate* owner and certain persons related to the owner must be aggregated; (4) sales must be made by the owner to a market maker in the stock or by a broker on behalf of the owner to purchase in unsolicited agency transactions; and (5) Form 144 Notice of Sale must be filed with the SEC and the principal exchange (if any) for the stock no later than the day on which the sell order is entered. (Note: After a holding period of *three* years has elapsed, restricted stock becomes unregistered and may be sold free from the requirements of Rule 144 so long as the owner is not and has not been during the prior three months an affiliate of the issuer.)

Rule 145: Stock received in connection with a merger, consolidation, or other reorganization by a person who was an affiliate of the disappearing company (and who does not become an affiliate of the surviving company), or stock acquired from such a person by a nonaffiliate of the issuer in a private transaction. Rule 145 stock is subject to some of the same selling restrictions of Rule 144 stock.

sale of deep-in-the-money call options: Investor partially monetizes and hedges restricted or clean stock position, retains control of stock, and avoids taxation; investor's downside price protection is limited to amount of premium received; no investor participation in upside appreciation beyond value of premium received; at expiration investor must pay counterparty any per share amount above the strike; investor's upside price exposure mitigated by eventual salability of stock position; moderate risk to investor.

sale of out-of-the-money call options: Costless yield enhancement strategy to investor; investor sells the option, receives cash, retains control of stock, and avoids taxation; price protection to investor up to the strike and downside protection equal only to the value of the premium received; investor suffers loss if the stock price declines below the value of the premium received; investor's upside price exposure mitigated by eventual salability of stock position; investor retains downside stock price risk.

sales credit: Part of the gross spread; the sales credit goes to the retail side of each firm involved in the offering, on a pro rata basis (i.e., based on the amount of securities sold by each firm). The broker usually receives 25–50 percent of the sales credit relating to his or her sales, the balance of which goes to the broker's firm. The higher a broker's production level, the higher the "grid" or percent payout he or she can demand. Sales credits are usually paid to brokers monthly.

sales of stock through a structured equity program: Provides public corporations, affiliates, and shareholders with a means to sell large amounts of stock over time in a cost-effective, consistent, and "quiet" manner; outright sale of stock through an SEC shelf registration.

Securities and Exchange Commission (SEC): In 1982, Congress amended the CEA and the federal securities laws dividing jurisdiction over options and futures contracts on financial instruments between the CFTC and the SEC. The SEC has regulatory jurisdiction over stock options, currency options, certificates of deposit, and stock indexes, among other securities; stock and option exchange; and investor matters.

security: The term is defined in Section 2(1) of the Securities Exchange Act of 1933 and Section 3(a)(10) of the Securities Exchange Act of 1934 and generally refers to any note, stock, treasury stock, bond, debenture, certificate of interest, or participation in any profit-sharing agreement or any option transaction entered into on a U.S. national securities exchange.

self-regulatory organizations (SROs): U.S. public marketplaces that regulate themselves under the auspices of the SEC or other regulatory bodies (i.e., national stock exchanges or, in the United States, the NASDAQ).

selling-group members: Those firms not invited to join as a comanager often participate in selling-group members. Selling-group members do not share in underwriter's liability but earn sales credits based on the pro rata amount of securities sold.

shadow book: A record of investor orders is kept by the lead manager during an initial public or private offering; it is built from indications of interest from each comanager. The shadow book provides information on potential demand that allows for a decision on whether or not to proceed with the offering.

shelf registration: A method of prefiling with the SEC for the issuance of new publicly offered securities so that, at such time as a takedown (i.e., use of the shelf) is required, issuers can do so with little or no delay in receiving SEC effectiveness.

short against the box: Investor fully monetizes restricted or clean stock, locks in price, has use of cash proceeds during the term of the position, and retains control of stock; investor runs the risk of borrowed stock being called away, but risk is mitigated by deliverability of stock held as collateral; presently not a taxable event but currently being reviewed and subject to change by the Internal Revenue Service.

short option value: The value of the call option embedded in a PERCS or ELKS.

short sale: Borrowing stock from another investor and then selling it.

standardized options: Exchange-listed securities that are issued and guaranteed by the Options Clearing Corp (OCC) in contrast to OTC options and warrants that are subject to the creditworthiness of corporate issuers.

standstill yield to maturity: The annualized rate of return earned on a PERCS, ELKS, or DECS if the common is unchanged at maturity. The rate of return includes the income earned on the security as well as any capital gain or loss. The higher the standstill yield to maturity, the better the risk/reward of a PERCS or ELKS relative to common.

stock basket: An index of stocks usually including a relatively small number of constituents (e.g., 5 to 50 stocks) and representing an industry sector or some narrow market niche.

strike: A specified starting point used in determining the cash settlement value of an option or warrant contract.

structured products: Financial instruments that are designed or engineered to meet specific financial or investment objectives and composed of derivative securities and contracts, the elemental building blocks of structured products.

structured shelf and equity distribution program: Allows issuers and shareholders to continuously sell large amounts of common stock into the market at such times and prices as desired off of a shelf registration filed under the SEC's Rule 415; issuers can raise funds through common stock sales by registering new shares on an equity shelf registration statement filed with the SEC or the common stock portion of a universal shelf; control persons and holders of restricted stock or stock received in an acquisition can sell their holdings through off-the-shelf transactions.

structuring: A nontraditional process of creating and fabricating a wide variety of financial products whose values are linked to or derived from one or more underlying assets, such as equities, bonds, commodities, currencies, or other economic interests.

suitability: A determination of an investor's qualifications for certain types of investments, such as net worth and investment experience and income; with regard to restricted stock transactions, an investor's relationship with the company who issued the underlying stock position, the number of shares proposed for a transaction, the daily trading volume of the stock, the length of time the stock has been held, stock trading price volatility, and other legal and regulatory constraints.

swap intermediary: The broker–dealer or other dealer who structures the transaction, values and prices the cash flows, documents the transaction, and collects fees from one or more counterparties involved in a swap transaction.

swaps: Private, unregulated, OTC, contractual agreements negotiated between two or more counterparties who agree to exchange periodic cash payments on an agreed notional amount and maturity, related to interest rate, equity price, currency exchange rate, or commodity price changes.

swaptions: An option contract on an interest rate swap with the swap having some future commencement date.

syndicate invitations: An offer from the lead manager of a securities offering to join the underwriting or selling group as a comanager or regular member.

syndicates: Group of investment banks that participate in underwritten securities offerings.

tack: Restricted stock may not be sold for two years after being granted; another investor taking the stock must hold the stock or *tack* the remainder of the two-year holding period onto any remaining time left before open market sale is permitted.

term: Specific period of time that an option or warrant is in effect.

theta (option time decay): The dollar amount by which an option price changes due to changes in time to expiration, often thought of as the amount of time value decay that occurs in the price of an option as it approaches expiration.

time value: The amount by which an option price exceeds its intrinsic value and represents that part of the value of an option relating to the amount of time left until the instrument expires. Time value declines over the life of the instrument and represents the option's potential to acquire more intrinsic value before it expires.

time value decay: The amount of decline of an option price as it approaches expiration (also called erosion or evaporation of time premium).

timing and exercise risk: Option contracts should expire on days (accounting for foreign holidays) and at times of day (adjusted for time zone differences) that allow traders to set or unwind hedges.

trust structures: Legal "containers" into which restricted stock can be deposited or pledged and resold as units to other investors; investor retains voting rights, partially monetizes a concentrated equity position, hedges price risk, and defers potential tax payments during the life of the trust.

trust units: The securities that represent ownership interest in a trust.

underwriter's liability: The obligations incumbent upon comanagers to share in their pro rata costs of an offering and, more important, in any potential damages claimed by and awarded (through arbitration or legal action) to investors, resulting from material omissions from or misrepresentations in the offering document (i.e., the "red herring" or prospectus supplement, if a shelf takedown).

underwriting: The process of organizing, registering, marketing, and selling securities by investment banks that oversee the offering process.

underwriting fee: Part of the gross spread; the underwriting fee is allocated to the lead manager's costs in bringing the deal, such as legal, printing, and other offering costs. Any amount over such costs are usually split among the comanagers. Any unallocated underwriting fees and the management fee are split among the comanagers on a negotiated basis.

unmatched positions: When the term or duration of a hedge is different from that of the related instrument or position, a loss is possible if the actual volatility at each roll-point over the term of the instrument is greater than the implied volatility assumed in the past when the hedge position was set.

unregistered stock: Stock that may not be sold to the public until it is registered with the SEC or otherwise meets an exemption from registration.

upstairs market making: The securities buying and selling activities engaged in by the trading desks or broker–dealers; contrasted against the market-making activities of an exchange floor specialist.

vega (traded volatility—a.k.a. kappa): The dollar amount of change of an option price with a 1-point change in the volatility of the underlying security.

volatility: A measure of the frequency and intensity of price changes of the asset on which an option is based. Of the problems in managing market risk, volatility is perhaps the most critical determinant because of its pronounced effect on option pricing and overall profitability of a structured instrument. The more volatile the price of an asset, the greater the price risk exposure and the greater the expense in hedging such exposure. Volatility and its effects on option pricing is evaluated using various proprietary mathematical "black box" models run on computers.

volatility spreads: The difference between the price a product can be sold for and the price at which a hedge can be purchased to partially or fully offset the risk of an obligation to the issuer/originator.

warrants: The economic equivalent of owning the underlying asset in the form of long-term options that can be privately issued or listed on worldwide stock exchanges; whereas standard listed options are guaranteed by an exchange or clearinghouse, warrants are backed by the credit of the issuer.

warrant valuation: The value of a warrant can be analyzed using standard option pricing parameters (strike, interest rate, dividend/coupon rate, term, volatility, and underlying security price); however, since the credit backing a warrant obligation is of a specific issuer and not an exchange or clearinghouse (which is usually considered to be a risk-free rate), the borrowing rate of the issuing or guaranteeing corporation must be added as an input in computerized valuation models.

yield curve risk: Risk due to shift in the slope of yield curves.

yield to maturity (YTM): A measure of a convertible bond's annualized return. A bond's YTM takes into account not only its current yield but also any capital gain or loss at maturity. If a bond trades below par, its YTM exceeds its current yield due to the capital gain at maturity. On the other hand, the current yield of a convertible trading above par exceeds its YTM due to the capital loss at maturity as the convertible declines to par.

"you choose" options and warrants: For investors waiting for certain events to occur between the present time and a specific date in the future before deciding what direction to play.

zero-cost collar transactions: Costless trade to investor seeking hedge protection of equity position without incurring any out-of-pocket costs (e.g., also referred to as "costless" or "cash-settled" collars); investor retains control of stock and avoids taxation; investor achieves price protection by selling a call and buying a put, therefore locking in gains between put and call strikes; investor's upside price exposure through the sale of the call option is offset by the ability to sell the actual stock position; minimal risk to investor.

zero-coupon bond and embedded option: Index- and asset-linked notes are designed to be the economic equivalent of a zero-coupon bond plus an option whose value is determined by reference to price movements of the underlying asset.

INDEX